THE MOTHER OF ALL DAYS

R HOUSE
   PUBLISHING

THE MOTHER OF ALL DAYS

*The True Story of a Fatal Break-In
and the Unexpected Path to Healing*

TENNYSON JACOBSON

The Mother Of All Days by Tennyson Jacobson

Copyright © December 2024 by Tennyson Jacobson

All rights reserved.

No part of this publication may be reproduced, distributed, or transmitted in any form or by any means, including photocopying, recording, or other electronic or mechanical methods, without the prior written permission of the author or publisher, except in the case of brief quotations embodied in critical reviews and certain other noncommercial uses permitted by copyright law. For permission requests or for information about special discounts for bulk purchases, book club editions, or academic use, please contact the publisher, addressed "Attention: Permissions Coordinator," at the address below.

R House Publishing LLC - JC Cochrane
2931 Ridge Rd. STE. 101 #169
Rockwall, TX. 75032

jc@rhousepublishing.co - www.jccochrane.com

Developmental Editing: JC Cochrane
Book Cover Design and Interior Layout: Emma Elzinga, Inksplatter Design

ISBN: 978-0-9976923-7-2 (paperback)   978-0-9976923-8-9 (hardcover)

This is a work of nonfiction. While the events and experiences described are true to the author's life, in order to protect the privacy of certain individuals and respect their boundaries, some names, identifying details, and events have been altered, fictionalized, or portrayed in a way that avoids harm. Not all names, characters, businesses, places, events, or incidents are used factually. Any resemblance to actual persons, living or deceased, or actual events is purely coincidental unless explicitly stated.

Printed in the United States of America

First Edition

CONTENTS

Forward IX
1 All By Myself 1
2 By Your Side 19
3 In The Light Of Day 39
4 Table of Three 55
5 In The Dead Of Night 63
6 The Story 75
7 Why Us? 89
8 My Safe Place 97
9 The Shepherds 107
10 The Face Of PTSD 113
11 Something To Be Grateful For 123
12 Trusting My Intuition 133
13 The Courage It Takes 143
14 Break Free 149
15 Sundays With Jeff 161
16 Whatever It Takes 171
17 All The Parts 185
18 Being Here Now 197
19 Does It Make Your Tail Wag 205
20 Angels & Spirit Guides 219
21 Hell, Yes 231
22 The Vortex 237

23	I Am	251
24	The Wonder Of The Woo Woo World	257
25	Putting It All Together	267

Epilogue By Tennyson Jacobson 277
Afterward By Kyle Jacobson 281
Acknowledgements 289
Connect With Tennyson 295

To Kyle, Lyla, and Skyler, I love you more.

To you, the reader, and those who make the brave decision to heal.

Lastly, to the parts of me that have never given up fighting to find peace, fulfillment, and purpose. This book would not exist without your persistence.

FOREWORD

When Tennyson first reached out to me, the voice on the phone was that of a 32-year-old woman who had experienced an unbelievable traumatic event—what some might call "big T trauma." However, despite the weight of her experience, I realized how eager she was to heal. Tennyson explained that she had been engaging in therapy and other methods to find relief but felt frustrated, stuck, and exhausted. Her voice was gentle, soft-spoken, and vulnerable. And yet, in her words, there was determination, resilience, and grit—all signs she was ready to do the work.

Even in the face of profound horror that entered her life, I noticed Tennyson remained remarkably grateful throughout her journey. From our first conversation, I recognized her quiet strength and deep desire to help others rather than succumbing to anger or despair. Over the past six-plus years, as I have gotten to know her better, I have learned how her childhood shaped her to be a caretaker—someone who puts others' needs before her own. Through our sessions, we both met parts of Tennyson that struggled to express anger, and instead sought to find the good in others. It became clear that a series of "little T traumas" had profoundly influenced her—shaping her identity and her response to trauma. As a positive, it left her with an unwavering commitment to uplift and support those in need, ensuring that others don't have to navigate their healing journeys alone. Hence, the reason she wrote this book.

Life presents each of us with challenges, moments of hardship, profound loss, the quest for meaning, and trauma of countless forms. This book is an invitation to walk alongside Tennyson on her journey. As you read, you embark on a parallel path, where you'll discover the power of your intuition and unearth hidden parts of yourself—parts that are courageous, resilient, and capable of overcoming life's adversities. These inner strengths guide us forward, deepening our connections and fostering compassion for ourselves and others—-setting the stage for healing. Witnessing Tennyson's journey has been an honor. Through these pages, you, too, will come to understand the power of determination, love, and healing—how they intertwine with intuition and staying curious while being committed to self-work. She shows us how healing is a process that unfolds over time, requiring patience, trust, and the willingness to continue showing up for oneself.

As you turn the pages, you may find yourself reflecting on your own hidden strengths and the profound impact they can have on your life and those around you. No journey is meant to be walked alone. Along the way, we encounter aspects of ourselves and others who extend a hand, offer a kind word, or share wisdom just when we need it most. These moments become beacons of light, guiding us through our darkest moments. This book is Tennyson's extended hand to you—a testament to the power of connection and support and a reminder of the courage within you—the quiet yet undeniable strength that pushes you forward, even in the face of uncertainty.

Tennyson's story is not a theoretical lesson on courage; it is a lived experience filled with raw emotion and profound discovery. Courage is not always loud; it is often the quiet resolve to keep going, face our fears with an open heart, and move forward despite uncertainty. She shows us how courage emerges when we step beyond our comfort zones, confront our deepest fears, and embrace new ways of thinking, feeling, and being. It is through this courage that we grow and realize the true extent of our potential. Through her journey, Tennyson demonstrates that true transformation flourishes in connection—when we allow ourselves to be seen, seek support, allow ourselves to receive, and offer that same grace to others.

At the core of the human experience is our desire and capacity to help others. We are not isolated beings but interconnected souls who thrive when we lift each other up. Acts of kindness—whether grand or small—create ripples of compassion that extend far beyond their initial moment. Helping others is not about rescuing or fixing; it is about showing up, being present, listening, lending a helping hand, or offering encouragement. Tennyson embodies this; her story reflects her lifelong commitment to empathy and support.

Whether big or small, trauma can alter the course of our lives in ways we never expected. Whether through the loss of a loved one, an unforeseen change, or deeply scarring experiences, trauma can feel like an unshakable burden. Yet, Tennyson will show you how it does *not* define us. The human heart has an extraordinary capacity to heal. The process is ongoing, requiring patience, self-compassion, and the courage to face what is broken while embracing the journey of becoming whole. Healing isn't about erasing the past; it is about integrating it into who we are becoming. It can look different for everyone. You are not meant to heal in the same exact way as another. This book illustrates how Tennyson carved her own path by staying curious about what would support her journey. She learned to trust her intuition, allowing it to guide her. This was not easy for her, as her natural inclination had always been to avoid disruption and follow the familiar, well-trodden paths of those around her. Yet, by embracing her inner wisdom, she found the courage to create a path uniquely her own. As can you.

As you read this book, allow yourself to reflect on your own journey. Like Tennyson, embrace your inner strength and your capacity to heal. Let your heart be your guide, and may you find inspiration, comfort and connection in these pages. You are not alone. This journey is yours to embrace, and within you resides the courage to keep moving forward, to heal, and to trust the path unfolding before you.

– Dr. Jeff D.

1

ALL BY MYSELF

Being alone in a room had become my greatest fear. I stood in the doorway of my in-law's guest bedroom, fighting to hold back tears. It was only a few weeks after that life-altering event. My heart pounded as every ounce of me didn't want to go in, but I knew I needed to.

I entered, sat down in the old wooden rocking chair and closed my eyes while I thought back to the most recent session with my therapist, where she gave me this homework called *exposure therapy: an exercise to confront one's deepest fears*. The homework itself sounded simple—spend twenty minutes in a room alone. But because my life had drastically changed a few weeks prior, it now took everything within me to get myself to do this "simple" task. By this point, I was desperate to feel even an ounce more normal than I did. I'd even take half an ounce or a quarter of an ounce. *Anything*. With lack of sleep, my body constantly reacting to every single little noise or person as if I was going to die, and worst-case-scenario thoughts that raced through my head nearly every minute of every day, I was drained physically, mentally and emotionally. So, I agreed to try her recommendation.

I would strategically time when I did this activity in the evening for two reasons: one, I wanted to do it when everyone was home, and two, nighttime made my fears ten million times worse. My body was already on high alert during the day, but at night, it felt like every single cell of my body was on guard and prepared to fight. In exposure therapy, you pick the situation that makes you face your deepest fear and there was no question—bedtime was the worst.

I closed the hollow oak door behind me as I walked into the room. Each time I did this, I knew what I was getting myself into—any comfort would be gone. Knowing I would have to sit in pure terror for the next twenty minutes as I followed my therapist's advice was the last thing on earth I wanted to do, as I knew it would be pure torture. Part of my homework was to fill out an exposure record sheet as I sat in this hell. I would rate my level of fear before and after the duration of exposure. I was also to add any notes of thoughts, feelings, or physiological responses that came up throughout the experience, knowing we would discuss those at the next appointment and, hopefully, show any improvement I was making.

My therapist was based out of Harborview Trauma Center in Seattle, well-known for treating the most severe traumas. I liked her, but I hated going to Seattle (which was exposure therapy in itself—driving into the city where crime rates drastically increased versus the small town I lived in). As someone with a mom who put me in therapy at a young age, mainly because I am a twin and learned how to manage twin dynamics, I could see how talk therapy had been beneficial. But this was different. I was showing up with a big trauma this time, more appropriately, a *huge* trauma. The kind that made the headlines in newspapers. It was nothing like being there to build relationship skills. I had hoped this therapist would help me find some relief and support, as I had back in the day, but instead, I felt stuck. My fear and anxiety felt so real and didn't seem to be getting any better. I was sleep-deprived from my body being in a constant state of hyperawareness, and I had no tools on how to turn it off. Even though it had only been weeks since the event, my body was running on empty, my mind was non-stop, and the combination was wearing on me more than I could manage—even as hard as I tried. Exposure therapy was helping a little, but certainly not fast enough.

Most importantly, I immediately didn't feel a connection with this therapist. This caught me off guard and scared me because I knew I didn't have the tools to figure this out on my own. I was at the place that was supposedly the best of the best, but our conversations only led me to feel misunderstood. I didn't know it then, but now I can see how things can only go so far with a therapist with the knowledge they have studied and the life they have lived.

If you were looking at me in this room from a bird's eye view, it would look like I was doing absolutely nothing in what seemed to be a dismantled guest room with no bed, two small dressers, a wooden rocking chair and a lamp. You'd see me walk into the room and sink down into the old rocking chair. Sometimes, I'd get up to double-check that the window was locked, but most of the time, I simply rocked back and forth for about 20 minutes before bolting out of there. The truth is, the overwhelming fear and the dark places my mind wandered to during those moments were the hardest things I have ever faced. It was exponentially more challenging than I had experienced just weeks prior, which was still making the national headlines. It was frustrating that our lives had turned in a whole other direction in less than ten minutes with a stranger, and now, sitting by myself in a room for twenty minutes in what should be a welcoming guest room scared me more than anything I could imagine.

This was all taking place in my in-laws' house. They had a cozy home in a safe neighborhood. It was where my husband, Kyle, had grown up. I was in his old bedroom. A room I remember visiting in high school when we started dating and couldn't believe we were a couple. He had been my high school crush all four years, even though he graduated two years prior to me, and I couldn't believe I was someone who got to see his bedroom. Not because of doing things that can happen in bedrooms, but because it was his intimate space and where you learn who a person is. At that time, his room held old wrestling and soccer trophies, pictures of friends, medals from half and full marathons he had participated in, a large collection of books, given he is an avid reader, and a nicely made bed with a blue, red, and tan flannel fluffy plaid comforter. Not that it was perfectly made, as he wasn't quite at that level, but he certainly knew how to keep a tidy space. It was a room that only made me think of my favorite memories of falling in love and the butterflies of getting to know someone, but today, it felt like a room in a psych ward.

Just outside the door and down the hallway, Kyle played

with our 8-month-old daughter, Lyla, as he lay with her on the carpet, surrounded by her favorite musical toys and stuffed animals. She would practice her tummy time as Kyle stroked her hair while smiling at her, making sure she had all her toys within reach. My in-laws, Norm and Mary, were sitting on the couch right next to them, enjoying the sweet moments of watching their son and granddaughter play together. The vision landed differently than before, realizing that this event had brought immense clarity in how legitimately grateful they were for all of us to have survived what we had.

It's so hard to explain the mind-f that a traumatic experience can do. You logically know you are probably safe, but your mind and body tell you a completely different story. And even as desperately as I wanted to turn it off, I couldn't. But Kyle knew exactly how I felt. He had been there that nightmare of a night and was experiencing similar struggles in his own way while also doing the same exposure therapy.

We were in no way prepared for the work we had to do after that night. But isn't that the case for all who endure big trauma?

In those first months, it was brutal watching Kyle, who only ever made me feel protected, traumatized. As a firefighter, he had faced trauma numerous times. He likes to joke that he hasn't, but I know that is his way of playing down things he sees and accidents he responds to. He had legitimately saved people's lives from horrific car accidents, suicide attempts and medical emergencies, but now, simply being alone was the most terrifying thing he was facing, too. He was a grown man—a *mentally and physically strong man*—who could barely stand the thought of sitting in the family room by himself after everyone went to bed. Like me, he was shocked at how messed up he was. He just wanted to go back to how things used to be, so he committed to doing the work.

Kyle had two exercises for his exposure therapy homework. One was to stay up after everyone had gone to bed while sitting in the dark living room for five to ten minutes, exposing him to a similar environment to what happened that night. The second was that he had to walk out the front door at night, go about twenty yards down the unlit driveway to the mailbox, and return. He didn't want us to watch him, so sometimes I watched him without him knowing. Opening the door and stepping on the threshold, he took a deep breath, preparing himself for what was coming. He knew that every second of walking down that driveway was going to suck. With adrenaline pumping through his body, he knew fear would completely take over, as he anticipated someone was going to jump out from nowhere and attack.

There were times when Mary, his mom, stood there with me, watching Kyle. We would look at each other with tears welling up in our eyes as we watched someone we admired so much, physically but more so in character, do something we knew was literally scaring him to death. He would be shaking, breathing fast, fighting back tears, while also subtly laughing at himself because of how uncomfortable he was, saying, "Dude. This is crazy…I can't believe how much I don't want to do this right now," as he worked up the courage to walk out the door. Here was a guy who beat almost anyone in any physical competition and now was terrified to walk twenty yards in the dark. There is something beautiful but completely heart-breaking about watching someone purposely expose themselves so vulnerably to something that should be such a mundane task, but for Kyle, it was the most terrifying thing he could imagine. To watch the person who always protected me and *did* protect me paralyzed with fear was absolutely brutal. I could see how it profoundly impacted him. I knew how brave he was, but I also had to wonder if being a man made it harder for him to feel just as paralyzed as I was. The truth is, we were a team, and watching him put in the work inspired me not to give up on my own.

Here we were, two weeks after the event, and he was supposed to compete as the team leader on our CrossFit team for a chance to make it to the CrossFit Games. Our team was so close to achieving this accomplishment the prior two years. But, on this day, instead of a bunch of heavy lifting and lung-crushing workouts, it's taking all that is within him to have the strength to walk to the mailbox of his childhood home—a house that held tons of his favorite and safest childhood memories. Observing Kyle do his work while realizing I was making minimal progress made it clear that it would be a long road for *both* of us.

I was shocked at how significantly this trauma was impacting us. I couldn't stop thinking, *Why can I not just feel better?* Part of me felt like a failure because I couldn't just "get over it." I know you're not supposed to compare, but if I had to, Kyle seemed to be doing a little better than me, but not much. I guessed it was because, while working as a firefighter, he was used to more trauma and tragedy than I and seemed to be able to compartmentalize in a healthy way. He is also physically bigger and stronger than I am and could protect himself easier than I could, which played a huge role in that evening. It was something that *saved our life*. After this encounter, I'm not sure if being "humbled" is the right way of saying it, but I sure became humbly aware of what protecting myself from someone much bigger and stronger than I meant. I had played a big role in my survival, but there's no denying that size makes a difference. The truth is, everything triggered me and even as supportive as everyone was around us, I was frustrated with feeling like a burden and having so many "issues." All I wanted was to feel normal. To *feel* the emotion of happiness again and at least somewhat safe again. Although those felt like such unrealistic goals, I wanted to do anything and everything I could to at least try to find a way through this.

Within minutes of starting exposure therapy, I had tears falling down my face. While rocking back and forth in the chair, I attempted to calm myself while taking some deep breaths. I was sweating, shaking and scared to death while the memories continued to come to mind. Almost always, I flashed back, thinking of his huge black eyes and the way he looked at me—a look of pure hate and evil. And oh my God, the smell. Each time I sat there, it was pure hell. It wasn't that I was experiencing the attack all over again. It was the anxiety that came from replaying how such a terrifying person had come out of nowhere, so what was to say he wouldn't come out of nowhere again? Or maybe someone else who wanted to finish what he started. That incident destroyed my belief system about safety. I felt like a fish out of water. As far as I could tell, I was never safe. Nobody and nowhere was safe. If it could happen to me in this sweet, quiet town I grew up in, it could happen anywhere and it could happen again. I sat there and noticed how my anxiousness shifted and I got pissed off because of what he did. Because of him, I couldn't even function sitting alone in this room. I grabbed the paper the therapist had given me and thought to myself as I wrote my notes—*Ok, lady, I'll rate myself* on the chart you gave me...I'm a 10 out of 10. I'm not improving. At all. What in the world do we do now? I imagined saying to her.

My mind raced to my next thought: *Oh my God.* I stared at the only window in the room. *Is it locked?* I jumped from the chair and rushed to the window, ensuring it was fully closed and locked. I flipped the latch back and forth to make sure I had no shadow of a doubt that it was secure. Then, even knowing I had secured the lock, I yanked on the window as hard as I could until I was convinced it wouldn't budge. As terrified as I was, I tried to gather all my composure and look *out* the window to see if anyone was hiding in the bushes or roaming outside, just waiting to break in. As I leaned toward the glass and looked out, I thought, *Come on, you got this, Tenny.* As insane as I felt, I also knew I felt this way for a reason... I had double and triple-checked the locks on every door and window on that horrible night, and somehow, he *still* got in.

I turned and looked at the clock on the nightstand—ten more minutes. *Fuck,* I thought.

I went back and sat down to resume my therapy. My assignment was clear, and if I was anything, I was a rule follower who never wanted to let anyone down. Until this point, I liked following the rules. But, I hated this assignment and rules, especially from someone I didn't fully trust and feel emotionally safe with. But this was her only tool, so I had to give it my best, even if I was tempted to rebel.

My therapist was educated but rather young. She had short brown hair, kind eyes, and a touch of Seattle's all-natural vibe. She wore jeans that opened wide at the bottom, an oversized sweater, and very little makeup. In the beginning, I was hopeful. I gave it my all, but there was a certain indifference in her approach, and the more I showed up, the more I felt unseen.

"What's coming up for you?" She gently asked.

Fighting back tears, I admitted, "I'm just so scared it will happen again."

Completely not acknowledging me, she responded, "I get it. I have an idea. Let's do this." Turning to her computer, she said, "Tennyson, I want to pull up actual statistics on the crime in Seattle."

She Googles.

As she finds the results she is looking for, she reports, "Ah, yes. So, what I have pulled up here are the crime rates in Seattle. As you can see, crime has decreased over the last few years. The likelihood of this happening again, especially in Seattle, is probably .00001%." Pleased with her findings, she looked up to see if I was relieved.

She continued, "The only reason I brought this up is to show you the facts. Statistically, it is nearly impossible, Tennyson."

I sank deeper into my chair and tried to believe what she was saying, but I just couldn't get there. Maybe she was right. But it didn't matter. I heard this same reasoning after I felt like he was coming back. Cops with decades of experience told me, "They never come back." But they were wrong. He did come back. Her statistics only increased my frustration, confusion, and hopelessness. Kyle and I were the outliers. All I could think of was, *You just don't get it.*

Not knowing what to say, I shrugged and nodded. I did not want to disrespect her, but I also felt invalidated.

Trying to encourage me, she said, "This is great news, Tennyson! I know what you went through was an absolute nightmare. But even these crime statistics aren't even for violent crimes. They are basically all for little robberies. That's reassuring, don't you think?"

We both just looked at each other. It was so awkward. I didn't know what to say. All I could think was that *this was making me worse.*

After several sessions I had had with her, sharing real fears and being so exhausted from my body being completely on overdrive all the time without being able to turn it off, I didn't know what to do or say anymore. I know she was trying her best, but her reasoning and statistics were not helping; they were the last things I wanted to hear.

I silently questioned myself: *Am I crazy? Am I missing something here?* I didn't feel crazy. I drove to Seattle for crying out loud. I was willing to put in the work, but we simply weren't on the same page.

She broke our silence, "Given this information, how are you feeling?"

I wished I could agree with her and that her reasoning was helpful, but I also needed to stay honest. I explained, "I'm so sorry, but I can't say that it does help. If I'm being totally honest, I actually feel worse. I don't know what's wrong with me. I wish I could feel relief with those statistics, but the fact is that I didn't even know these statistics before today, so this only makes me more aware of all the crime that *is* happening. We were told we are already the one-in-a-million statistic."

I paused and said, "I don't know…I'm sorry. I am just so scared."

I turned away, trying not to cry and not wanting to look at a face where I didn't feel I was being received. I could feel her looking at me, not knowing what to say. I felt terrible I wasn't just "getting it." She was trying her best, and I was trying, too, but nothing she said comforted me. We had hit a brick wall. I felt guilty that we were in this awkward situation, and I just wanted to get back home.

On top of the challenges within those sessions, going to Seattle was the worst. I don't like to use the word hate very often, but at that time, I utterly hated it in every respect. I grew up in a small community just 30 minutes outside the city. Those 30 minutes made a huge difference from city life to rural communities that lined the foothills of the Cascade mountain range. Even though it was a short distance, it felt worlds apart, from busy streets and dark parking garages in the city versus acre-sized lots, horses as neighbors, and beautiful mountain views. Driving into the city sounded like a stupid idea, as I felt like I was just asking for someone to attack me. Frankly, the worst part was getting in the elevator in the parking garage to get to my appointment, where I'd be locked in with total strangers. I had to give myself a pep talk every time I got out of my car before taking the short walk to the elevator, genuinely praying I wouldn't see someone walk to the elevator with me. I would come up with a backup plan if I did. I didn't want to have to analyze every move they made and their facial expression and then have to decide whether they were safe or not.

As much as I hated Seattle and felt disconnected from my therapist, I did at least see tiny improvements from the exposure therapy, which made me silently feel somewhat hopeful and even proud of myself. I had heard mixed reviews on its effectiveness but was willing to keep trying—anything. I looked at the clock again—*two more minutes. Thank God. Almost there*, I thought.

Knowing I was almost done, I sat back and relaxed in the

chair and could feel the slightest shift on my scale of 10 coming down to a 9. As I looked around the room, though, I couldn't help but realize how creepy this guest room felt. The missing queen-sized bed mattress and bed frame had left four dents in the plush carpet. I gently rocked in the old wooden chair and studied the two empty dressers and the feeling of vacancy in the room. I felt guilty as to why that bed was missing. *We should be staying in here.* I thought back to our first night after the incident and how Kyle and I had come into this room, thinking this was where we would stay for a while until our new house was built. But that's not what happened. We ended up pulling the queen-sized mattress off the frame and moved it onto the floor of my in-laws' master bedroom. We simply were too afraid to sleep in this guest room alone. It was on the complete opposite side of their small, one-story rambler, tucked back by the garage. There was no way in hell we would sleep in what felt like an entire continent away from someone. My mother-in-law graciously brought the whole frame in the following day, doing everything she could to make us feel as comfortable as possible and somehow knowing we wouldn't be ready to be on our own for quite some time.

Our mattress faced their king-sized bed and while I lay there, I often thought, *I cannot believe I am sleeping in my in-law's bedroom.* As weird as it was, truthfully, there was nowhere else Kyle or I wanted to be. I remember questioning: How is it that we are grown adults who run a successful business and have a baby, yet we are sleeping with our parents in the same bedroom? I'd like to think our sleepover would only be a few days, but little did we know it would take three months before we were willing to try moving across the hall.

This was such a confusing time. Kyle and I were like little kids, scared of the boogie man coming to get us and wanting to be safe in Mommy and Daddy's bedroom. I loved Kyle's parents, but it also made me think of my parents. I loved their bedroom growing up, and I always looked forward to running in there with my sister to wake them up on holidays or special days. Life looked different than it did when I was a kid, but, in a way, I also longed for my parent's room I was trying to find comfort in. On these nights, going to sleep was the worst as it just reminded us of how vulnerable we were—not being conscious to hear if someone was lurking in the house and if we needed to protect ourselves.

There were times, though, when we'd occasionally crack up laughing at the fact that Kyle and his parents would put on their headlamps for their nighttime reading while I scrolled my phone to distract my constant worry-filled thoughts. We'd realize how somewhat weird it was that we were basically having a grown-up slumber party. The quick moment of laughter was a nice break from the seriousness we seemed to be stuck in. We were mainly in survival mode, so our joking, lighthearted side had practically disappeared. And due to how awkward it was to sleep right next to my in-laws, as I am sure it was for them too, it was superseded by the sense of safety we needed. My pajamas consisted of workout shorts and a tank top with a bra because there was no way I would make things more awkward than they already were. Not that that wasn't my bedtime attire already, but it's just different having to be aware of this comfort level while all being in the same room together.

As if things weren't uncomfortable enough, I knew I'd have to pee in the middle of the night. This meant I had to get out of bed and quietly walk past the foot of their bed, hoping they were fast asleep as I listened to their deep, steady breathing. On top of that, I would use their bathroom, a tiny bathroom that made it feel like I was invading their personal space, making me feel doubly uncomfortable. I'd silently question myself, *What do I do? Do I flush?* Oh my gosh, so awkward. I'd do everything possible not to wake them, so I would tiptoe around the close quarters so they wouldn't wake up. There was a guest bathroom down the hallway, but walking the hallways at night was a hell NO. I often felt guilty that we might be putting them out. However, I could tell that every bit of them wanted to be there to help us in whatever way they could. So, even as awkward and ridiculous as it all felt, we knew we were genuinely welcomed.

My timer finally went off, and I wrote down a few notes and couldn't wait to get out of there. With my sheet of paper in hand, I got up and walked into the family room to be with Kyle and Lyla. Often, leaving the room, I would be fighting back tears. Half of me felt relieved it was over, but the other half knew I would have to do it again the next day—and the next, and the next.

I only recently saw this quote, ten years after sitting in the room alone, that perfectly embodies what exposure therapy was for me:

"Bravery is not the absence of fear. Bravery is feeling the fear, the doubt, the insecurity, and deciding that something else is more important." Mark Manson

For me, all I wanted was to feel normal again. I wanted my life back. I hated what this trauma had done to both Kyle and me and how it had left us. It was shocking to both of us how, in a span of twelve hours, we went from competent individuals to people who couldn't even go to the grocery store alone.

Our world tends to highlight big moments of courage. Things like a firefighter running into a burning building, a soldier confronting an enemy on the battlefield, a woman who speaks up about sexual abuse...And I suppose, our moment of big courage.

But I have learned that there is another side to courage—soft courage. It's about being brave in every day small moments that no one else sees but you. And it's these moments that truly shape our lives.

Yes, what we experienced was life-altering, but there doesn't have to be a life-altering event to cause challenges and struggles. Jeff, who is now my current therapist, who has truly changed my life and who I will share later about in this book, has said this, "I believe that every little experience that we have is a little tiny T (little t trauma). And I think we are made up of millions of little T's, and that's who we are. And how we learn to respond to them, deal with them, become resilient, and develop grit is all about how we have grown up and learned to deal with these little T's."

Most people reading this book may not have experienced a big T trauma. Still, every person reading these words has experienced everyday moments that impact who you are, how you show up, how you speak to others, how you speak about yourself, how you talk to your kids, etc. Our event cracked me open to gain awareness of the millions of moments I had experienced *before* this event and how they have been holding me back from living the life I dream to live.

I didn't know how I would ever feel safe again, but more than anything, I wanted to. This deep desire fueled my commitment, even if that meant taking the tiniest baby steps. I was scared as hell, but I would force myself out of my comfort zone because I knew it would be the only way to see progress.

I didn't realize it then, but sitting in this room alone was, hands down, the hardest thing I had ever done. The amount of fear I felt, and *feeling* it show up in my body from my heart pounding, sweating, tingles all over my body, adrenaline pumping, and feeling dizzy, left me wanting to rate myself higher than a ten if I could have. It was insane to experience what my body did without being able to control it whatsoever. And as uncomfortable as it is for me to admit, I know it was one of the bravest things I've ever done. I would be completely exhausted afterward…my body reacted like it just did the most intense workout ever and all I did was sit in a chair for 20 minutes! It was truly physically, emotionally, and mentally exhausting. I wish I could tell you this came from some deep awareness of a bigger picture, but truthfully, I did it because I was desperate to feel normal and happy again.

In the beginning, I didn't know if I would ever get better. We lived through what many people and newspapers have called "Your worst nightmare." Little did I know that this event would be the catalyst for me to not just heal from this event but to heal from things I had no idea were ultimately holding me back from embracing who I authentically am and all that I seek to be. I didn't purposely choose this path, but as I took steps to heal, I now see how it has been part of my unique life journey, as it has brought people and experiences into my life that I wouldn't trade the world for. The truth is, I wouldn't be writing this book with the hope of helping others if I hadn't experienced it.

I'm far from an expert, and I don't claim to have it all figured out. What I share here comes from an experience I've *lived* through and what I've *learned* afterward. One thing I do know for certain is that I never could have done this alone. Like I said earlier, Kyle was right there with me that night. I hate that he had to go through it, too, but I also recognize that it's a gift we were able to face it together. No one else in this world can truly understand what we saw, what we experienced, and what we fought against that night. I wouldn't be here without him and I suppose he wouldn't be here without me—as cheesy as that sounds.

Thinking back to ninth grade, maybe I had a sense of what was to come when I wrote his name in my binder, surrounded by a big heart...

2

BY YOUR SIDE

Not everyone loves their high school years, but for me, they were some of the best. Middle school was awkward, filled with trying to fit in and navigate the emotional rollercoaster of pre-teen life. High school felt like stepping into a new world, a mix of nerves and excitement. I loved the energy, the upperclassmen who intimidated me yet made me feel cool by proximity, and, of course, the excitement of football games, pep assemblies, and the possibility of new crushes.

My twin sister and I weren't like the other inseparable twins. We were as different as could be, and even in the womb, my mom swore we occupied separate worlds—Jessie, the chatty and bold one, while I quietly kept to myself. In high school, I was the people-pleaser, the rule follower, the one who strived to excel academically and fade into the background so as not to add to my parents' stress. They ran a small business, working long hours, and while they were amazing parents, their focus was on trying to not let the business fall apart. Looking back, I realize I frequently felt lonely during those years. Maybe that's why I so badly wanted a boyfriend—someone who made me feel seen and someone who made me feel special.

On one of those ordinary high school days, I saw *him*. Walking in the opposite direction, talking to a friend, glowing like a spotlight in a crowded hall. His smile was the first thing I noticed—big, genuine, full of joy. The kind that radiated warmth and pulled you in, pulled everybody in. He had bright blue eyes, tan skin, and bleach-blonde spiked hair straight out of an early 2000s boy band, complete with a puka shell necklace. He was effortlessly cool. And I was immediately all in.

One day, as we passed each other in the hall again, I heard his friend say, "See you at practice, Kyle!" And just like that, I had a name to match the face. My first high school crush had officially begun. *Lucky you, Kyle.*

I would see him in the halls, always laughing, always surrounded by people who had fun being around him. He was a junior and a star athlete—starting on the wrestling team at 153 pounds and a standout soccer player. I daydreamed about catching his attention, doodling his name in my binder with a big heart around it like a true teenage girl. But then reality hit.

Every day, on my way to grab my clarinet before heading home, I would see Kyle standing at the bottom of the staircase—holding hands with a pretty cheerleader in her uniform, him in his wrestling letterman jacket. They were the perfect cliché. My stomach would sink every time. I tried to hide my clarinet, worried he'd think I was a nerd. And in the most embarrassing of teen girl moves, I even wore the same sweater I once saw her in, hoping, ridiculously, that if he liked her in hers, maybe he'd like me in *mine*.

Years later, when I finally asked Kyle if he remembered me from high school, he said, "I remember you from the assembly when you were pretending to be Christina Aguilera...you were wearing tight white pants." Out of all things, that's what stuck. Typical.

For the rest of high school, I stayed single. It wasn't that I didn't want to date—I was just selective. Or maybe naive. Maybe both. I wasn't interested in drinking or experimenting like many of my peers, and I was completely clueless when it came to relationships. What I do know is that I was willing to wait for the right guy.

Senior year arrived, and to my surprise, I was elected as one of the homecoming princesses. I wouldn't say I was necessarily in the "popular" group of girls, but I was friends with girls in all different groups. When it was announced, I had to step away from the band and sit with the other homecoming princesses and princes elected onto the homecoming court for a chance to be King and Queen. At least now, as a senior, I had no shame about being in the band and was actually proud of the fact that I felt like I bridged this gap between what may be classically defined as "nerdy" and now being on the homecoming court which I always thought was only for the "popular" kids. Our Senior class of 2004 was pretty special as we all seemed to get along and be more of one big group versus the typical cliques.

Part of being on Homecoming court was that the whole school voted on who the King and Queen would be at this assembly. Once they called our name to be on the court, all ten of us (five girls and five guys) had to go to the front of the gym, and a teacher would ask us a question or act out something to help the rest of the school vote on who the King and Queen would be.

Perfectly enough, I was asked by a teacher to act out with our school mascot, a Wildcat, what I would do if my homecoming date went in for a kiss, which was perfectly awkward because here I was, the only one who never had a boyfriend and literally had NO idea what the heck I would do. I was freaking out, but you have to act so fast that I did the only thing I could think.

As our mascot pretended to move in for a kiss, I stood there, put my hands up, waved my hands back and forth to block him, and said, "I can't do this. I can't do this."

Everyone laughed, and I laughed because my unintentional rejection of the mascot came across as well-played and entertaining. Maybe it was because everyone could relate, maybe it was because it made the crowd laugh, or maybe it was something else, but I was voted the Homecoming Queen.

During my senior year, while hanging with friends at youth group, I opened up to my youth pastor about being frustrated that I still didn't have a boyfriend. And then he said something I least expected. In complete seriousness, he looked at me and said, "You know, Tennyson, God does make some people stay single their whole life."

My heart sank. And I wanted to punch him in the face. As someone who deeply desired to be in a relationship, it made absolutely no sense. Maybe he was trying to make me feel better, but it did the complete opposite. His comment sunk deep and caught me completely off guard, making me really second-guess if I was really made to be single. *God, please not let that be me,* I begged. I was seventeen, for crying out loud. I decided his advice was crap, and chose to have hope, even though his opinion stuck with me.

Then, out of nowhere, two months before high school graduation, he walked into my youth group. *Kyle. Freaking. Jacobson.* The same smile, the same energy. But now, he was here. And not just visiting—he had joined as a volunteer. I couldn't believe it.

We started playing tennis together through youth group meetups, then just the two of us. We talked for hours on the phone about everything and nothing at all. It was effortless. One night, he casually asked, "Hey, I was wondering if you'd want to grab dinner and a movie sometime?" My heart nearly stopped. Had I just been asked out on a date? Had my years-long crush actually materialized into something real? After all four years of never dating a single guy as I waited for the "right one", now the guy whose name I wrote in my freshman year binder is actually asking me out on a date. Holy. Crap.

Our first date led to many more. Kyle would show up at the Taco Time drive-thru where I worked, always making an effort to see me. Sometimes, he'd run ten miles from his house to mine as his prep for a marathon, just to say "hi." He'd stop by Starbucks and bring me my favorite drink at the time, a White Chocolate Mocha. And every night, he'd call, and we'd somehow talk for hours.

Then, one night, he said it. "Tenny, I love you. This was so unexpected. But if I am honest, I see myself marrying you."

And just like that, everything I had imagined four years ago—staring at that boy in the hallway—was coming true. But there was a catch. When I got into the college I had dreamed of, four hours away, Kyle told me he didn't want to do a long-distance relationship. My heart sank. Wasn't this the same guy who told me he could see us getting married?

Initially, I was pissed, but after some thought, I chose the college closer to home, following what I knew in my heart to be right. We made it work. Every weekend, we made the drive to see each other. Through college demands, my work at a fine dining restaurant at a luxury resort called Suncadia, and Kyle becoming a firefighter, we stuck together.

My initial goal in earning a nutrition degree was to help women with eating disorders—something I had firsthand experience with. But after taking a specialized class, I realized I didn't have the gift for that work. My passion was nutrition, but this was much more complex.

My struggle began two years into college when I dropped to ninety-four pounds—dangerously low for my 5'7" frame. It all started as a way to improve my tennis game and spiraled into obsessive control. I hadn't realized how bad it had gotten until my body started shutting down—I lost my period, my digestion failed, and laxatives became a crutch. A visit to a GI doctor was a wake-up call; the shock on her face mirrored my own disbelief and I had no idea how to fix it. The nutritionist's meal plan felt physically impossible, leaving me in tears. I wanted to get better but was overwhelmed at how to find a way to overcome it. But the turning point came at a firefighter BBQ, where Kyle's colleagues and wives quietly voiced their concern to him. I was embarrassed that I was the subject of concern. Their respect meant so much to me, and their worry was the final wake-up call I needed.

Recovery was slow, but I began eating more and regaining weight. I realized eating disorders stem from a need for control, but I hadn't yet understood why I craved it so desperately. Around this time, Kyle introduced me to CrossFit. Watching strong, athletic women inspired me—I wanted to be powerful, not just thin. My competitive drive pushed me to improve, and before long, I was back to 125 pounds, not just healthy but thriving.

And then, five years after I fell in love with my crush, Kyle proposed. When people questioned our young engagement, I smiled and said, "If you met him, you'd understand." On July 18, 2009, we got married. Our first dance was to "By Your Side" by Sade. And, in true Kyle fashion, he farted during our dance. That moment—me laughing, him laughing, the world disappearing around us—that was us. As newlyweds, we planned to wait five years before starting a family. We wanted to build something for ourselves first. I continued serving at fine dining restaurants while struggling to figure out a career in nutrition that excited me. Until Kyle, ever the entrepreneur, had the idea to open a CrossFit gym, something we could do together as he maintained his firefighter position.

Our gym became a second home to so many, a place where people pushed limits and found unexpected friendships. We built a community, not just a business. The friendships and bonds we formed there shaped us in ways we never imagined. Kyle's only request for our website? That "Eye of the Tiger" would automatically play when someone visited us online. It was perfectly ridiculous and perfectly us.

I found myself helping to run the gym while unexpectedly stepping into motherhood sooner than planned—our lives shifted the moment we discovered I was pregnant. Lyla was born, changing everything. I was terrified but in awe of her. She was sweet, happy, and easygoing. She fit seamlessly into our world, coming to the gym with me, nestled in her car seat as I worked out and even sometimes when I coached. Gym members called her "itty bitty Lyla" and always wanted to hold her. It was the perfect balance of being home with a new baby while still being able to do my duties working at the gym. I coached, signed up new members, managed people's accounts, helped with programming and nutrition coaching, organized social events and handled the marketing on our social media page. At the same time, we were building a house on Kyle's parents' property. To save money, we had moved in with my mom—back into my childhood home. It was bittersweet. That house held so many memories—the music room filled with candlelight, the jazz albums playing late into the night, holiday family get-togethers often with dance parties, my sister and I playing ABC store or dialing onto AOL in our "kid wing." My parents' dream home, which they had worked hard for so many years to build, was a reality. But things were different in this house now; my parents were newly separated, and the house held sadness, too.

My parents designed the one-story home with the center of the home as the music room. My dad's one inheritance from his late parents was a baby grand Steinway piano, which sat right in the middle of the music room. I loved the music room so much. It was the heart of the home. The music room split both sides of the home. One side had the bedrooms and kids' rooms, and the kitchen, dining, and family room were on the other. There was a large fireplace made of river rock hand-picked from our local river. It reached the top of the sixteen-foot ceiling. My mom covered the mantel with large candles of all different shapes and sizes—there must have been at least twenty of them. When they designed the music room, they made eight custom wingback chairs with patterns of musical instruments and musical notes. My dad went all out on the speaker system, purchasing five-foot speakers for each side of the room and bass speakers in the back of the room. We would turn out the lights, light the candles, and turn the music up. Loud. We listened to all types of music by Linda Ronstadt, Diana Krall, Nat King Cole, and Dave Brubeck. While my parents loved various kinds of music, their favorite was classical jazz. They had a CD collection of probably 200 or more, including Sade, my favorite of the collection. There was something about her soulful, beautiful voice combined with the candlelight that was just perfection. Because my parents invested a lot into the music room, it meant our living room would have old patio furniture for a while until we could afford the couch, and not one of us complained.

One of the things I loved about this house design was that they had designed a "kid wing" for my sister and me. We felt grown up having our little section of the house just for us. There was a door off the main hallway with four rooms… our two bedrooms, a playroom and a study room. We'd close the door to our kid wing and often be in our own little world. In my younger years, that would be playing store or spending countless hours playing board games like Candyland or, my favorite, DreamPhone with our friends. We'd plop mattresses on the floor in the playroom and watch all the classic movies of the 90s like Sixteen Candles, My Girl, Now and Then, Titanic, The Wedding Singer, My Best Friend's Wedding…the list goes on. We'd create dances and little skits in the playroom. As different as Jessie and I were and as challenging as it was to relate to each other sometimes, these were the moments when we did have fun together.

Kyle and I moved what little furniture we had from our little 1100-square-foot home into the house, making it feel like a storage facility at times. We put our huge, brown, microfiber L-shaped couch in the music room, which changed the vibe from the perfectly laid-out plan my parents had designed the room for. We took over the kid's wing, which was filled with "stuff"—boxes, bins, clothes, tools, and TVs, far from the cozy kid's room where we played Candyland and watched movies.

My mom was also trying to organize the home and sometimes, with her "organization bins," it felt a bit overwhelming. She'd use bins to store towels, photos, scrapbooking materials, CDs, and glassware.....it led to bins being stacked up all over the home. The vibe was weird—two families, each with all their stuff, trying to cohabitate in one space.

We turned my old bedroom into the nursery, and Kyle and I moved into my sister's old bedroom. Jessie's room had always been so dark as the light fixture never worked. Our only lamp was a rinky-dink light that barely put off any light. There was no dresser as Jessie had always used a bookshelf to store her clothes, so since we temporarily moved into the house, that became our "dresser." I remember lying in bed and thinking, *Maybe it's no wonder my sister went through more challenging phases when we were young.* She was always trying to figure out her own style. We watched her style over the years as a skater, punk, and then her gothic period. One year, when we visited family in Florida, I remember my sister being adamant that she did not want to expose herself to the sun. It wasn't from a place of skin protection, but rather maintaining her look of pale skin against dyed black hair.

After moving in, I felt a bit of the grunge vibe while staying in that room; however, I also remembered the raves our family would do in her room for holiday get-togethers, which was done to support the things Jessie was into. I can't say I didn't hate them, as we'd all have so much fun when we turned out the lights, put up a strobe light, and recruited many of our cousins to dance together as we blasted whatever music she was into.

My old room felt bright, which was a better fit for the nursery. We furnished it with a used white crib and a white changing table off Craigslist that helped keep the space bright. I found an inexpensive white floral rug and decorated the corners of the ceiling with the pink paper flowers you would find at a party store to help decorate for a party. I had very little design expertise at twenty-five years old and a very low budget, so the party decorations seemed to be the perfect idea. The one piece of furniture I begged Kyle to splurge on was a nursery glider. I desperately wanted something comfortable to sit in, knowing that frequently being up in the middle of the night would be a reality for quite some time, but I also wanted one piece of "new" in the room. I found this beautiful, off-white, plush glider that felt like I was sitting in a cloud.

Living with my mom wasn't always the easiest. First off, it's hard to "move back home." I was a grown adult and wanted to figure out things on my own. But on top of that, our sometimes rocky relationship had more challenges than I hoped for. On the flip side, though, there were a lot of times when my mom was incredibly helpful. I know she wanted nothing more in this world than to take care of the three of us. She would offer to make us dinner, do our laundry and watch Lyla. There were even times when she asked me if there was anything I could teach her so she could help with anything related to the CrossFit business.

To this day, my mom would give you the shoes off her feet if you needed them. She has one of the most generous hearts of anyone I know. My mom is the person who, if I had asked her to stay awake all night singing to Lyla, she sure would have tried. She's not a singer, but she would find classical music on her iPad and play it for Lyla as she slept in her bassinet. Classical–because, supposedly, it helped develop the baby's brain—every choice my mom made was very intentional.

I remember when, just two and a half months after Lyla was born, we attended our annual Cascade CrossFit Christmas party. This had been a tradition for the previous three years, and I was excited that I could now partake in some festive adult beverages and let loose a little bit after being pregnant. Our CrossFit Christmas parties became what our clients and I looked forward to every year and it was a place I felt comfortable to have fun. After all, our people joined because we blasted "Eye of the Tiger" on our website. We were a group that worked hard in the gym but didn't take ourselves too seriously. We appreciated the times when we could get together outside the gym and have fun.

I definitely seized the moment. Three—maybe four drinks, plus someone's brilliant idea of a fireball shot, were all offered to me, and I gladly accepted. When you haven't consumed alcohol in almost a year, it certainly lands differently than when you're used to it. While Kyle was responsible because he had a CrossFit competition the next day, I let go, getting caught up in the fun of all my favorite people around me. And I paid for it. To this day, Fireball always sounds like the worst decision ever.

While Kyle left around 6 am the next morning to head to his competition, I woke up around 9 am, next to Lyla, who was also just waking up. Feeling an immediate pounding in my head and like I might actually be dying, I had an instant wave of guilt rush over me. *Good God. I'm the worst mom in the world.* I felt like a pile of crap. It was going to be an incredibly long day of figuring out how to get through this hangover and take care of a two-month-old baby.

Oh God. I felt my stomach churn, and I knew I was about to be sick—I needed to get to the bathroom fast. Lyla was wide awake, and I couldn't leave her alone in her bassinet, so I scooped her up and sprinted to the bathroom. Desperate, I placed her in the mesh bath seat—the one we usually kept outside the tub—conveniently stored next to the toilet. And so, poor Lyla had the unfortunate front-row seat to her mom's brutal payback from a little too much fun.

As Lyla lay in the seat, I immediately hunched over the toilet and started throwing up. I can count on one hand the number of times alcohol has made me sick—it's rare. *But this? This was a disaster.* Throwing up is, quite literally, the worst. And as I emptied every ounce of fun from the night before, a new wave of guilt hit me.

When I finally caught my breath, I glanced at Lyla—only to find her laughing. Every time I heaved, she let out the biggest, most joyous belly laughs, as if I were putting on a comedy show just for her. I couldn't believe it. *This has got to be a joke.* Here I was, my daughter's first witness to the aftermath of a night out, and she thought it was hilarious. Was I entertaining her? Traumatizing her? Who knew? But one thing was clear—I had officially entered a full-blown shame spiral.

I eventually felt a small wave of relief, scooped up Lyla, and made my way back to my bedroom, apologizing the entire time.

"I am so sorry, sweetie. I'm so sorry you had to see that. I'm so sorry I'm sick today. Oh, Lyla, sweet girl, I'm so, so sorry." I held her tiny body close to my chest, hoping she could somehow feel how much I meant it.

Laying her gently on the bed, I collapsed beside her, staring at her sweet, smiling face. *Oh my God, how in the world am I going to take care of you all day?*

As if on cue, my mom emerged from her bedroom and walked into mine. Taking one look at me—pale, exhausted, and clearly wrecked—she offered a knowing smile and said, "Good morning! Tennyson, are you okay?"

"Oh my gosh, Mom. I threw up, and I feel *awful*," I groaned, my voice weak. Tears welled up in my eyes as I lay there, stomach twisted in knots, drowning in exhaustion and shame.

Then, with the gentleness only a mother can offer, she said, "Tennyson, I would absolutely love to have Lyla to myself today. Would it help if I took her for a while so I could spend some time with her?"

She might actually be an angel.

Relief washed over me. *Are you serious? Oh my gosh.* I could've cried from gratitude. "Thank you so much. Yes, please. That would help so much. Thank you, Mom."

It was hard for me to appreciate her so much and then find ourselves in another spiral. I was beyond grateful for her support. But, conversations about the past—about my dad, their marriage, the struggles with their business—seemed to surface every day, pulling me into a history that wasn't mine to hold. I wanted to ease the weight for both of them, to be the bridge between their pain, but the truth was, I wasn't meant to carry it. I was exhausted from being the dumping ground for all her pain for the past decade.

But Kyle, as always, was my constant. He easily made himself at home in all of this, which made me appreciate how easygoing and laid-back he was. He always knew what to say and how to get me calm when emotions were high with me and my mom. We'd walk our neighborhood with Lyla in a stroller and our two Yorkies, Lola and Lily, trailing alongside, talking about the future and planning our next steps. Even though the weight of my family's past sat heavy, I knew—deep within—that Kyle and I were building from all of the good we had grown up with but then also something different. We wanted to keep the best parts of our upbringings and add all the good things we wanted for our family now.

Our conversations revolved a lot around the building of the house and needing to make small but critical decisions about certain things. We were just about to break ground. We'd walk and talk and play peek-a-boo with Lyla while Lola and Lily equally loved their walks outside. As we made our way through and around the neighborhood, I couldn't help but think back to my memories of walking around that same neighborhood when I was a kid. My sister and I, with our friends, would spend our hours every day making friendship bracelets, which we would then organize in tackle boxes and go door-to-door selling them for five cents, ten cents, or if it was really a good one, twenty-five cents. I guess I had a little entrepreneurial spirit back then, but I loved the accomplishment of working on something that someone would buy. I smile, thinking about the innocent ten-year-old version of myself walking around doing this while my sweet neighbors graciously supported our small business. While we took these walks, the one thing that always came up was that we were excited that our future house would be in a neighborhood very similar to this one—safe and surrounded by wonderful neighbors.

Needing a break from the layers of grief, sadness, and pain that consistently bubbled up living with my mom, we decided a getaway to the sunny and blue skies of Crescent Bar, Washington, would be a much-needed reprieve. I looked forward to getting away for the weekend. The plan was to hang out with Kyle's parents, come back early on Sunday—my first Mother's Day—and spend time with my mom. After that, Kyle, Lyla, and I would head out to dinner.

The getaway was perfect in every way. Kyle's parents owned a condo there and it was about a two-hour drive from our home. We'd visit it frequently as it was a short drive to escape the cloudy and rainy western side of WA versus the dry, sunny, and warmer eastern side of WA. Our trip was exactly what we needed, especially in the month of May. In fact, all Western Washingtonians, by the month of March, are desperate to see some sunshine and have a break from the constant rain and clouds that inevitably make Washington so beautiful. By Sunday, we had had tons of pool time and many golf cart rides with Lyla in her car seat blasting music, and we felt relaxed and refreshed. There is something about sunshine and feeling the temperature hit above seventy that fills your soul.

With Lyla only seven months old, I felt lucky to have in-laws who were so supportive. Mary was always in the kitchen cooking up healthy meals, and she never missed a chance to offer up childcare—basically nudging us onto a date night so they could focus all their attention on their only granddaughter.

We headed home early Sunday morning since Kyle had to

get back to CrossFit practice for an upcoming competition. As we pulled away, Mary called out, "Drive safe, you guys. Tenny, enjoy your first-ever Mother's Day dinner out tonight!"

Driving home from Crescent Bar never loses its magic. The view is unreal and I can't help but fall into this trance-like state, imagining my dreams and goals or sorting through whatever is on my mind. Crescent Bar sits right against these massive cliffs by the wide, winding Columbia River. On the way home, you pass by those breathtaking cliffs, the sparkling river, and after passing countless farms and rolling hills, the Cascade Mountains come into view. Huge lakes, endless evergreen forests, even a winter ski resort—all pass by like scenes from a movie. There are little mountain streams that fall like mini waterfalls and a large bridge built so animals can cross through their territory and over the freeway safely. Living here is pretty spectacular, and every time we make this drive, it reminds me just how lucky we are.

As we drove home, we couldn't stop laughing about watching Lyla giggle in her floaty. She was just so darn cute in her little sun hat, and those chunky legs peeking out made it even cuter. We kept talking about how lucky we were to have that spot to hang out for free, anytime we wanted. The community was full of friendly faces. The kind way that people looked at Lyla made it feel so welcoming. It was such a great weekend of laughs, relaxation, and much-needed sunshine, literally and figuratively.

As Kyle pulled my car down our long driveway, I couldn't help but take in the property I grew up in. It made me a little sad. Things had changed. The once nicely manicured lawn was no longer because my dad was gone and the funds to care for the house were different than in the past. It didn't look like it did back in the day.

What I did love about this home was that it was tucked at the end of the road with three other properties, our home sat on a one-acre lot—just like the others—all built with the same vision: to face the mountain and take advantage of the incredible view. Across from us, an old farm stretched out, where horses grazed lazily or galloped through the fields, adding to the peaceful charm of the place. Each property had a long driveway leading to the back, where the houses were set, leaving massive front yards open to the beautiful landscape. Tall fir and maple trees lined the driveways, giving each home a sense of privacy, making it feel like our own little retreat. My dad, the golf lover that he was, had turned our front yard into his personal practice course, complete with a golf hole, a flag, a putting green, and even a sand trap—so he could tee off right from our porch. Ours was the kind of neighborhood where you never saw a stranger, but you didn't see much of anyone either. Everyone had their own space, tucked away on their big lots, enjoying the quiet, just as it was meant to be.

My parents had specifically selected this property to build their dream home, passing on several other properties once they had found this one. Years went into the A-frame design so that it would perfectly respect the environment while taking full advantage of the incredible mountain view. The inside had an open-concept living space that felt warm but also expansive. The kitchen had a blend of modern and rustic elements. So much work and love had gone into this place. Even though my parents were going through a challenging time and living here today was definitely different from how I felt during my childhood, the home was still a reminder of happier times and a lot of love. As I think back to us unloading our luggage that day, it's wild to think that was the last day we would ever return. Life has a way of throwing you the unexpected when you least expect it. Little did I know that weekend would be the last bit of normalcy before everything changed in our lives.

3

IN THE LIGHT OF DAY

Once we got inside, I was looking forward to some quiet time with Lyla and a little time with my mom. Holidays have a way of shifting the energy, making everything feel a little more meaningful. It was like a reset—an unspoken agreement to put aside any stress or frustrations and just be present. My mom especially wanted this day to feel special for me since it was my first Mother's Day. And even though I knew money was tight for her, she somehow always found a way to go above and beyond for moments like this—birthdays, Christmas, any day that mattered. She's the kind of person who truly lives by "going the extra mile," not just in words but in the way she shows up for the people she loves.

When we returned around 12:30 pm, Kyle quickly packed up and was back out the door in ten minutes and headed to the gym to practice for the regional CrossFit competition. Our gym had a group of athletes, three men and three women, who qualified for Regionals and Kyle was the team captain. Every year since our gym opened in late 2009, our team has been close to qualifying for the CrossFit Games—an opportunity I hear less than 3% of CrossFit gyms qualify for. And this year, it felt like it was finally our year to qualify after barely missing in the past several years. Our Cascade CrossFit community was always so pumped for this, as it was such an exciting time of year and certainly no small feat. Our gym knew how to have a lot of fun, but we also had many extremely talented athletes.

Like many of us, I didn't think much about my spouse leaving—especially not for something as routine as a workout. Between his shift at the fire station, working overtime, and coaching and operating the gym, Kyle was always in and out of the house.

Unfortunately, the time I had hoped would go smoothly with my mom—where we could set everything aside, even just for the day—didn't go that way. Looking back, it's obvious that the weight of her trauma, both big and small, wasn't something she could just push down or ignore. With no real outlet—no close friends, no family to lean on, no therapist to help her unpack it—I became the place where it all landed. While the conversation turned south, as it had many times, I finally tried to set a boundary—something I had tried before but always struggled to do. But my mom begged to have her perspective understood as I begged to not talk about the past. Tensions flared, emotions boiled over, and she broke down just like many times before. She took off to her room, sobbing, and a few minutes later, I heard the shower turn on. I hoped that would help her reset her emotions and that we could come to an understanding later. But God, it hurt. I hated that this often happened, and that this was my relationship with my mother. I was always left thinking: *How could two well-meaning, good-intentioned people who love each other end up like this over and over again?*

Frustrated, heartbroken, and completely drained from yet another painful moment with my mom, I needed to shift my focus—anything to keep from spiraling. I set Lyla down on a blanket, surrounded her with toys, and threw myself into cleaning. My mind was a wreck, so at the very least, I needed my space to feel calm. I picked up her toys, wiped down the dining room table, and started unpacking from the weekend, hoping that if I could create a little bit of order around me, I'd feel a little less chaotic inside.

As I was straightening up, through my peripheral vision, I caught an image of someone approaching our glass front doors, which faced the back of the house. While my initial reaction was to head toward the front door to greet the visitor, I quickly realized this was odd. Within just two steps toward the door, my brain had already processed several small details that registered something was seriously off. It's wild how fast your mind processes things. I thought, *This is weird. People never just drop by our house. Especially on a Sunday. Especially on a Mother's Day.* As I took one more step toward the front door to open the door, I realized this was not just weird. This someone was a man and he immediately felt dangerous to me.

The man approaching my door was a complete stranger. He was moving fast—too fast—and I could tell he had no intention of stopping to knock. Before I could react, he burst the door open and came straight for me.

Holy. Shit. I didn't even have time to think, let alone process what was happening.

My brain knew the whole fight, flight or freeze thing, but at that moment, my body had only one instinct—run to Lyla. She was still sitting on the floor, just ten feet away from me… and twenty feet away from him. He was heading straight for me. Everything about him was terrifying—not just his size but his presence. His energy was off, something dark and dangerous. And his physicality sure as hell didn't help. He loomed over my 5'7", 125-pound frame like a giant, easily over six feet tall, probably 215 pounds, built like a man who did hard labor every day—the kind of strength you could see just by looking at his hands. His clothes were filthy—his shirt stained, his brown hair matted under a dirty trucker hat, his pale faded jean shorts stiff with grime. But the worst part? His black eyes. He didn't blink. He didn't hesitate. He just locked onto me and took huge, deliberate steps forward, closing the space between us in seconds.

I was just two steps from Lyla. Two steps. But he got to me first.

Before I could reach her, I felt a violent yank on my ponytail. His right hand ripped my head back, dragging me into him, his body pressing hard against mine. In an instant, he had me pinned against the back of the couch, his chest crushing into me as he shoved me forward.

Then came his left hand—dirty, massive, rough, and calloused—secured over my mouth, covering half my face in his grip. He kept me locked against him, his hold on my ponytail tightened as he bent me over the couch, his weight bearing down, trapping me in. Every muscle in my body tried to fight, but he was too strong. He pulled my head back, forcing my face next to his. That's when I smelled it. It wasn't just body odor. It was something worse—filth, decay, something rotten and unavoidable. A thick, suffocating stench filled the air around him like a cloud of contamination. Breathing it in made me sick to my stomach. I had never smelled anything like it in my life. It was so heavy, so disgusting, that it made me feel like it was seeping into my skin as he used his body to pin me down.

This had always been my greatest fear—a feeling I know many women share. In the past, I would think of how I might respond if I found myself in a situation where someone was trying to hurt or take advantage of me. I knew I was small, but given that I owned a gym and tried my best to keep up with the women who were way stronger than me, I was fairly strong for my size. And from a one-off time of trying to pin Kyle—a wrestling coach at our high school—I learned to get scrappy because he was way stronger than me. I thought that if I were ever in a situation like this, maybe, just maybe, I could find a way out. I figured I could bite or find areas to dig my fingers into sensitive spots—anything to get free. "Where there's a will, there's a way," my parents' voice echoed in my mind from childhood. But this man was different. He was big and strong—far stronger than me—and I quickly realized he had complete control. I kicked, tried to scream, and squirmed as best I could, but his position made it impossible to break free. I was terrified and, at that moment, felt completely at his mercy. It's odd to say this, but I felt humbled. The level of helplessness I felt at that moment was something I could have never imagined.

My heart pounded, and my mind raced. I immediately imagined him taking me and kidnapping me. *What would he do with me? Would I be away from my family forever? Would he rape or kill me? Will he make me take Lyla with us?* The fear was raw and real, and I had no idea what I would do to get out of this.

As he pulled me in close and kept his disgusting, dirty hand over my mouth, he firmly yet quietly said, "I won't hurt you. I just want your money."

It caught me off guard, but I felt the slightest sense of relief when I heard him say that. It felt like I was being given a small window of opportunity that would allow me to get out of this situation if I had money to give him. I never carry cash. But by some amazing coincidence, someone had paid me $41 for a hoodie at our gym just before we left for Crescent Bar, and I had that in my wallet. *Thank God.* I couldn't believe I had cash and maybe something that would give him an excuse to leave.

With his hand still over my mouth, I mumbled, "I have money. It's over there. In the diaper bag by the door."

He yanked me up from the couch as if I was completely at his mercy, his grip on my ponytail so tight it's like he treated it like a leash, controlling my every move. Dragging me toward the front door, he led me straight to where my diaper bag sat. By now, Lyla knew something was wrong. She had been just a couple feet away, watching it all unfold—seeing me scream, kick, and fight with everything I had. She wasn't crying, not yet, but she could sense something was seriously wrong. I couldn't see her face, but all I knew was that I was relieved to be moving away from her. He kept his grip tight—one hand still yanking on my ponytail, the other locked around my waist, holding me in place. I could feel his breath behind me as I fumbled desperately through my oversized diaper bag, my hands shaking as I sifted through swaddle blankets, bottles, formula, baby toys, diapers, extra onesies—every bit of baby gear I always carried. My wallet, the heaviest thing in the bag, had, of course, sunk to the very bottom. It felt like an eternity digging for it. *Why the hell did*

I load so much stuff into my diaper bag, I thought as I fumbled through the bag. When I finally found it, I braced myself, fully expecting him to rip it straight from my hands. It was a big wallet with a zipper wrapping all the way around, easy to grab and run. But he didn't. He just stood there. Waiting. Holding me. I unzipped it, pulled out the cash, and handed it to him, continually expecting him to rip it all out of my hands. And as terrified as I was, something about the whole thing felt off. *If money was what he wanted, why was he waiting for me to hand it over? Why not just take the entire wallet—credit cards and all? Or the whole damn diaper bag?*

Something wasn't right.

I handed him the money, and finally, he let go of me.

For a moment, we just stood there—three feet apart—locked in a stare as I waited to see what he was going to do. His eyes weren't just dark; they were black, like something out of a horror movie. Empty. Otherworldly. I had never seen anything like it before. It wasn't just unsettling—it was pure hatred steaming out of him. It was as if his stare alone was telling me, *I hate you.* What disturbed me the most—though I didn't understand it at that moment—was that there wasn't even a flicker of fear or hesitation in him. No panic. No confusion. Nothing human. He wasn't second-guessing his actions or worried about getting caught. He just stood there, radiating something I can only describe as pure evil.

Then, without warning, he wound up his massive hand and hit me across the left side of my face and jaw.

The force sent me crashing to the floor, my ankle twisting painfully as I landed on my side. My vision blurred for a second, and my skin burned where he had smacked me. It's strange how time can stretch and collapse all at once. From the moment he burst through the door to the second he vanished, it couldn't have been more than a few minutes. But in those moments—being pinned under him, suffocated by his disgusting stench, my mind racing with terrifying questions about what he was going to do to me—it felt like forever.

And then—it was over.

He turned away, walked straight out the front door, then—with eerie ease—hopped over the handrail of our patio and disappeared. Not in a hurry. Not panicked. No signs of adrenaline, no frantic escape like you'd expect from someone who had just stormed into a stranger's home, assaulted them and stolen from them. He simply walked away, calm as ever, vanishing completely out of sight.

And then, just like that, he was gone.

Everything that followed was pure chaos. I stumbled to my feet and ran for the front door, slamming it shut and fumbling with the lock. My hands were shaking so badly I could barely get the dang thing to work—it was one of those old, finicky locks that never clicks in on the first try. But I fought with it until I was sure it was bolted shut.

That's when I realized my ankle was actually hurt. A sharp, burning pain shot through my ankle the second I put weight on it. I hadn't even noticed in the moment, but now it was impossible to ignore.

"FUCK. FUCK. FUCK!" I screamed, the pain, shock, but mostly pure panic hitting all at once. It wasn't my usual vocabulary—but it was all I could yell after the terror of what had just happened.

Hearing me, my mom rushed out of the bathroom, still

wrapped in a towel, her face filled with fear. "Tennyson—Oh God, Tennyson! What happened?! Are you okay?! WHAT HAPPENED?" she sobbed, her voice as frantic as I felt.

And then there was Lyla. Poor, sweet Lyla. She had already started to cry, but now, hearing me scream and my mom panic, she was wailing, her tiny lungs working at full force. Through the chaos—through my mom crying, through Lyla screaming, through the absolute terror still pumping through me—I choked out the only thing I could manage: "SOMEBODY JUST BROKE IN!" And then we all just stood there—crying, shaking and completely stunned. I immediately called 911.

Dispatcher "911. What are you reporting?"

"Some guy just came into my house. He just walked right up to me and wanted money."

I talked and cried at the same time, my words coming out in broken, breathless gasps like I had just sprinted a 400-meter race. My heart was pounding so hard. I struggled to calm myself, console Lyla, explain everything to my mom, and dial the 911 dispatcher all at once. Through my sobs, I kept repeating, over and over, "Oh my God. I'm just so thankful he didn't hurt my baby."

Looking back, it's surreal to think about. Lyla was right there in the room with me. Yes, my mom had been in the house, too, but my seven-month-old baby was the only actual witness to what happened. That fact haunts me. Did he know she was there? Had he planned for that? Or was she a surprise? And if she hadn't been there—would things have gone differently?

I must have called Kyle before dialing 911 because while I was still on the line with the dispatcher, he was already on his way home with one of his best friends, the co-owner of the gym. My mind was scattered, barely processing what was happening as I held Lyla tightly, rocking her, whispering, "Oh my God. It's okay, honey. It's okay." But even as I tried to calm her, my body wouldn't stop moving. I paced between every door and window, checking, rechecking, triple-checking that everything was locked.

At one point, I wiped the tears and mascara from my face and felt it—the pain of where he had hit me. My fingers paused against my cheek as I flashed back to him staring at me and how much this complete stranger seemed to hate me.. *How could this have even happened? In my childhood home, of all places?*

I snapped back to the moment and urgently asked the dispatcher, "Are they coming soon? Where are they coming from? Should I go outside and get in my car?"

Dispatcher: *"Just lock your door."*

"My baby is in here!" (Lyla was still crying, her little body shaking in my arms.)

Dispatcher: "Just lock your door and stay inside, ma'am."

I was still crying, still gasping for breath when the next question came.

Dispatcher: "Did he smell like alcohol?"

"No."

Dispatcher: "What did he look like?"

I hesitated. My brain was still in survival mode, still focused on the fear that he might come back. It took me a second, and my voice was shaky, but I surprised myself with how much I noticed about the man, given the circumstances. In fragments, I finally answered: "Tall. White. Not long hair. Age…50-ish. Blue sweatshirt. Jeans. White sneakers."

Given that we lived just outside of town, while wonderful for views and privacy, it also meant it took people extra time to reach us, specifically the pizza deliverer. We had never previously had to call emergency responders, but it felt like it was an eternity as I frantically waited for someone to arrive. When the first police officer arrived, I went outside to wave to him, letting him know he was at the right house. He came partially down our long driveway, rolled down his window, and yelled out that he thought he may have seen someone running and said it might be the intruder. So I watched him back out and go look for him. Although that sounded relieving and somewhat encouraging, I didn't want him to leave. I desperately wanted someone there who felt like they could protect us. Frankly, someone with a gun. I nervously glanced around the property and immediately ran back into the house. After a few minutes, he came back with no findings and his return marked the beginning of the initial investigation.

Additional police officers quickly arrived. They asked if they should call medics to look at my injured ankle, but I begged them not to. It felt ridiculous to call an ambulance for what felt like a sprained ankle. I had heard all the stories of calls Kyle went on, where I was surprised people even called 911, and I didn't want to be that person. They kept nudging me to at least have the medics come, and I continued to try to tell them no, but they insisted. They must have been inside my brain because they finally told me, "It is smarter to have someone at least just look at it, and we suggest this all the time. I promise it's not a big deal." I finally gave in.

Shortly after the investigation started, Kyle's truck pulled into the driveway. No words can really describe it, but I'll give it a try. Seeing Kyle—the one person I never realized made me feel so safe—coming down our driveway was the most profound relief I've ever felt. He couldn't have gotten out of his truck faster than he had. At the same time, I jumped up and ran from our couch to the front door to get to him as fast as I could. And when we stood face to face, I saw something in his expression I had never seen before—something I'll never forget. For a moment, he stood still with his eyes wide and fixed on me. He had a look of deep concern but also deep gratitude. Today was a reality neither of us had ever imagined. It left us speechless.

Anyone who knows Kyle knows he's a strong guy, not just physically, but in his character and how he carries himself. He's kind, funny, confident and caring. He has this way of making people feel safe and comfortable, always stepping up to help in a way that makes it seem like no big deal. It's just who he is. Maybe that's why he's such a good firefighter—he's steady, always able to compartmentalize, never letting the weight of a situation rattle him. But more than anything, Kyle appreciates the simple things in life—family above everything else. What you see with him is what you get. No pretense, no ego. Just a great man with a pure heart. And that's exactly why so many people, myself included, love and respect him the way we do.

But at that moment, I saw something different in Kyle. His eyes—bloodshot, welled with tears—told me everything before he even said a word. As he walked toward me, arms open, I saw it all: the relief and gratitude that I was okay, the love so deep it didn't need words, and the relief from the fear of what could have been. Kyle has never been an overly expressive, "share-your-feelings" kind of guy, but that *look* on his face said everything.

As terrifying as that afternoon was, it's still this moment I go back to the most. It was a gift. A strange, sharp moment of clarity—one of those once-in-a-lifetime shifts where everything you take for granted suddenly becomes crystal clear. In the span of a few hours, we had gone from living our normal, happy life to staring at the reality of how fragile it all was. How lucky we were that we hadn't lost each other. It's one thing to see these kinds of attacks in movies or on the news, but when it happens to you, in your own home, in your own life—it shakes you awake. It makes you feel gratitude in a way you never have before. I ran straight into his arms, and he grabbed me tight. We've always been huggers, but *not* like this. Not like we were afraid to let go. But this time? This hug was different. I felt it instantly—his need to hold on, to ground himself—almost feeling like he was doing it to make sure I was really there. And for the first time since it all happened, I felt safe. I felt protected. And I felt, more than anything, like he never wanted to let go and neither did I.

Our friend and fellow gym co-owner had a completely different expression. His wide eyes said exactly what everyone else was thinking: *What the hell just happened?*

It was surreal because this kind of thing just didn't happen—not in our town, not in our neighborhood. I didn't know the man who had just barged into my home and attacked me. I had never seen him before in my life. Nothing about this made sense.

By early afternoon, with the area secured and statements being taken, investigators combed through every piece of evidence they could find. The only tangible evidence being the intruder's filthy brown trucker hat had fallen off when he bent me over the couch, and the police bagged it as evidence. They even brought out a K-9 unit, explaining how violent offenders release pheromones—adrenaline, sweat, fear—that dogs can track. They found some bent blades of grass and only a few footprints behind our house. No clear trail. No answers. The man had disappeared. But as I answered their questions, my mind kept circling back to one thing: how intense yet calm he had been. He had walked in, taken control, and left—no urgency, no panic. The only emotion he had shown was that cold, dead look of hatred when he stared at me. That blackness in his eyes…it gives me chills just thinking about it. I prayed the dogs would pick up his scent, but something deep inside me figured they wouldn't. Even with a small army of emergency responders swarming the property and Kyle now home, I felt uneasy, even though I wasn't alone. There's something about being violated in your own home—your safe place—that shatters you. It wasn't just that he had overpowered me. It was him. There was something deeply, deeply disturbing about him that I couldn't get out of my head.

But then there was something else. A thought stuck in the back of my mind—clear, steady and constant. It wasn't fear. It wasn't panic. It wasn't paranoia. It was just a quiet, neutral knowing. *He's coming back.* I couldn't get it out of my head and it took everything in me to say it out loud. I had no proof, no logic to back it up, but the feeling was undeniable. *He's coming back.*

The officers were professional, kind, and patient. They listened carefully, reassured me, and followed protocol exactly as they should have. So when I kept voicing my fear, "What if he comes back?" "I think he's coming back." They did their best to comfort me with the most logical response they could: "We've never seen that happen before. They never come back."

One officer, a seasoned cop, looked me straight in the eye and said, "In thirty years of experience, I have never seen anyone ever return after doing something like this." Another added, "Of course, we don't have a crystal ball, but the likelihood of that happening is almost impossible."

I wanted to believe them. I really did. Their logic made sense. They weren't dismissing me—they were speaking from decades of experience. They were simply trying to reassure me and ease my fear with statistics and probabilities. But every time they told me it wouldn't happen, I thought: *They've never seen it happen. But that doesn't mean it won't.*

The investigators suggested the intruder may have been homeless, one of the few people living in the large woods behind our house, drawn to the area because of nearby churches offering hot meals. That was a surprise to me—I had no idea there were people potentially living in the woods behind our home. And while it was the only theory that made even partial sense, it still didn't fit. I couldn't help the feeling that something deeper was at play—that I was missing a piece of the puzzle. My gut was screaming at me, sending signals I didn't know how to read yet. I wasn't practiced at listening to my instincts, so I fumbled through it, trying to make sense of the mess. The whole thing felt off. The randomness. The way he waited instead of grabbing my wallet. That black, soulless stare. The way he hit me, even though I had already given him what he wanted.

Always considering others, Kyle offered his friend his truck so he could head home since the investigation had gone on for hours. By the time the last officer wrapped up their report and wished us a good night, it was 5:00 pm I stood there in a daze, holding Lyla, exhausted and emotionally drained, still trying to process.

My first Mother's Day had turned out quite differently than

I could have ever imagined. And worse, I was left with nothing but questions and a bad feeling. And not a single answer.

4

TABLE OF THREE

Given the day's events, I couldn't wait to get out of the house. I no longer felt safe in what should have been our safe place. I didn't want to even look or touch the couch he had bent me over. The glass front door scared the heck out of me, as well as every single unlit room in the house. I had no idea how in the world I would sleep after all that had happened. My mom had left during the investigation to spend some time with her mom for Mother's Day. So, when Kyle asked me if I was still up for going out for dinner, I couldn't get dressed and get out of there any faster. I quickly fixed my messed-up makeup, threw my clothes in the wash (even though I preferred to burn them), changed, and got Lyla ready. I was still freaking out inside and just tried to keep telling myself, *Come on, keep it together, Tenny.* At the very least, I hoped we could go out and enjoy the Mother's Day dinner plans Kyle had made.

As we were seated, it was strange to sit in a room full

of people who were so happy and so comfortable. Everyone laughed and smiled while celebrating the special mom at their table. I was such a mix of emotions. I wanted to be like them and everyone around me, but I felt like I was this massive wet blanket walking into the restaurant. I felt guilty that I felt this way as Kyle put effort into this dinner and did not want to make him feel bad, but I couldn't have felt more uncomfortable. I hoped the change of scenery from our house to the restaurant would help, but it didn't. It only highlighted how out of place I felt. I tried my best to maintain normal conversation and shrug off what had happened, but it was all a mask. My mind was fixated—all I could do was try to make sense of how everything happened. I wanted a reason for this. I wondered, *"Why me?" "Why our house?" and the most consistent, "What if he comes back?"* would not stop repeating in my head.

There were moments in the conversation where I could pull myself out and think back to how Kyle looked at me, realizing how bad things could have been and how grateful I was for still sitting with them. These moments helped ease the fear as I genuinely felt thankful for an amazing husband and a beautiful, adorable baby who was still safe and sound with us. That sounds so cliche, but feeling like this man could have effortlessly abducted, hurt, or killed me and or Lyla made me hyper-aware of how unexpectedly life can change. Occasionally, I would look at Kyle across the table, and he would smile. I felt he acknowledged how I felt, as he was doing everything he could to make things feel normal again. He played with Lyla, made funny faces and kept her busy, giving her random things to play with that allowed her to explore her curiosity. Kyle always made me feel like everything was okay just by how he handled things confidently and calmly. Not to mention, he always knew how to lighten things up.

At one point, Lyla started choking on a piece of lettuce and we both jumped up to help her. Lyla had never choked before and today was a great day to do it while we were in hyper-aware mode. Within seconds, she was fine and returned to playing with the food on her tray, but dang, that threw both Kyle and me into a loop. My heart was racing, as I'm sure Kyle's was, too. We eventually relaxed in our seats and I thought, *Whew, that could have ended worse.*

After the day we had just had and the choking scare, I didn't know what to talk about. But Kyle, being Kyle and always knowing how to lighten things up, said, "Wow, what a day! Kind of crazy how just yesterday we were hanging out by the pool and then taking a golf cart ride blasting the music."

I smiled, knowing exactly what he was doing and appreciating his effort even though I was so freaking over this day. "Hey, I need to go to the bathroom. I'll be right back." I said.

I made my way through the dining room, looking at all the happy people who seemed to be extra happy and enjoying themselves and their families. The restrooms were in the worst location, tucked away at the end of a long, dark hallway. Catching me off guard, a waiter busted through two silver doors connected to the kitchen, holding multiple plates for a table nearby. With my nervous system still in overdrive, I pressed my back against the wall, hands spread out to the side, as he unexpectedly flew by me. I stared him down, taking a second to process if he was someone "safe" to be near. I had never even thought of that kind of thing before. I gave myself a pep talk. *He was wearing an apron. He works here. He has plates in his hands. It's OK, Tenny.*

He's safe. I'm safe.

I pulled myself together and then looked down the ridiculously dark hallway where the women's door was. It was my next hurdle. I love some ambient lighting to set the mood, but why in the world did it need to be *this* dark? I thought about going back to the table. Did I really need to pee *that* bad? I considered holding it. I kept studying the hallway and decided to give myself another pep talk. *Come on, Tenny, you got this. It's just the bathroom. You're in a restaurant surrounded by people—only a few more steps. You can do this.* I could feel myself start to sweat as I stayed close to the wall, trying to minimize as much potential as possible for someone to grab me from behind. Walking down the hallway, I probably looked so strange trying to play it cool as I glued my back to the wall. The hallway was dim and I couldn't help but think *that the intruder had appeared out of nowhere today. What's stopping him from hiding around any other dark corner? I know they haven't found him. What if he followed us? What if he is here?*

Once I made it to the women's bathroom, which was brighter, I felt a slight sense of relief. However, as I heard the door close behind me, the thought of being alone in this cave-like room started to freak me out. Determined to not let this day's events take over, I left there quickly and practically ran down the hallway back to Kyle and Lyla.

Since previous plans had been made with one of my best friends from California to get together after dinner at the house, I was glad to have another perfect distraction. When she arrived, it was wonderful and, at times, helped me feel normal. It felt good to be with a girlfriend and talk about old times. *The times where only good memories surrounded this house.* She was my main best friend through my middle and high school years.

We had many memories of being in this house together, having countless sleepovers growing up, doing homework together, and practicing our instruments. We had a couple of glasses of wine and caught up on each other's lives. I shared some details about the day with her but brushed it off as I tried to stay focused on the positive things unfolding in her life and ours since I rarely ever got to see her. I desperately needed this time with one of my closest friends, but the later it got, the harder reality set in—eventually, I'd have to go to bed—to lay down in the dark and close my eyes.

And then the thought I had from that afternoon returned. *He's coming back.*

After my friend left and it got closer to bedtime, all the feelings from the day came back up, and I started to panic. I rushed around the house to recheck every single door and window. Even though I had just seen my mom make a round before bed, I wasn't going to believe anything unless I did it myself.

I made my way down the hallway to Lyla's bedroom. She had been put down hours prior and was sound asleep. After checking her window lock and ensuring her baby monitor was on, I paused to watch her sleep. She was so cute as she was snuggled in her swaddler with her little arms resting peacefully at her side. *Thank God he didn't take you.* After a few minutes, I headed to our bedroom.

Kyle went to bed that night completely unafraid as he tends to stick to the facts and leans on trusting the experts. He had peace of mind that I absolutely did not have. It surprised me how calm and seemingly unaffected he was, but it was also nice to have someone who felt so confident sleeping right next to me. Once I finally climbed into bed, I thought, *What if I missed a lock?* So I got out of bed and did another round around the house. It took a while, as there were so many windows in my parents' house, but I finally made it back into bed. Yet, even after just a couple of moments, I couldn't get the thought out of my head that maybe I didn't try hard enough to check the locks, so I decided to get up another time. I could tell my activity was not helping Kyle sleep, and could sense Kyle noticing me getting in and out of bed. *He must think I am a total freak.*

Since Kyle's sleep schedule as a firefighter was challenging, I usually slept on the side of the bed closer to the door so I could get to Lyla if she woke up in the middle of the night. But that night, I insisted on switching sides. The last place I wanted to be was on the side of the bed, close to the door, where someone could sneak in at any moment, leaving no boundary between me and the door. After a third and final check of all the windows and doors, I finally stayed in bed with Lola and Lily snuggled in close, who always slept in the middle of the bed between Kyle and me.

Thoughts raced through my head about our past discussions on gun ownership, debating whether or not it was right for us. I was the one who struggled with the idea of having a weapon. I honestly didn't think, even if faced with an extreme situation, that I'd actually be able to kill someone. I have saved insects before, so the thought of actually using a gun for how it is intended felt the farthest from reality as possible. Chances are, my own weapon could be used against me.

Because a police friend of ours suggested wasp spray was better than pepper spray, we went with it. We kept a can of spray on my side of the bed and a solid wooden Louisville Slugger baseball bat on Kyle's side. Thinking back now, I can't believe we even had those items. I can't say many people I know have wasp spray sitting on their nightstand and a Louisville Slugger bat on the other side, especially in a community where nothing ever happened.

Since Kyle always goes to bed before me, I thought he might just *say* he was tired but find him having a hard time sleeping, but no. He had no trouble falling asleep; he was out like a light. Part of me was slightly annoyed that he could fall asleep so quickly after everything that happened that day, but part of me knew he wasn't there to experience it. Once I was settled into bed for a while, I lay there listening to Kyle breathing heavily, signaling he was in a deep sleep. Meanwhile, I stared at the baby monitor, wanting to make sure that if he *did* come back and chose Lyla's room before ours, I would catch him. At this point, I knew there was no way I would sleep that night, so I surrendered to the fact that I would just stay up all night watching the monitor.

We had not heard anything from the police or the canine unit, so earlier thoughts were still running through my mind. *What if he comes back?*

Around 1:30 am, Lola and Lily started wiggling their little bodies, signaling it was time to go to the bathroom. This was common. Usually, I'd take them outside to do their business, but that night, there was no way in the world I was going to go out at 1:30 am by myself. Let alone walk into the dark hallway by myself.

I rolled over to Kyle, gently rubbed his arm, feeling awful that I was waking him up, and said, "Babe, can you please take Lola and Lily out? I really don't want to go outside."

Since our dogs did this to us almost every night, Kyle woke

up slightly annoyed and said, "Come on, girls. Let's go out."

"Babe," I told him as he climbed out of bed. "You should take the bat."

Because the bat was now on my side of the bed, it would take extra effort for him to walk all the way around. Probably knowing I would fight him if he didn't take anything, he appeased me by grabbing the wasp spray. He led the dogs out of the room, and for about ten seconds, I lay there alone in the dark. But then, the dogs raced right back into the bedroom, shaking and growling. *Weird. They'd just left. And they are acting so scared.*

Lola and Lily were never like this. They were high energy and sweet but never shaky and nervous. Not to mention, they immediately burrowed right into me.

It took me a second to wonder why they were back so fast. *If they're back, where's Kyle?* That's when I heard rustling. I immediately knew what was happening. I threw the covers off, jumped out of bed, grabbed the baseball bat, and rushed out of the room. The dogs didn't even want to follow. There, wrestling with my husband in the dark hallway, was the familiar, huge figure. I could smell him. I couldn't see his face, but I didn't need to. I was right. *He was back.*

5

IN THE DEAD OF NIGHT

I ran as fast as I could to get to Kyle. I had no idea what I would find, but at the same time, it was like I knew exactly what I would find. After rushing out into the hallway, it only took a second for the details of the situation to become clear. I didn't process anything intellectually; it was as if my body knew exactly what to do and I just followed all the little cues I had been picking up on, how disturbing he was, the feeling that he was coming back—all pieced together in what felt like milliseconds. My heart was pounding out of my chest and I felt something I had never felt before in my life—complete and utter rage. The hallway was dimly lit with recessed ceiling lights, but I didn't need bright lights to know what was happening.

He was here to finish what he had started earlier that day.

I knew Kyle was strong and he'd be able to fight this guy, but the evil I had seen in him earlier made me subconsciously aware that *all* of our lives were at stake on this night and I needed to do whatever I could to support Kyle.

His disgusting smell filled the hallway—heavy and foul. There was barely any noise from him, but I wasn't surprised. His calmness and the intensity I experienced earlier matched the exact energy in the hallway. I saw their two bodies fall to the ground in the middle of the hallway. Incredibly impressed but not surprised, Kyle managed to get the guy into a headlock and have the upper hand. Their bodies were meshed as Kyle wrapped his arm around the back of the guy's neck, who was now on all fours.

Kyle would later testify that he turned right out of the kid's wing to take the dogs outside to pee. Lola led the way but quickly started growling as they approached the front door. She turned, still growling and immediately took off, heading back to our bedroom. Lily followed. Frustrated that the dogs may wake someone up, Kyle turned to quiet them, but only to look up and see a man standing at the end of the hall. It appeared that he had passed the door to our kid's wing, where Lyla and I were, and was headed toward the last door in the hallway—the master bedroom, where my mom slept.

With the bat still in my hand, I watched them fight. In wrestling matches, they pair you with someone in the same weight class to make it a fair fight. As much as a stud as Kyle is, the 6'2" and roughly 215-pound guy would naturally have a bit of an upper hand on Kyle's 5'10" and 185 pound frame. Besides that, Kyle was wearing mesh workout shorts and no shirt—hardly dressed to fight for his life. Statistics aside, there were a lot of underlying layers between these two. The hate and intentions this man came with, along with the shock and reality of what Kyle realized about this situation, left a heaviness in the room that can't be put into words. All I knew was this was going to be one hell of a fight.

Kyle described their first recognition of each other: Just like the intruder had done with me, he bee-lined it straight for Kyle. He walked fast, taking huge, giant steps toward him. In total shock after the events just twelve hours prior, reality hit and Kyle let out, "Oh…my…God." The intruder stared directly into Kyle's eyes and he noticed exactly what I had seen earlier that day—his eyes and his facial expression were completely absent of any emotion. Kyle later expressed, "It was as if he was possessed."

All of the little things came together for Kyle at that moment. He had agreed with the cops earlier and could not believe this guy was now standing in our home. There is no world where a stranger inside your house at 1:30 in the morning could mean something good. He certainly wasn't there for a cup of tea. As if his possessed look, aggression, and pace weren't freaky enough, as he headed straight for Kyle and reached out his hands to attack him, Kyle noticed that he was wearing gardening gloves that made his huge hands look even bigger. And if that wasn't disturbing enough, he had gone the extra mile and duct-taped them to his wrists. *What in the hell?* That was all Kyle could think. The situation was perfectly clear to Kyle. He instinctively knew that it would be "him or me," which would only mean the rest of us would follow.

Before wrestling him to the floor, Kyle raised the wasp spray toward the intruder, spraying it directly at his face as the man charged. The man didn't break his possessed look or flinch as wasp spray flew directly toward him and into his eyes. It actually seemed to piss him off even more. He kept bull-rushing toward Kyle, passing the front door he could have left out of, and showed no signs of backing down. By this point, Kyle knew he had no choice but to fight him physically.

At first, the man tried to tackle Kyle. Kyle grabbed his shirt with his left hand and punched him with his right. Their fistfight only lasted a few moments until they fell to the floor, which is when I showed up. Knowing how hard it can be to get someone into a headlock, I couldn't help but thank God that Kyle had wrestling skills not just from being a wrestler in high school but also from the years that followed, where he spent coaching the high school team. That, coupled with owning our gym and the daily workouts of heavy lifting and workouts that crush your lungs, where he often lifted the heaviest and had the fastest time, Kyle would be *the one* you would want in this situation. He is competitive, strong, and calm under pressure from his years in the fire department, but he also despises people who unfairly try to take advantage of someone else. Little did we know how all of this would come together in this moment *for him* to try and save our lives.

It was surreal watching Kyle fight this guy. Not many people get to see how their spouse would show up for them in that situation and to see how deeply they are protected…and loved. And here I was, watching it right before my eyes. And as horrible as the situation was, this feels weird, but I'd be lying if I didn't say part of me was excited. Maybe that was the adrenaline talking. But having known that this man was coming back and now he was here, inside my house, I felt some relief because I wouldn't have to fight him alone. Kyle was here when he could have easily been working a shift like many other nights.

Once they got to the ground, Kyle's first attempt to cause damage, while simultaneously holding him in a headlock, was to knee him in the face. He tried several times, but his knee kept skimming off the top of his head.

Holding the Louisville Slugger bat in my hand, I got close and quickly reviewed the positioning to see how I could use the bat best. It's almost as if Kyle knew I would have the bat as he had the guy in a headlock, on all fours, leaving his back wide open and perfectly positioned for me to swing down on him. There was no talking between me and Kyle. I didn't even know if he knew I was there or not. I made sure Kyle's head wouldn't be in the way, but it's almost as if he also knew to put his head where it wouldn't be in my way.

Fueled with rage and instinct, I took an extra moment to make sure this bat would have the maximum impact possible when I hit him. I was aware that I was small and that this man seemed out of this world mad, so I had to be intentional if my hits would be productive. I reached the bat as far as I could above my head, stood as tall as possible, extended up on my tippy toes, and then used my core to crunch down and slam down as hard as possible on his wide-open, massive back. With every ounce of my lungs, I screamed, "FUCK YOU!" as the bat slammed on his back.

Nothing. No "Ow!", no "Ugh!", no "You bitch!" Completely nothing. The intruder had taken a decent blow and was totally unmoved.

I wound up the bat again, taking an extra second to bring all my strength even though I somehow knew seconds were precious, and slammed the bat down equally as hard the second time, again yelling, "FUCK YOU!"

The sound of the thud and the feeling of hitting his body were foreign, intentional, and rage-fueled. Something I had never experienced before, using a word I never used. I didn't know Kyle's plan, but I just wanted to try to help. As I watched Kyle fighting to maintain the upper hand, all that went through my mind was that I wanted to hurt this terrible man as much as possible to stop him. I wound up the bat again and again, always taking the extra second to make sure I was hitting him as hard as I possibly could. I continued to drop F-bombs every time I hit him—fueled with so much adrenaline and unleashed anger.

The whole time, he didn't make a noise. Which is insane because later, we learned that my swings were impactful. Apparently, I had created what they call 'railroad tracks' on his back as the blood pushed out to the sides where each swing had landed. I knew I was giving it my all, but I was even surprised to learn the impact I had, as were the detectives.

On my sixth swing and my sixth F-bomb, the bat split in two on its final impact to his back. I wish I could have seen my face at that moment, as I remember being completely shocked and caught off guard. This was an adult-sized solid wooden bat and whatever I had done over the last minute caused it to break. The image that comes to mind is the rare moments in a baseball game where a bat breaks in two, leaving two pieces with jagged ends. That was exactly like the bat I was now holding. The immediate thought was to take one of the pieces and jab it straight into his still wide-open back, but I couldn't. I thought, *I can't actually put that in his back, stabbing him.*

Unfortunately, the intruder showed no sign of slowing. He had been army crawling, inch by inch, forcing Kyle backward and across the carpet into the family room. There were no words, no screams, and what seemed to be barely any movement, but the amount of energy consumed between Kyle and him as they fought for the upper hand was more than intense. He was punching between Kyle's legs, trying to bite Kyle, break his fingers, grab his balls—he was attempting anything possible. It's like he was a freaking animal. Kyle had a tight hold on him, and I could tell how hard he was fighting to maintain that. I couldn't see what was happening on the ground, but I could tell this guy wasn't going to stop. Realizing I wouldn't do anything with the broken bat, I did the next most logical thing that came to mind. I decided to kick him in the balls.

He was still on all fours secured in Kyle's headlock, so his hips were somewhat high and his legs just slightly spread, which meant I had a decent opportunity to take advantage of this. Immediately, I tried kicking with my dominant foot, my right, but because I had sprained it when he hit me and I fell earlier, it intensely hurt every time I kicked him. I gave up on my right and switched to my left, which was even more pathetic.

Trying to figure out what else I could do, I saw the can of wasp spray lying on the floor just a couple of feet away. Knowing this guy's head was down while Kyle's head was up, I knew I would be able to spray him in the face without worrying about spraying Kyle. I picked up the can of spray, crouched down low to get under his body, held down the trigger and sprayed him point-blank in the eyes. I moved the stream back and forth continuously, not letting up on the trigger.

While I've never gotten a stream of wasp spray shot straight into my eyes, I can imagine that it doesn't feel good. But, just like everything else we were doing, there was no response. No screaming. No yelling out in pain. I held that trigger down for a long time, and there was still no reaction at all. I couldn't hear it, but Kyle later said the only thing he could hear from the guy was grunts and growls as they fought.

I didn't piece it together then, but his continued non-response made things much scarier. His lack of feeling pain or acknowledgment when a bat broke on his back or that the wasp spray in his eyes didn't even seem to bother him meant we were dealing with someone extremely disturbed.

By that point, the intruder had progressed by pushing Kyle down the entire length of the hallway, over fifteen feet through the dining room, and to the side of the couch, where he'd thrown me just hours earlier.

If you've watched wrestling or boxing, you know there is a reason the rounds are so short (often less than 3 minutes). It's because they're three minutes of full intensity—giving everything you've got to win. This to say, Kyle was absolutely exhausted. All that we were doing wasn't stopping him. The intruder wasn't just going to "tap out." I wasn't sure how long the wasp spray would last, even though it had been a full can, and it wasn't making a difference anyway. Kyle had maintained the upper hand all this time, but even with our combined efforts, this guy *still* showed no signs of quitting.

With my finger firmly holding the sprayer, I felt the wasp spray become lighter. I continued directing the last of it into the guy's eyes. It was then that I heard Kyle say calmly and clearly, "Tenny, I need help."

Four words I had never heard Kyle say before.

I could hear the exhaustion in his voice. He was known for being great in times of crisis. I had listened to the stories of his Lieutenant, who shared proud moments of witnessing

Kyle lead fires and how direct Kyle was while remaining calm and collected. So, for me, those four words meant how critical the situation was. That was all I needed to hear. It was like a light switch flipped in my brain. I wasn't cognitively processing anything as it was all happening so fast, but never in my life had I heard Kyle ask for help, *especially* when it came to something physical. It made me know something was seriously wrong and I'd have to look for something more impactful than a bat and wasp spray.

I'm not a man, so I can't say this from that perspective, but while it seems like most people struggle with asking for help, it seems like asking for help is even more naturally challenging for men. I say that because Kyle asked for help and the awareness and courage it took to do so, I believe, is the pivotal moment of this evening. If he hadn't said those four seemingly simple words, I honestly don't know if that switch in my brain would have happened. Kyle *knew* that if this guy got loose for even a second, he would not survive, nor would I, or my mom and, heaven forbid, Lyla. And instinctually, deep down, I *knew* the same.

The second Kyle said those words, there was no second-guessing or hesitation. I immediately knew I needed to get something more effective than everything else that had failed at that point. So, without any more dialogue with Kyle, I ran to the kitchen.

I have to admit, it was a surreal experience seeing how fast my mind processed the next steps, especially given the magnitude of what I was about to do. I knew we had two big, ten-inch kitchen knives stored on opposite sides of the kitchen. One was newer, sharp, and typically stored in a drawer; the other was flimsy and dull and most commonly stored in our old butcher block of knives. Occasionally, someone would accidentally switch where the knives were stored. I wanted to get back to Kyle as fast as possible, aware of how critical things were, but I grabbed both knives to be positive I had the sturdy and sharp one.

While I was in the kitchen, my mom showed up to the scene. It all just happened *so fast*. She had shown up right as I ran to the kitchen. She had heard my F-bombs, something she had never heard from me, especially in the middle of the night, and she wasted no time joining the fight as she tried to whack the intruder in the balls with a piece of the broken baseball bat. While fighting with the intruder, the only other thing Kyle said during his fight was, "Rosalyn, call 9-1-1", so she ran back to her room to get her phone.

I set down the flimsy knife on the counter, moved the solid one into my right hand, positioned it in my hand in a way I have never held a 10-inch kitchen knife, and rushed back to Kyle to find that the intruder's back was still wide open. And, without second-guessing what I was about to do, I wound up just as I did with the baseball bat, and drove the huge blade directly into his back.

Even writing this, it doesn't feel real. The whole thing felt completely insane. I don't think I fully realized the reality of what I was doing while doing it. Not that I ever imagined what it would be like to stab someone, but hearing of stabbings or watching it in movies, I would randomly wonder, *How does that work? I mean, there are ribs, a spine, and so many bones.* But the knife went in with no hesitation and that was shocking. I continued to stab him over and over again. As I pulled out the knife on the fourth or fifth time, I noticed the huge 10-inch knife was covered in blood and a chunk of the knife had broken off—a small piece in the middle of the blade. Somehow, seeing that chunk missing from a sturdy, solid kitchen knife made me realize what I was actually doing. *Maybe it got caught on his ribs? I don't know. Oh my God. What am I doing? This is literally crazy.*

I then heard my mom on the phone with the 911 dispatcher; she sobbed and screamed. "She's stabbing him! Oh my God, she...she...she stabbed him!"

I stabbed the man in the back eight times. I had no plan of stopping as I was now, more than ever, completely jacked on adrenaline and, I imagine, experiencing what some call an out-of-body experience, totally overcome with all of the fear, emotions, instincts, and intuition that were playing out. I could not know if what I was doing was truly hurting him. Again, none of my other efforts had done anything, so by this point, it felt like he was invincible. So, I stayed at it.

Kyle knew what was happening, though. By the time I had stabbed him on the eighth stab, Kyle could feel his breathing shift to agonal breathing. Something I didn't know anything about, but Kyle did. It's what happens when someone isn't getting enough oxygen and they are near death. Kyle could also feel his body go lifeless. At this point, he said, "Tenny, stop."

I didn't want to, though, as I didn't believe he was done attacking Kyle. *Wait, I killed him? Do you mean he is dead?* I was terrified that, like in the movies, he would rise and come back after us.

As Kyle flipped him over, letting the man's back lay against the carpet, he let his body fall to the floor right next to him. Unsure of whether he was dead, I surprised Kyle when I stabbed him one more time in the stomach, still not believing he was going to stop.

"Tenny, stop!" Kyle insisted.

I stopped but stood there waiting and ready, anticipating he could get up any second and resume the attack. Even though it was the last thing in the world he wanted to do, Kyle climbed on top of him and laid on him, every bit of him completely exhausted. Even though Kyle logically knew the guy was gone, he, too, felt like the guy could come back to life at any second.

Still holding a death grip on the bloody knife and now staring down at what seemed to be a lifeless body, I finally saw his face for the first time that evening. I was in total shock, not fully realizing what I had just done. I looked at the still body, glanced over at my mom, who was screaming and crying to the 911 dispatcher, and watched as my husband lay on top of him, completely drained after the fight for his life, for all *our* lives. My heart was pounding out of my chest as I tried to catch my breath.

I just stood there, frozen. This wasn't a bad dream that we would wake up from. This actually just happened and my mom had just watched her daughter stab a home intruder in the middle of their family home.

The 911 dispatcher asked my mom, "Did you say that someone is dead, Ma'am?"

Hysterically, my mom replied, "YES! She stabbed him! He's DEAD!"

I stood there stunned. *How in the world did I just kill someone?*

6

THE STORY

"Ma'am, can we speak to your daughter?" the dispatcher asked. I slowly walked across the room and held the phone to my ear. The male dispatcher's steady voice asked for my name and location and for me to recount what had happened. I retraced the past few minutes, trying to remember every detail. My voice—young and uncertain—probably made me sound no older than fifteen. I told him that the police had been here just twelve hours earlier—and that I was the one who had called then. When he asked for my full name, I recited it letter by letter as if preparing for an interrogation. Then, when he asked my age, I was so flooded with adrenaline that I answered incorrectly.

"Twenty-seven," I said, only to quickly realize my mistake. "Sorry…I'm twenty-six. I'm so sorry, I didn't mean to lie."

He remained calm and professional as he noted that I had stabbed him, though I assumed he'd eventually understand that I acted in self-defense—even if that hadn't registered at the moment.

"Where is the knife?" the dispatcher asked.

"It's in my hand," I replied.

"Can you put it down?"

"I don't want to put the knife down. What if..." I began, tears welling up. "I—I can put it down, though."

"Can you put it down?" he repeated.

"Yeah, of course."

I started crying again. "Okay," I managed, pausing to catch my breath. "I didn't know what to do," I cried, each sob emphasizing the overwhelming rush of emotions.

Describing the events was easy, even as I struggled to catch my breath. "My husband got up to take the dogs out, and then I heard fighting, and I told him to take the bat, but he took the wasp spray with him, and it didn't phase the guy. I found my husband fighting with him, and I grabbed the bat because I heard them fighting, and I just started hitting him, and it wasn't doing anything! It wasn't doing anything at all!" I started to cry. "So all I could think of was to grab a knife," I said as I started sobbing.

While on the phone, I stood there, covered in blood—panting, crying, trembling from adrenaline—shocked as my body had at one point switched into survival mode, and then it hit me: I could potentially go to jail. I knew it was self-defense, but would they see it that way? During the fight, Kyle and I never planned a strategy. It didn't even register to talk; he was focused on handling his part while I did whatever I could to help. There was no communication or direction—we just worked silently together. Kyle later testified that he had no idea what I was about to do.

"Is all your family OK?" the dispatcher asked.

"Oh my God, yes!" I burst into tears as soon as he asked, relief mixing with the fear, knowing that Lyla and my mom were safe, as I realized how differently things might have turned out.

"Ma'am, is all your family ok?" he asked again, double-checking.

"Yes, we're *all* OK," I panted in response.

Then, Kyle signaled that he wanted to speak to the dispatcher. He had stayed, trapping the intruder with his body, but he pushed himself off from the intruder, stood up, and headed toward me.

"Oh, my husband is grabbing the phone," I said.

When Kyle was on the line with the dispatcher, he sounded completely exhausted. When the officer asked, "Are you OK?"

Kyle slowly replied, "I'm ok. Oh man, I got…ugh…ugh…yeah," struggling to catch his breath. "I'm just kind of freaked out right now, to be honest," he added, still panting and out of breath from fighting—not just for his life, but for all of our lives.

Kyle barely spoke while he was on the phone. It was instinct, muscle memory—connecting with the dispatcher as if he were on duty. Emergency calls were his thing.

The dispatcher's first priority was ensuring the weapon was secured. Kyle hesitated before finally asking me to move the knife, admitting he didn't want to step away. He stood just five feet from the body, eyes locked, cautiously preparing for the impossible—for the man on the floor to rise. He relayed every detail with the steady professionalism of someone who had done this a hundred times before. His voice was calm. Articulate. Guiding them to our house as if this were just another call—just another scene.

I stood frozen in the middle of the dining room. My pajamas—white tank top, light blue workout shorts—soaked in blood. I didn't know where to stand. Where to look. What to do. I kept asking, "Is someone coming? When? How soon?" My voice shook between sobs, my body shaking so hard I didn't understand what was happening to me.

Hours ago, I knew he was coming back. Somehow, I felt it. And yet—I still couldn't believe this was real.

In less than twelve hours, he had broken in, attacked me, left, and returned. And now... here we were. I watched as Kyle stood at the window, still breathing heavily, flashing the porch lights to guide the officers in.

His gaze stayed fixed outside as he spoke into the phone. "You know what? All these people were here at one o'clock today. You can tell the officers that." I could barely see his face in the dark, but watched as his head dropped. "Oh my God, that creeped me out. Fuck!" He kept trying to steady his breath, closing his eyes as his chest kept rising and falling. After a long pause, he shook his head. "Those dogs knew. They fucking knew." His voice cracked as he breathed deep, fighting back emotions and tears as pieces came together for him. "Because... this fucker broke in earlier today, you know. God." He paused and took a breath. "Thank goodness..." He held it together and quickly refocused just as the first patrol cars pulled up. Their guns looked drawn.

Eight minutes. That's how long it took for emergency responders to arrive. The longest eight minutes of our lives.

As officers and detectives arrived, they carried an energy of control—calm, deliberate. There was no chaos, no shouting, no dramatic entrance—just a quiet understanding of what needed to be done. Still, I wasn't convinced this man wouldn't get back up. As the officers stepped in to relieve Kyle and me from standing guard over the body, I couldn't shake the instinct to keep control. "Where's your gun?" I demanded. "Point your gun at him!" I couldn't understand why they weren't as terrified as we were. *Why didn't they seem to grasp what this man was capable of?* It hadn't fully registered that *I* was the one who had just stabbed him.

Kyle and I were led to the entryway and told to sit on the same bench where my diaper bag had rested. The same spot where I had seen the hatred in his eyes. Where he had hit me. Where I had fallen. Now, we sat far from his body as firefighters and medics worked on him. I know now that first responders are trained to prioritize the most injured person. In this case, that was *him*—the man we had fought to save ourselves from. I overheard someone say they were performing CPR, and confusion crashed over me.

Why? This was a monster and we had just done everything in our power to end this fight. We had survived. *And now they were trying to bring him back?*

I don't know how to describe what we felt other than complete shock. But weirdly, I wasn't panicked. There was a strange calm about me, almost a giddiness. Maybe my brain was desperately trying to grasp onto something *normal* after the nightmare we had just lived through. Even in that moment, I recognized how odd it was.

Two officers stood nearby, keeping watch over us. And, true to my ability to try and lighten the mood and sometimes be completely awkward, I turned to the female detective in a uniform jumpsuit and asked, "Wow, how in the world are you able to go to the bathroom in that thing?"

She didn't miss a beat. Instead, she shared a funny story about struggling to figure it out during a call. For a brief moment, we all laughed. She was kind and warm—an unexpected comfort. Later, I realized how strange it was to ask that question *then*, but in that moment, it felt natural.

Kyle and I knew we were innocent, but it was surreal how quickly the officers knew it, too. Not a single one treated us like suspects. In fact, they were compassionate, almost protective.

Somehow, we had made it through the night. As the morning hours crept in, we made calls—me to my dad, Kyle to his parents. My mom, thank God, had gone to be with Lyla. She had miraculously slept through everything, but now she was waking up as detectives moved through the house, gathering evidence. After what felt like an eternity, the CPR effort ended. It hadn't lasted long—his injuries were too severe.

Capt. Ben Lane walked over to Kyle and me. He knelt in front of us, silent. He didn't need to say anything. There's something about a person of rank kneeling in front of you. It strips away the titles of authority. In that moment, I didn't see a Fire Captain. I saw *Ben*—a man who understood the weight of what had just happened. A man who carried his own shock, and his own compassion for what we had endured.

Capt. Ben Lane, and now Fire Chief of a large multi-city department, had responded to the first break-in. He said, "When the call came through dispatch, it was flagged as MEDIC WEAPONS (a weapon was on the scene) and I saw that same address pop up again all I could think was, holy shit. It's Tennyson. Again."

While sitting there, I glanced down and saw myself—*really* saw myself. My white tank top and workout shorts were soaked in blood—not just stained—*soaked*. The fabric clung to my skin, still wet in some places and cracking in others as it dried.

It covered my arms, hands, legs, and feet. It was suffocating. It wasn't just *his* blood. It was his filth, his stench. It filled our house. And all over my body. Everywhere. I needed it off. Now. Uncomfortably aware of the blood covering my skin, I asked if I could take a shower. An officer checked with the lead detective and escorted me to my bathroom. He walked with me as I grabbed fresh clothes and then stood guard at the bathroom door as I walked in and shut the door behind me. The last thing I wanted was to shut myself inside a room, only to have to open the door again, not knowing who—or what—might be on the other side. The fact that they instinctively understood that impressed me. I felt protected. What I didn't know was that this extra attention wasn't necessarily just kindness. It was because, at that moment, I was a murder suspect. But I didn't understand all that yet—I just needed the blood off of me.

I turned the water on and cranked the heat just past my threshold, hoping the scalding water would burn away every trace of him. As I waited for the steam to rise, my eyes caught Lyla's little mesh bathtub, stored off to the side. *God. This could have been a different situation.* I grabbed a loofah and poured half the bottle of body wash onto it, scrubbing as hard as my skin could tolerate. Bloody suds trickled down my body, pooling at the bottom of the tub as the slow drain struggled to keep up. I scrubbed harder. And then again. And again. I needed every speck of him gone.

Not long after, Detective Bartlett, the investigator assigned to our case, showed up on the scene. At that point, Kyle and I were still working through the shock, and exhaustion started to creep in. It was only 3 am, only two hours after everything went down. The skin on Kyle's kneecaps was almost completely gone, rubbed raw from being shoved across the carpet. His chest had open wounds—marks that, to this day, have scarred over. And we still have no idea how he got them.

Detective Bartlett needed statements. One by one, she took Kyle, my mom, and me to her car. I don't remember who went first, but I *do* remember the walk to her vehicle. For a moment, I had forgotten the weight of what I had done and forgotten that I was walking toward a police car *as the person who had killed a man*. I had no idea how they saw me. I had no idea what this all meant for my future.

And then she asked her first question. *"Are you okay?"*

I hadn't expected that. I had expected interrogation, not empathy. The relief was instant.

My voice shook as I answered. "Yes… I… I just don't want to be in trouble." I kept repeating it, the words tumbling out between tears. "I just don't want to be in trouble…"

Later, Detective Bartlett would tell us there was never any doubt about what had happened. The evidence spoke for itself, and the break-in just twelve hours earlier only made it more transparent.

Everything we did was self-defense. Still, there was protocol. A man was dead in my living room, and *I* was the one who had killed him. That fact alone meant that, legally speaking, I had been arrested for murder.

And so had Kyle.

I didn't grasp that at the time. Even as Detective Bartlett read me my Miranda Rights, it still didn't feel real. I wasn't being dragged away in cuffs. I wasn't being treated like a criminal. Instead, she placed me in the front seat of her car—a simple act that, as a close friend in law enforcement later told me, was *"a class act.*" Another detective sat in the back, but nothing about the interaction felt like an interrogation. Detective Bartlett wasn't just professional—she was *human*. I don't think she or anyone else there that night will ever fully understand how much that meant to us: to be treated with respect and kindness. Especially after what we had just lived through.

There are specific people in my life that I have met who feel like angels. People who feel like they have a unique and special role to play in my journey through life. Detective Barlett felt like one to me. She did everything she could to make me feel heard and obeyed the law while treating me compassionately. As she looked at me before reading me my rights, it felt like she was looking into my soul. She probably was…using every bit of experience and training to study my body language to put the clues together. But it didn't feel that way. It felt like she saw my innocence and had compassion for me, knowing this would be the start of a very long and challenging journey. I can't imagine what things would have been like if she hadn't been the one helping us through it all.

At one point during the interview, she pulled out her business card, handed me a pen, and told me that she wanted me to write something down. "I'm going to give you the name of a book," she said. "I want you to read it."

Surprised that a homicide detective recommended a book to me after reading my rights, I was intrigued to read what she would recommend. It was the book *The Gift of Fear* by Gavin de Becker. I can't say I loved the book's title when she told me about it. Fear was about the last thing I wanted to experience any more of, and I certainly didn't understand it to be a gift. But I made note of it. When I reconnected with her ten years after our event, I learned that she didn't even remember doing this as it's not something she ever does.

Around 4 am, after Kyle and I had both given our testimonies in the Detective's car, it was my mom's turn. While Mom went off, we were able to catch up on making calls.

Kyle called his parents. I can't imagine what it was like to be on the other end of that call—to hear your son say he had to fight for his life…and that we had killed someone. It was incredibly emotional in a way that wasn't typical for his family. But it was also super productive. We had to figure out *what's next?* We needed to plan where to go and what to do with Lola and Lily, as there was no way in hell we'd spend another night in that house. Not that we *could* even if we wanted to. It was now an active crime scene, taped off and under investigation.

I called my dad. He still owned the house and had only recently moved out, living less than a mile away. He came back frequently to help my mom with things. When I told him what had happened, he couldn't believe it. In the eighteen years they had lived there, there had never been a single concern. This was the home they had built in a safe neighborhood, surrounded by wonderful people. How was this happening *here*?

He rushed over immediately, but they wouldn't let him on the scene.

Kyle also received another call from his fire chief, filled with emotion: "Kyle, we are here for whatever you and your family need. Just let me know, and we will take care of it."

I have to say, there is nothing like being a part of the first responder community. To feel like you have a whole second family who would genuinely be there for you and do anything you need, especially in a moment like this, was something we were deeply grateful for.

After my mom's testimony, Detective Bartlett returned. She approached me and asked, "Tennyson, do you have a camera?"

I was surprised she didn't have a camera, so I said, "Yeah, I have one. Do you need one? I can go get one for you!"

I didn't even register why she had asked, but paused slightly, wondering why these professional investigators asked me for equipment.

She smiled at me softly. "OK, thank you. No, we are good. We don't need a camera."

Which, of course, confused me more. *If they didn't need it, why were they asking?*

That's when more details from the crime scene started to come up—things we hadn't noticed while doing everything we could to stop him.

They asked us if we had brought out a roll of duct tape. *What the f&#!* No, I definitely did not grab duct tape.

That's when they explained: Not only did the intruder have gardening gloves on his hands duct taped around his wrists, he had brought extra duct tape, a camera, a flashlight, and a tripod.

This guy came with a plan.

They also found his car about half a mile down the street with the driver's side and passenger seats lowered. That detail was terrifying and didn't make sense until others helped explain it. Presumably, he was preparing to transport something or someone. The rest of the details would emerge slowly, piece by piece. We'll never know what was in his head or what he had planned for that night, but based on what the investigators could piece together, his intentions were clear and pure evil.

No one could explain how he got into our home that night.

There were no broken doors, no shattered windows, no forced locks. Someone suggested that maybe he had snuck in earlier while we were out at dinner—hiding somewhere inside, waiting. But I just couldn't believe that. Our dogs would have sensed something. They would have known. And yet, they hadn't reacted until the moment he attacked Kyle. Some speculated that he was caught off guard when he saw Kyle in the hallway. Because Kyle had loaned his truck to our friend earlier that day after the first break-in, it looked like I was alone.

The timing of everything haunted me. Our dogs woke up *exactly* when they did. Kyle was home—*the first time* his truck was ever gone, and he was still there. It could have all so easily led to a different headline. What if he had found Lyla first? Her room was only a few steps from where Kyle first saw him. What if he had reached our bedroom instead of meeting Kyle in the hall?

As someone who sometimes struggled to believe in a higher power, make sense of faith, and accept life's randomness, these details destroyed all my doubts. *Something* was protecting us. There was no other explanation.

One of the most common questions I get is, "He had to be on drugs, right?" People assume that's the only way to explain his deranged strength, his complete lack of fear, and his inability to feel pain. *But no,* toxicology reports showed no trace of drugs or alcohol in his system. And that didn't surprise me at all. The only crime on his record was stealing a can of chewing tobacco from a local gas station. On paper, he wasn't dangerous. But, the detectives came to a chilling conclusion: This was a full-blown *psychotic break*. It was the first time any explanation actually made sense. They explained that during a psychotic break, a person's mind disconnects entirely from reality. Their perception is twisted, their thoughts are demented, and their strength—superhuman. It was like facing a monster—a human shell, driven by something beyond reason.

What we did learn was that this man had a history of terrorizing the people closest to him. His own family had been afraid of him. His wife had finally escaped after enduring his abuse, but the divorce sent him into a downward spiral. He isolated himself in a trailer, walls covered in beer boxes, writing his own version of the Bible, feeding his bitterness. Also, detectives told us that at one point, he had told his mother that monkeys had dragged him down the trailer and aliens drug him back the other way.

He despised women. *Detested* them. Hate isn't even a strong enough word for it. He saw women as the scum of the earth—a belief he ranted about endlessly online. Even his own mother, the only person who occasionally checked on him, was terrified of him. If she brought him food, he would berate her over something as small as a bruise on an apple. He had a YouTube channel filled with misogynistic rants. In one video, he claimed that women had only one goal: to *destroy* men. That was how they gained power.

"Women are horrible, miserable... evil, evil creatures," he declared. "And they must be stopped."

The hate I felt from his stare was *real*. I had looked into his eyes and seen nothing but blackness. He was already living in hell. And then there was the final piece of the puzzle—the reason the canine unit couldn't track him. A psychotic break like his would have disrupted the usual adrenaline spikes and pheromones that tracking dogs rely on. He wasn't running on fear or rage like a normal person. He was running on something else entirely.

This experience forever changed us. Our world flipped upside down, impacting every part of our lives moving forward. The headlines told *one* story. But what happened to us—the aftermath, the toll, the unrelenting fear—was so much deeper than words could ever capture.

It became the story after the story.

And we had no idea how long it would take to put the pieces back together.

7

WHY US?

Why me? Why my family? Why that night? The investigators suspected he had seen me around—maybe at the local grocery store or Starbucks—and that I reminded him of his ex-wife. Even if that wasn't the case, I represented everything he despised. Later, it became clear he had been watching me. They found footprints behind our home, deep in the woods—trampled ground, broken branches—the place where they believed he hid, waiting. It was terrifying to think about, especially in a neighborhood that had always felt so warm, welcoming, and safe.

That morning, there were more protocols to follow. The police told us we needed to go to the hospital to have our wounds checked—both of us had open cuts that had been exposed to the intruder's blood, something they took very seriously. Around 6:00 am, we finally gathered some of our things, grabbed Lyla and the dogs, and headed to Kyle's parents' house. His mom, Mary, took care of Lyla and the dogs while his dad, Norm, drove us to Kyle's fire department so his fellow firefighters could take us to the hospital. The moment we got into the car, though, the weight of it all hit us—we were terrified to even be on the road. The same streets we had driven many times now felt exposed and dangerous, like nowhere was truly safe.

As we pulled away from the scene, we had no idea the media was waiting. They had been kept at a distance, but as we drove past, reporters tried to flag us down for an interview. Our story had already hit the early-morning news, and word was spreading fast. My phone started blowing up—texts, voicemails, and Facebook messages pouring in as the community I had known my whole life learned what had happened. The news hadn't shared our names, but they didn't need to. They showed our house, gave vague descriptions, and in a town this small, it was obvious who we were. Everyone who reached out said the same thing: "HOW could this happen here?" They were in total shock as they saw our home on their TV screens—it didn't seem real. In a place where I had deep roots and knew so many, we were the last people anyone expected to go through something like this.

When we got to the fire station, Kyle's lieutenant, Troy, was already there waiting. He had driven an hour and a half on his day off just to be with us. Troy wasn't just close to Kyle—I knew him well, too. Anytime I visited the fire station, we'd have deep conversations about life, unpacking whatever was on our minds. He had a way of making people feel seen, like he truly cared. I had always found firefighters intimidating, but Troy never made me feel out of place. He welcomed me in, and I could tell he actually enjoyed our talks. He also adored Lyla. I'd watched him, more than once, pick up a guitar and sing to her at the station's dining table, not for show, but because he loved making her smile.

The second Troy saw Kyle, he rushed to hug him and then turned straight to me. He had spent decades holding it together in moments of crisis—first responders have a way of burying the weight of what they see—but this moment hit differently. He kept his composure, but I could see it all over his face. *I freaking love you guys.* He didn't have to say it—we both felt it.

Troy, along with Kyle's Battalion Chief, had arranged for us to be taken to the hospital in an aid car. It wasn't something we would have thought to ask for, but they knew it meant faster care. They had come in on their day off, making sure we were taken care of in every way possible. That kind of loyalty, that level of brotherhood—it's something you don't fully understand until you experience it in your most vulnerable moments. Firefighters, medics, police officers—it's more than a job. It's a family. And in that moment, when we felt lost and unsure of what came next, that family surrounded us. We had no idea what to do, but they did. And they made sure we never had to figure it out alone.

When we arrived at the hospital, the staff separated Kyle and me, placing us in different rooms. We went along with whatever they told us to do, too exhausted, too numb to think differently. But the last thing I wanted was to be alone without him. Without hesitation, Troy stepped in. He gathered the nurses and quietly explained what had just happened—why we *needed* to be together. The nurses didn't question it. In a moment of deep understanding, they wheeled my hospital bed into Kyle's small room, squeezing me in beside him so tightly there was barely any space for them to move.

It felt ridiculous—two hospital beds crammed into a single

room—but the pleaser in me couldn't have cared less as all I wanted to be was right next to Kyle.

The emergency room director stopped by to check on us, reassuring us that they were there for whatever we needed. It meant something. Kyle had spent years bringing patients to this very hospital as a firefighter. Now, he *was* the patient. It was another moment of feeling so deeply taken care of.

And God, we needed it.

We felt like two little kids—traumatized, in shock, confused, and now also possibly facing a murder investigation.

They took Kyle for an X-ray, worried he had broken his hand from punching the intruder in the head. When he returned, they treated his knees—raw from the fight—before giving both of us a thorough look-over. That's when they told us we needed to go directly to an infectious disease doctor a few blocks away. I hadn't even *thought* about *that*. But because we both had open wounds—Kyle from the fight, me from where the knife handle had rubbed my skin raw from the friction against my fingers—they needed to test us for exposure. HIV, Hepatitis, and God knows what else. The second they said it, something snapped inside me. Up until that moment, I hadn't processed much beyond survival. I was still running on shock, still in a haze of *just do the next thing*. But now—now, I felt my first real wave of anger.

This whole thing had already been a nightmare. The first break-in had been the most terrifying for me—alone in my own home, ambushed by a stranger who looked like pure evil. Then, just as we tried to believe it was over, he came back, forcing us into the fight of our lives.

And now, on top of everything else, we had to worry about

this?

The possibility of a life-threatening disease? *You have GOT to be kidding me.* I was furious. And terrified. All I could think about was how awful he *smelled*. The filth of him. And how that alone made me believe our risk had to be higher than normal.

We had arrived at the hospital around 10 am, and by noon, we were scheduled for testing. They squeezed us in immediately, recognizing the urgency of our situation.

The waiting was the worst part.

I thought back to my shower, to how I had scrubbed myself raw in scalding water, doing everything I could to erase him from my skin. I prayed that it had been enough.

When the results came back *clear*, I nearly passed out with relief.

I would have bet money that wasn't the case. It felt like we had somehow lucked out again.

But the relief was short-lived. Because while this was *one* hurdle, it was just the beginning.

We had barely begun to process what had happened, and now, real life was still moving forward, dragging us with it. We were grateful to be alive. But everything was a disaster. We had to navigate being arrested for murder. We had to figure out where we were going to live. How to run our business. How to get through each day with this crushing weight of fear and anxiety that left us feeling completely paralyzed. Survival mode had carried us this far. But we were about to find out—it wasn't enough.

Once we returned to Kyle's parents' house, the four of us sat down and made the decision—we would stay with them. There was no other option. We started mapping out our next steps, returning missed calls and texts, and figuring out how we would move all our things in. What we didn't know—what Kyle's dad hadn't told us—was that the media had already found their way to the house. News crews had been waiting outside, trying to get interviews. Supposedly, someone from the Today Show even showed up. I have no idea how the news spread so fast. But suddenly, everyone wanted to know what had happened inside my childhood home. Everyone wanted to understand how something this horrific could unfold in a quiet town in Washington. Within hours, the headlines were everywhere:

Intruder Fatally Stabbed.

Washington Woman Fatally Stabs Home Intruder to Defend Family, Police Say.

Washington Mom Defends Family Against Intruder.

I hated that they focused on me. We were a *team*. I didn't want to be a headline. I didn't want to be their made-for-TV hero. I understood why it was a story—a 125-pound blonde woman stabbing a man to death wasn't something you heard about every day. But the truth was, Kyle had done the real work. *He* had saved our lives that night. Without him, I wouldn't have been able to do what I did.

He had fought a man in the midst of a psychotic break and somehow survived. And all I could think was—if I had been alone, I wouldn't have stood a chance. But the headlines didn't tell that story. They barely scratched the surface of what actually happened. And this—*this*—was where the media's version of events ended:

Intruder breaks in. He's killed. The family is safe.

But for us—for Kyle, for me, for Lyla, for my mom, for our

entire community—this was only the beginning. The shock, the aftermath, the unraveling of everything we thought we knew. And the eventual growth and perspective that unfolded as the years followed. This is why I had to write this book. To tell the story *after* the story.

There were so many layers of life colliding at once—Living with in-laws. Building a new home. Being new parents. Running a business. Grief from my parents, still fresh, separation. My deeply hurting mom, who now lost her dream home. And now, surviving a traumatic home invasion, coupled with a murder investigation and sudden, relentless PTSD. *It was utterly devastating.* There's no other way to put it. It forced us to confront things we never could have imagined. To face some of the hardest work of our lives just to find our way through it.

Detective Bartlett had been right. This was going to be a long road. It would take years.

And what I didn't know then—what I *couldn't* have known—was that this moment would become a catalyst. Not just for healing. But for self-discovery. Looking back, I realize those twenty-four hours were a time when my instincts and intuition had done exactly what they were meant to do. I *knew* he was coming back. I *felt* it. And when it actually happened, it confirmed something I would never again ignore:

Listening to that voice is critical.

I need to say that again—*listening to that voice is critical.*

I had always been aware of intuition in a vague, abstract way.

But that night changed everything. It reshaped my understanding of it, my respect for it.

It gave me a new awareness that I hadn't acknowledged before.

And from that moment on, it became one of the most important forces guiding me forward.

8

MY SAFE PLACE

We jumped right into the endless to-do list. We had to figure out our shifts at the gym and manage programming, membership, and emails—every little backend detail we were responsible for. The foundation for our new house had just been poured, framing had started, and we had to keep up with contractors. And then there was Kyle's firefighting schedule, layered on top of everything else.

But the most concerning part? The unknown of being in a criminal investigation.

Could we somehow go to jail?

I had a certain peace about it knowing what I did was pure self-defense, and after experiencing how all the law enforcement treated us. Not to mention, the care and compassion that Detective Bartlett had shown us in the early morning hours, but continued to as she kept us up to date with the investigation. Yet, that thought couldn't help but sit in the back of my head.

And then there was the trauma—an all-consuming weight that clouded every thought, action, and moment as the shock slowly started to wear off.

It was a relief to have a safe place to land, here at my in-laws, but it came with difficult decisions—like what to do with Lola and Lily.

I knew we couldn't stay in Kyle's parents' small house with two high-energy dogs, and I understood their concerns. But I was *heartbroken*.

People had always told me, "You can't compare your love for your dogs to your love for your child." And before having Lyla, part of me thought, *maybe that's true for you, but I don't know if that will be true for me.*

Now, I understand the difference. But I also knew that Lola and Lily had participated in *saving our lives that night*. If they hadn't woken us up when they did… if Lola hadn't bolted back to the bedroom, showing signs of danger and making Kyle turn around. Everything could have ended so differently.

It felt like I was abandoning them after they had *protected us*, but I had no idea how to fix it. And with so many moving pieces, I didn't have the bandwidth to process it. So we found them a temporary home—first with friends from our gym, and then, more friends from our gym, and eventually, with my dad—until we could figure out a long-term plan.

As we sat in Kyle's parents' kitchen, shortly after arriving back from the infectious disease doctor, his phone rang. It was his fire chief. "Kyle, within thirty minutes of your story hitting the department, firefighters were already calling in to cover your shifts." His chief paused, his voice thick with emotion. "Kyle…"

Kyle looked at me, unsure of what was coming next.

"Your shifts are covered for three months. Take all the time you need to be with your family. And if there's anything else you need, just say the word. You have a family here, too. We're here to support you however we can."

After the call, Kyle and I just sat there.

I didn't know what to say. I hadn't even thought about something like this happening, but the relief that hit me was overwhelming. They knew what we didn't know yet—this wasn't something we'd bounce back from quickly.

To this day, it's still the part of our story that makes us the most emotional.

A twenty-four-hour shift at the fire department is *a lot*. It's long days of unexpected calls, a crappy night of sleep, and a full day away from your family. These firefighters weren't just being *kind*—they were *sacrificing*.

And they weren't getting paid for it.

The fact that so many of them stepped up, without hesitation, to cover Kyle's shifts so he could focus on recovering... I still don't have the words for what that meant.

Kyle had served his community and responded to save the lives of others. Now, his brothers and sisters at the fire department were giving him his turn to receive.

Messages kept flooding in, and we couldn't keep up. Before we knew it, one of our gym members had organized a MealTrain for us. I had never heard of it before, but I quickly learned how wonderful it was. If we had been asked, we probably would have declined—but there wasn't even time to think about it. Between back-to-back appointments with doctors, detectives, and trauma therapists, the last thing on our minds was cooking.

So we accepted. And tried not to feel guilty.

The food was helpful. But the real impact of MealTrain was the *connection*. It was opening the door to a friend or community member, no words needed—just being seen. I still remember the faces of those who showed up. The way they looked at us. The warmth in their eyes as they handed over a meal they had either cooked themselves or gone out of their way to get for us.

Those moments can't be bought.

It's something else entirely.

As time passed, we struggled to figure out how to adjust. We were completely traumatized. *Unsafe*—everywhere, all the time. It took weeks before we felt like we could even drive by ourselves. Even something as simple as sitting in our car outside the gym made my heart race. Every day was exhausting—lack of sleep, paralyzing fear, worrying about whether we would go to trial, trauma therapy, managing the gym, coordinating the new house build, and even grocery shopping scared the crap out of me as I studied every single person I passed to assess if they were safe or not.

It would take six months before I could walk into a store without my head on a constant swivel, expecting to be attacked.

One of the biggest lessons I learned in this season was something I think a lot of people struggle with—receiving. Kyle and I were not the type to accept help. We never felt like we needed it, so asking for it felt foreign. But this experience changed that. It forced us to get comfortable receiving. And it taught us something crucial—it's not just a gift for the person receiving. It's a gift for the person giving. People wanted to help. If we had shut them down, we would have been rejecting their genuine desire to show up for us. I know I would feel the same way if the roles were reversed. If someone I cared about was suffering, I would want to help in any way I could.

Deepak Chopra puts it best:

"To graciously receive is an expression of the dignity of giving."

About a week after the event, we received a basket of handwritten letters. Our gym members had set out paper and pens, inviting people to write us notes of love and encouragement. These letters helped us get through each day. Because even though the intruder was gone, the fear wasn't. I couldn't just turn off the panic, the hyper-awareness, and the exhaustion. Every moment was a fight.

Walking down a hallway? I had to pass three doorways, and with each one, my body expected an attack.

Going to the bathroom? I would cautiously open the door, poke my head out, and check both directions before stepping back into the hallway.

Hundreds of these moments. Every single day. And then, every night, we'd climb into bed, *try* to relax, *try* to sleep… only to wake up and relive it all over again.

Two weeks after the event, Kyle and I took our first drive alone. We had errands to run—the bank, the grocery store—and decided to stop at Starbucks. I pulled up to the window, rolled it down, and was met with the soft, kind smile of the young barista.

"Hello, how are you today?" she cheerfully said.

I'll never forget her face and genuine smile. I had driven through this Starbucks countless times before, but on this day, that small interaction meant everything. She had no idea what we had been through. But her smile gave me hope. Her kindness reminded me that there are good people in the world. It's amazing how such a simple gesture like that can carry a powerful impact.

I thought, *she's happy. Someday, I will be, too.*

It was a small, quiet reminder that things could and would get better.

As the days stretched on, the exhaustion, the sleepless nights, and the relentless anxiety started to take their toll.

Everything felt dangerous: Getting in a car. Taking a shower. Walking into a room. Stepping into an elevator for therapy appointments. Opening *any* door.

My body was still convinced an attacker was waiting on the other side. At the advice of others, Kyle and I scheduled an appointment with our doctor. After hearing everything, he prescribed me Xanax—three times a day or as needed.

I panicked. I'd only ever heard horror stories—people getting addicted, and relying on something outside of themselves in order to feel normal. Or how casually people joked, "Just give me a Xanax!" like it was nothing. I didn't want to be a person who couldn't live without it. I had never imagined taking anything like this. I liked my feet on the ground and my mind clear. I hated the thought of losing control. I fully believed that little pill would turn me into some sort of zombie, numb and emotionless. Exposure therapy, while brutal and exhausting, was helping *a little*. But it wasn't enough. I wasn't functioning. I was barely making it through the long, draining days. And with the constant cycle of sleepless nights, I hit a breaking point. I had to try something. So, I chose to trust my doctor. And I was wrong about Xanax. I didn't turn into a zombie. Instead, I felt relief. Small, short-lived glimpses of what it felt like to be normal again. I'd walk past a door and—for the first time in weeks—not feel shivers rush down my spine. I'd sit in a car alone, and if someone walked past, I wouldn't immediately feel electricity shoot down my arms. My nervous system had been fried—locked in fight mode for weeks. This was the first time I could actually feel it settle, even just a little. I knew I didn't want to rely on it forever. But for now, I took the help where I could get it.

A few days later, a friend from our MealTrain offered to come to Kyle's parents' house and make us dinner. It was comforting to have a friend over just to feel some normalcy for a while. She made baked chicken, roasted vegetables, and potatoes—simple but right up our alley. More than the food, it was nice to have a friend to have a conversation with and distract ourselves from the day-to-day routine that constantly was clouded with trauma.

As she moved around the kitchen, I asked, "What can I do to help?"

She waved me off. "Oh, Tennyson, you seriously don't need to help. I got it! You guys just sit back and hang out."

I shook my head. "Don't be crazy. I'm very capable of helping. What can I do?"

Recognizing I wanted to be useful, she thought for a second before saying, "Ummm, okay. I guess you could chop the chicken."

Without thinking, I walked over to the butcher block, grabbed a large kitchen knife—and everything came rushing back. The fear. The terror. It was as if my body was reliving that night all over again. My hands gripped the handle, my eyes stuck on the raw chicken in front of me, and suddenly, I froze. I didn't know what to do as my heart started beating out of my chest, my mind raced in a million directions, and shivers ran all over my body. I didn't want to cry. I was strong. But I was also tired and concerned at how my body consistently did things I couldn't control.

I set the knife down slowly, carefully. My stomach sank with embarrassment and frustration as I turned away, hoping to walk away without anyone realizing, instead seeing it all unfold. They watched, unsure of what to do, unsure of how to help. I didn't say a word. I just walked straight to Kyle, buried my face in his chest, and bawled.

No one spoke. No one needed to. We all knew this was unlike anything we'd ever faced before. And we had a long road ahead of us.

This wasn't the only time it happened. Not long after the attack, we left for a trip we had planned months before—a long weekend at a lake house in Eastern Washington for Kyle's 30th birthday. We debated whether or not to go. But everything at home was so heavy—getting away, even just for a few days, felt like a much-needed distraction. The weekend was full of cornhole battles, walks to the lake, morning coffee on the massive porch overlooking Lake Chelan, and, somehow, a spontaneous decision to recreate the viral Harlem Shake video. For the first time in days, I felt like *me* again.

Until I found myself back in the kitchen, helping with dinner. Without thinking, I reached for the knife again. And just like before, it *hit*. The panic. The fear. The full-body wave of anxiety. I swallowed hard, forcing back tears, frustrated that I was still so weak…that I was still at the mercy of this uncontrollable fear and anxiety. I set the knife down, moved out of sight, and quietly snuck into the bedroom. I shut the door behind me. Walked straight to the closet. Let my back hit the wall and slid to the floor, tucking my knees to my chest and burying my head, I let the tears flow. *God, am I ever going to feel normal again?* I couldn't believe how triggering it was to do something so simple.

Would I ever be able to pick up a knife without feeling this rush of panic? Would I ever stop *reliving* it? Would I ever stop feeling trapped in this constant loop?

I had always known community was important. I'd always valued being a good friend and a good contributor. But this? This changed everything. Our friends, our community—they *carried* us through this. They made meals. Checked in constantly. Sent letters and messages. Slept over at Kyle's parents' house when his parents were out of town. Slept with me once Kyle was back at work. Took care of our dogs when we couldn't. Updated social media so we didn't have to. I can't even begin to describe how much it meant. They were, and are, amazing.

But not everything was going smoothly.

My mom was struggling. More than anything, I knew she wanted to stay with us and Lyla—to be with family after what we all had just been through. But staying at Kyle's parents' house wasn't an option. For us all, there were too many layers of trauma. Too many emotions heightened all at once. For the first time in my life, I had zero capacity to take care of someone else. It felt foreign to me. But I had no choice. I had to protect my energy for Kyle, for Lyla, and for myself.

She stayed with a neighbor the first night—someone we barely knew but who graciously opened their home. Then, she went to her mother's, but that wasn't ideal, either. She had already signed up for a trauma retreat in California, so the plan became: she would go there and then figure out her next steps. Between the financial strain my parents were under, their relationship falling apart, and now their dream home becoming a crime scene, everything was a disaster. I wasn't involved in handling it—I couldn't be. I was barely holding my own life together.

My mom ended up in a crummy monthly rental hotel in Sacramento. It broke my heart to see her living situation, alone and much different than the home she had loved so dearly. Meanwhile, my dad moved back into the house, along with my sister, who had been living in and out of the house, to oversee repairs. I didn't realize that after something like this, there wasn't some magical cleanup crew that came in and fixed everything. It was *our* responsibility. The blood had soaked through the carpet and the subfloor. The walls were stained. The baseboards were ruined. I avoided that house like the plague.

At that time, we just lived life one day—sometimes one hour—at a time. The light at the end of the tunnel? Our new home was still being built. We would have a fresh start. And even though we had no idea how we'd ever live alone again… We were *slowly* working our way toward it.

9

THE SHEPHERDS

A month or two after the event, one of Kyle's firefighter colleagues reached out with an unexpected question: "Would you be open to getting a protection dog?"

By this time, we had learned that the investigation had been closed. Thoughts of going to trial or ending up in jail could be behind us as all the evidence, testimonies, and toxicology reports were reviewed and undoubtedly proved our actions as life-saving self-defense.

Through our endless conversations with law enforcement and detectives, we constantly asked them how to protect ourselves better. One of the things they repeatedly told us was that having a dog was one of the biggest deterrents to intruders.

"Most criminals want an easy target. Dogs make things complicated."

Of course, our intruder wasn't operating under normal logic—he was in a full-blown psychotic break, which made me feel like he probably wouldn't have cared. But still, it was valuable information.

And the thought of getting a protection dog? It was the first thing that had made us feel excited in a long time.

Since we were still sleeping in my in-laws' bedroom, I thought, *Maybe—just maybe—a protection dog could help us finally move back into our own space.*

Without us even asking, the fire department had already done their research. They had connected with a highly respected local trainer who specialized in Schutzhund—the intense sport of training German Shepherds, Belgian Malinois, and Dutch Shepherds for personal protection. In other words, dogs trained to *neutralize* a threat. Kyle's department offered to sponsor us to get a dog. Another completely unexpected gift that left us speechless. Around the same time, Kyle's fire department and a local CrossFit gym launched a fundraiser on social media—friends, family, acquaintances, and even total strangers who had been shaken by our story generously donated. Because everything was happening behind the scenes, we had no idea how much was raised. Years later, when I finally had the mental space to process it all, I learned that a top-tier protection dog could cost upwards of $40,000.

I couldn't believe it.

Things were falling into our laps exactly when we needed them—even when we didn't know we needed them. People seemed to anticipate our needs before we did.

Eventually, Kyle would go back to work and I would be alone in a new house. To be completely candid—I wanted a dog that would *annihilate* anyone with bad intentions who stepped one foot inside my house. The thought of having a protection dog became our biggest source of hope in feeling safe again. Eleven years later, as I write this, my next generation of German Shepherd is lying beside me. And to this day, a protection dog is still the single biggest reason I feel safe at home.

This idea of a dog also forced us to have some brutally honest conversations about Lola and Lily. We still had months before moving into our new house, and my dad could only keep them for so long. As much as I loved them, we had to be real with ourselves. Two little Yorkies—high-energy, accident-prone—on top of a protection dog, a baby, and a still-traumatized family? It wasn't possible.

It broke my heart, but we had no choice. We knew we had to find them a forever home.

With the funds in place, we were connected to the trainer. We were warned it could take time to find the right dog. But since our house wasn't ready yet, the timing was perfect. The trainer, Les, drove three hours to meet us. Les was a retired police officer and K-9 handler with decades of experience in narcotics detection, Schutzhund, police K-9 training, and family protection dogs. He had hundreds of awards under his belt. We could not have been connected to a better person. Les insisted on bringing the dogs to us instead of having us come to him. He had prepped Kyle with a bite sleeve—so Kyle could see firsthand what these dogs were capable of. Kyle stood on one side of the yard. Les stood on the other, holding the first dog back. Then, with a single command—Les released him. My jaw dropped as the dog exploded across the yard at full speed, launched into the air, and clamped onto Kyle's arm. It was unbelievable. I actually laughed in shock and out of sheer disbelief at how powerful these dogs were. *Hell freaking yeah.*

Kyle looked at me, and I knew we were both thinking the same thing.

The first two dogs Les brought out were Belgian Malinois.

Absolutely beautiful—lightning-fast, extraordinarily trained, but… high-maintenance. Les explained their energy levels. These dogs needed miles of running every single day. With our already overwhelming lives—new parents, running a gym, rebuilding from trauma, endless appointments—there was no way we could keep up.

And then Les brought out Kiitos. Kiitos wasn't for sale. He was Les's personal dog—a Dutch Shepherd, all muscle, sleek brindle coat, pure power. The second he turned the corner with Kiitos, the energy shifted. And then—Kiitos surprised all of us. Instead of being intensely focused like the other dogs, he walked straight up to Kyle and melted into his lap.

Kyle and I stared at each other. This is it. We joked about taking him, knowing he wasn't available. But the moment was not lost on us.

About ten minutes after Les left, Kyle's phone rang. "Hey Kyle, I've been thinking ever since I left your house…I know how much you guys loved Kiitos. You need him more than I do. If you want Kiitos, he's yours."

Kyle looked at me in disbelief. "Dude. There's no way we can take *your* dog."

"No, I mean it," Les said. "It feels right. And I'd be honored if he were part of your family."

We were completely blown away—by his generosity, his belief in us, and this gift we never could have imagined.

As sweet as Kiitos was, after about six months, we realized we weren't a perfect fit. Kiitos needed a *job*—something we couldn't give him. He was meant to be working, not lounging around with a baby. We were devastated, but we knew the right thing was to find a better home for him.

Les helped us transition and found us Ludo, a protection-trained dog who had experience with kids but didn't require as much high-level stimulation. And Ludo was perfect. He made the decade after the event livable. There are pets. And then there are animals that seem to see your soul.

Ludo was my soul dog.

When Kyle was on shift, Ludo slept outside my bedroom door. When Lyla was scared, I would find Ludo sleeping outside her door. Ludo would patrol the yard and run the fence line with the horses next door. And every night, after everyone was in bed, Ludo would find me on the couch and lay right at my feet. He was always there. When we had to put him down ten years later, all I could say was:

Thank you.

Thank you for protecting us.

Thank you for loving our family.

Thank you for being exactly what we needed—when we didn't even know we needed you.

Thank you, Ludo. You will never know the extent of what you gave us.

10

THE FACE OF PTSD

When we first moved into my in-laws, the plan was to stay in Kyle's old childhood bedroom. But Mary immediately picked up on our hesitation.

Without missing a beat, she gently suggested, "If you'd like, you two can stay in our bedroom with us for a few nights and see how you do. It's no trouble at all. We'll just slide the mattress from Kyle's room onto the floor. You can move into another room whenever you're ready."

After nearly *three* months of sleeping next to my in-laws—tiptoeing to the bathroom at night, trying not to wake anyone—we somehow got used to the extreme awkwardness of four grown adults sharing a space meant for two. Our mattress sat on the floor close by, and while it should have been unbearable, the comfort they provided in feeling like they protected us was all that mattered.

But eventually, we knew *it was time*. We had to try sleeping in a room alone.

So, on Kyle's day off, we dragged our queen-sized mattress into Norm's office—a tiny room with a built-in desk right next to Lyla's room and across the hall from Kyle's parents' bedroom. It was Kyle's brother's old bedroom. Their actual guest bedroom was larger, more private, and even had its own bathroom, but it was on the opposite side of the house. And that was a hard *no*. At least in the cramped little office, we were close enough to still feel protected.

The setup was tight. Our mattress was wedged between the built-in desk and the closet, leaving zero space on Kyle's side of the bed and inches on mine between the bed and the closet. In a weird way, I liked it—being "packed in" felt safer, like there was no room for anything—or anyone—to hide next to the bed. But the window tortured me. A giant sliding glass window faced the front yard and one of the main streets in our small town. It wasn't a busy street, but it didn't matter. It felt exposed. Vulnerable. Like an open invitation for someone to watch me. Or worse.

Every night, as I lay in bed, I imagined someone lurking in the front yard. Someone crouched in the bushes below the window. Someone waiting for the perfect moment to slide it open and come inside. Then, my thoughts would jump—to the bedroom door. *What if someone found our room? What if they snuck in while we were sleeping? What if they killed us before Kyle's parents even knew what was happening?*

Lying there in that room, night after night, felt like exposure therapy in itself.

I was exhausted. My system was fried. Done. Every single thing in my life—sleeping, driving, showering, grocery shopping—felt like exposure therapy. Xanax was helping in spurts but would wear off and my system would be on high alert all over again. I was trying to remain positive and be patient as time moved on, but it was wearing me down little by little.

Right around the time we moved across the hall, Kyle went back to work. Technically, his shifts were forty-eight hours. But his Lieutenant, Troy, had an idea. He suggested Kyle come home at night—just from 7 pm to 7 am—because he knew nights were still the hardest for both of us. And firefighters volunteered to cover Kyle's night shifts for months. Again, this wasn't something Kyle or I ever would have thought to ask for. Everyone had already done so much. The idea of asking for more hadn't even registered. But here they go again, always anticipating our needs before we did.

I don't know if it was from pure exhaustion or if it was some kind of forced exposure therapy finally working, but after a few nights in the office, I actually slept. And then another night. And another. It wasn't ideal. And they certainly weren't glorious nights of uninterrupted sleep and blissful dreams. But we did it. We had slept alone for the first time in three months. And it felt like a victory. I was so proud of us. Kyle's parents were proud. *Maybe time really did help.*

After three months of Kyle coming home at night—six months after the break-in—it was time for him to go back to full shifts. And I wasn't ready for it. I knew it had to happen, but the thought of sleeping alone in that room next to that massive window made me terrified.

Troy, again, had an idea. "If you and Lyla want, you are more than welcome to sleep at the station when Kyle's on shift."

And for a second—I actually considered it. *Would it be*

crazy to bring a baby to a fire station? Would she wake up if the alarms went off in the middle of the night? Honestly…maybe? Lyla was a good sleeper. But then reality set in. Even if I did bring her, what about when I had to go to the bathroom? I'd have to walk down a brightly lit hallway in my pajamas, makeup-free, looking like death, and who knows who I'd run into? *God, that'd be embarrassing.* I knew the answer. I had to figure this out.

As soon as Kyle's full shifts started, the sleepless nights returned. No matter what I did, I couldn't sleep. His parents were so kind, offering to let me sleep in their room again while he was away. But at this point, it felt even weirder to sleep alone with them and I knew I needed to push myself to figure it out.

I tried everything:

- Listening to sleep music designed to calm the nervous system. *Didn't help.*

- Buying a gratitude journal to shift my focus to positive things. *Nice… but it didn't stop the nightmares.*

- Writing about Lyla in a journal—all the sweet, funny things she was doing to focus on the positives. *Didn't stop the panic at night.*

- Using Xanax, essential oils, prayer, breathing exercises—*Nothing was stopping my mind from racing, my heart from beating out of my chest, and anxiety coursing through my body as I lay in bed.*

I felt hopeless. And that was when I finally admitted it. I needed more help.

I reached out to a close friend whose family had connections with top local psychiatrists. I didn't know what a psychiatrist would do for me. I just knew they were the heavy hitters. And maybe—just maybe—they had some idea that could help me sleep.

Walking into the psychiatrist's office for the first time, shame hit me hard. *Why can't I figure this out on my own? I'm doing the exposure work. I'm going to therapy. I'm trying everything I can, from essential oils to journaling to prayer to gratitude....I'm taking baby steps every day. Why is my body still betraying me?*

I looked around at the sterile waiting room, the fluorescent lighting, and the chairs that had probably been there for thirty years, and I hated that my journey had brought me here. I had seen movies that inaccurately portrayed those who went to psychiatrists. And now, I was one of them. The psychiatrist was nice. Extremely intelligent. And as he explained dopamine, serotonin, and how trauma affects the brain, I realized I had no idea what he was talking about. I tried to follow. I had taken Organic Chemistry in college. I hated it but eventually figured it out. But his explanation was completely catching me off guard. All I knew was that it led to this: "Hormonally, you are depressed, Tennyson."

Wait. What? *I'm depressed?*

His recommendation: antidepressants.

Hearing that word destroyed me. I wanted a different answer. Some magic talk therapy. Some breathing exercises I hadn't tried. Something that would snap me out of this.

But the way he explained it made sense. He explained to me the function of antidepressants and how they help support hormones properly so that my body can start to relax when it is supposed to and not stay stuck in this fight-or-flight state. This is a massive simplification of what he told me, but that understanding was actually helpful as it allowed me to have a very basic awareness of what was going on in my body at a cellular level. So, no matter how much therapy, exposure, or gratitude journaling I did—those were not tools that were going to get me out of a trauma response. I didn't want to take it. But I wanted to sleep.

That first night, I was terrified to swallow the pill. *Would I get high? Would I start hallucinating? Would I turn into a potato sack?*

So, I didn't. I was too scared to. I thought maybe, if I tried just one more time, I could figure it out on my own. Yet, the past repeated itself.

Tired, hopeless, and frustrated, the next night, I took it. And I waited. And nothing happened, except...I finally slept.

I share this story cautiously. Medication is a sensitive topic, and this isn't about promoting or condemning it. It's about being honest with my own experience. I learn different tools I wish I would have known at this time so I may not have had to pursue taking antidepressants, but it's not how my story played out. And the biggest lesson I've learned? *No one else knows you better than you.*

Healing looks different for everyone.

And there is no timeline for it.

After four months of sleeping in Kyle's parents' office, our home was finally finished.

Kyle, using his time off from the fire department, built a six-foot fence around our entire half-acre property—one more layer of protection to help us feel safe. And then Kiitos jumped right over it. So that was fun. We'd have to figure that out, but honestly, we were impressed. Along with the fence, we installed security cameras and an alarm system, obtained concealed carry licenses, and, yes, purchased firearms—choosing bullets that would be particularly effective. We even added air conditioning, something that wasn't in our budget, but there was no way in hell we were cracking a bedroom window open at night. Between Kiitos, our security system, and every safety measure in place, we should have felt safe.

But PTSD doesn't work like that.

Moving in was bittersweet—a mix of relief and fear. This home had been two years in the making. It was something we had dreamed about for years. But it was also the first time in seven months that we would be sleeping alone in a house. Everything about it felt new and unknown. Thank God for the white noise fan we had become dependent on—it helped drown out every little sound that would have otherwise sent us spiraling. And thank God for Kiitos—sleeping right outside our bedroom door, positioned at the top of the stairs, protecting both us and Lyla. He was the biggest reason we could even begin to adjust.

Kyle was back at work full-time. And even with all of our safety measures and the medication helping regulate my nervous system, I still couldn't sleep alone with Lyla. Thankfully, our friends stepped in. Just as they had done when we were at Kyle's parents' house, they continued to stay over on nights when Kyle was on shift. Some slept on the couch. Some took Kyle's place beside me in bed. They did whatever made me feel the most comfortable.

Part of me felt guilty—like I was putting people out who had their own families, their own lives. But they *never* made me feel that way. They usually beat me to it, already knowing Kyle's schedule and offering before I could even ask. And now, with more life behind me, with people who have come and gone, I see it even more clearly— *There are friends for a reason. Friends for a season. And friends for a lifetime.* These were lifetime friends. The kind that sees you at your most vulnerable and responds with compassion, patience, and love. The kind that reminds you—you are not alone.

By this point, life *looked* fairly normal. We were in our home. Kyle was back at work. We were running the gym and coaching classes. (Granted, a member would still meet us early or stay late so we wouldn't have to open or close the gym alone.) I ran errands. I went to appointments. We were sleeping, for the most part. But the thoughts never stopped.

Whether I was walking through my house, driving to run errands, coaching at the gym, or lying in bed—my brain was constantly scanning for threats. Being in the car was particularly triggering. If I pulled up to a stoplight and glanced over at another driver who didn't look friendly, I immediately wondered if they were going to pull out a gun and shoot me. If a car followed behind me for too long, I became convinced they were tracking me. If a driver was aggressive—tailgating or cutting me off—I assumed they hated me, that they were going to follow me home, that they wanted me dead. I ran through escape plans. *How would I lose them?*

What would I do if they followed me to my destination? And even now—over a decade later—I catch myself having these same thoughts.

Just the other day, I was being tailgated. I tapped my brakes lightly, hoping they'd back off. They didn't. And just like that, my body went on high alert. You'd think these thoughts would be gone by now. They're not. And accepting that? It's been brutal. For so long, I believed that if I just did enough work, if I just kept pushing myself, I'd get there. But here's the truth— healing is *not* about "pushing through." It is *not* about "just getting over it." It is *not* about "time healing all wounds." Time helps. But time alone doesn't heal. And I didn't know that then. Society is full of messages like: "Just take action." "Move forward." "Focus on the future." "Stop dwelling on the past." And while those messages might work for some things, they grossly miss overcoming traumatic experiences that leave their mark.

At this point, I didn't even fully understand PTSD. I knew I had been through trauma. I knew I was still stuck in fear. But I didn't know how deep it ran. The National Center for PTSD describes PTSD as "A mental health problem that can only develop after you experience or witness a life-threatening event. It's normal to have stress reactions, and most people start feeling better after a few weeks. But if symptoms last longer than a month and cause problems in your life, it could be PTSD."

They outline four core symptoms of PTSD: If you have each of these symptoms, you meet the criteria for PTSD.

1. Reliving the event (re-experiencing symptoms). Flashbacks. Nightmares. Memories that feel real.

2. Avoiding things that remind you of the event. Avoiding places, conversations, people, or even thoughts about what happened.

3. More negative thoughts and feelings than before. Feeling disconnected from others. Struggling with self-worth. Seeing the world as dangerous.

4. Feeling on edge (hyperarousal). Constantly scanning for threats. Feeling jittery, irritable, or on high alert.

I wish I had heard this definition during that time. Maybe I wouldn't have beat myself up so much for not feeling better faster. I wish I had known then what I know now.

That trauma doesn't just live in memories.

It lives in the body.

And no amount of willpower can override an unresolved nervous system response.

One of the most accurate quotes I had found was from Dr. Gabor Maté, a renowned physician and author:

> ***"The attempt to escape from pain creates more pain. The willingness to accept pain as part of the healing process creates the possibility of a genuine healing."***

In the coming chapters, I'll share what actually helped—what truly made a difference—and what I learned about healing beyond time alone. Because if there's one thing I know now that I didn't then—You cannot *think* your way out of trauma. You have to *feel* your way through it.

11

SOMETHING TO BE GRATEFUL FOR

If you passed me on the street during this time, I would have looked completely normal. Maybe a messy ponytail, dark circles under my eyes—but *normal*. I smiled. I laughed. I worked out. I ran a business. I kept up with all the mom things. But under the surface, there was a mess I didn't know how to clean up.

I was happy in so many ways, yet a constant undercurrent of anxiety *never* left me. It was like living with an invisible weight—one I couldn't just take off when I wanted. The antidepressants helped me sleep, but they didn't quiet my nervous system.

A year had passed, and reality hit hard—*What if things never change?*

I was exhausted. Not the *tired* kind of exhausted. The kind of exhaustion that comes from spending every waking moment assessing threats, creating *exit plans*, and strategizing how to minimize danger. I tried to push the thoughts away, to fight them off. But that didn't work. Instead, I judged myself. *Tenny, you're lucky. You're so freaking lucky. Why are you still struggling?*

I had everything I ever wanted: A beautiful home we had dreamed about for years. An amazing fire department supporting Kyle. A tight-knit gym community we loved. Lyla—sweet, easy, an actual angel of a baby. And Kyle.

I was still as into him as the day I wrote his name in my binder. *Maybe even more*—after everything we had been through together. It was interesting that our first dance at our wedding had been "By Your Side," knowing we'd have hard moments to walk through together, but not knowing how literal all those lyrics would mean. Or that the *real* battle would be surviving the aftermath together. Often, I felt weak for still being so paralyzed by fear—for feeling like I was somehow failing at happiness. So, I'd force myself into the grateful mindset. *You should just be grateful, Tenny. People would kill for this life. You have everything you wanted—so why do you feel like this?*

And the truth? I *was* grateful. But gratitude didn't erase the fear.

My biggest fear was that someone else—some unknown stranger—would hear our story, relate to the intruder, and want to finish what he started. This man had come out of nowhere. I didn't know him. There was no warning. Like the Detectives said, they believed he saw me somewhere and that I might have reminded him of his ex-wife. Which meant that, at any moment, in any place, another stranger could see me. And maybe I would trigger them just as I did for the intruder.

Being alone made me feel small, vulnerable, and like an easy target. I knew I couldn't spend my life glued to Kyle's side. So I developed a new habit—I assessed every man I passed.

Was he safe? Was there a cue that put me on edge? Did he move in a way that seemed off? If I felt even a hint of unease, I watched him like a hawk—making sure I had a plan. And if we made eye contact, I carefully calculated my facial expression. Not too friendly, so it wouldn't be misinterpreted. But not *too* cold, in case that might make him angry and want to attack. I felt this because I still didn't know what I had done to set the intruder off. And so, if I made a mistake in just being seen to set someone off, I was going to do everything in my power to prevent that from happening again.

While at grocery stores, Target, the bank, and walking down a sidewalk—I watched people move through the world with so much freedom. And I *craved it*. I remembered that feeling. But it felt so far away now.

I will never forget the day it hit me—the exhaustion, the frustration, the sadness, and the hopelessness.

Kyle was at the firehouse, and I was home alone with Lyla. She was her usual happy self—sitting in her little bumbo seat on the kitchen island after lunch, playing with her stuffed toy. I stepped away to use the bathroom. Bathrooms still felt unsafe—the only time I was truly alone, the only time I had to open the door to the unknown when I was done. I shut the door quickly. And, like always, my mind went to the worst-case scenario. Someone was waiting for me. Someone was about to attack. Someone was going to rape and kill me and Lyla. I have to get out of here.

I tried to push the thoughts aside, but they wouldn't stop. And then—a thought appeared.

A surprising and foreign thought. *Man, it would be nice to not wake up one day.*

I froze. *Did I really just think that?*

It was so out of character. But it also felt true. Tears welled up in my eyes. I bent over, my elbows on my knees, head in my hands.

I had done everything I could to heal. And I was still drowning in fear.

I wanted to go back to Lyla. But I also had to sit with what had just happened because the thought of *not being here* had felt like relief. And that scared me.

I washed my hands, avoiding looking at myself. But when I finally looked up, I saw *her*. This tired girl who had tried so hard. I felt heartbroken for her, but I didn't know how to help. I left the bathroom and walked back down the hall.

Before Lyla even saw me, I caught a glimpse of her—sitting there. Happy. Content. Completely at peace. The second I turned the corner, she looked up—and lit up. Her whole face radiated. She flapped her tiny hands excitedly, smiling from ear to ear. And in that moment—I tried to snap out of it. *What the hell, Tenny? Get it together. Re-focus on what's good. Smile. Be happy.*

Suicide was not a stranger to me. I had lost family members and friends. And I had seen firsthand how it shattered those left behind. I had *always* felt deeply for people who got to that place. *How much pain did they feel to feel life was better off without them?* I never saw it as selfish. But now—I understood it in a way I never had before.

I didn't tell Kyle. I should have. But I didn't want to worry him. Besides that, the thought woke me up. I now had an awareness to pay attention to and trusted I was taking steps forward and that just because I had the thought didn't mean I was going to do anything about it. I wasn't in therapy at the time, other than my psychiatrist appointments—which felt more like doctor's visits than actual talk therapy. So, I stayed the course. I leaned on my friends. I stuck with the meds. Remained aware. And—bit by bit—things did improve.

People say, "Your trauma doesn't define you." And while I agree in some ways. In other ways, I don't. My trauma *does* define me. Not in a *victim* way. But in a *this-changed-me-forever* way.

The best metaphor I've heard? *A wound vs. a scar.* Trauma is a wound. Unhealed wounds get triggered easily. Healed wounds become scars. Scars never disappear. But they also don't bleed.

And healing—that's been my work. Not just from *this* trauma—but from all the little wounds I didn't even realize I was carrying.

I've also heard the phrase, "It's not your fault, but it is your responsibility." And that has never rung truer. Healing wasn't just about working through this one event. It was about everything else—all the small traumas I had never realized. If I had to describe it, it's like someone rolled up in a garbage truck, dumped a ton of crap in my front yard, and then escaped to Canada. (Nothing against Canada—it just felt far away.) Now, I had two choices. I could chase them down, demanding they come back and clean up their mess. Or—I could accept that it was my yard, and if I wanted it clean again, I had to figure out how to clean it myself. Sure, family, friends, and the occasional really nice neighbor could offer support. But no one else could take full responsibility for clearing the mess except for me. Because it was mine now.

Life can be brutal. I know I got lucky in so many ways. I see people losing their children, their spouses, their parents. I see the weight of addiction, abuse, trauma, devastating diagnoses, and grief so deep that it seems impossible to crawl out of. And that's just big T Trauma—the obvious, undeniable kind. Then, there are the smaller traumas, the ones that quietly shape us in ways we don't even realize. "You're so lazy." "I can't believe you did that." "How could you spill that?" "That's so stupid." "Why can't you be more like your brother/sister?" "Wow, that's what you wore?" "You're too sensitive." "You're too loud." "You're too much."

Or worse, the absence of positive reinforcement. Not just for achievements but for simply being who you are. We all experience it. It's all relative. And no one's pain is more or less valid than another's.

What kills me is watching people suffer—either because they're too scared to face their pain or because they don't even realize how much it has shaped their lives. They've got that pile of garbage rotting in their front yard. And instead of dealing with it, they just try to ignore it— letting it sit there, slowly making everything worse. Because healing is overwhelming. It's complicated. It's misunderstood. It requires getting uncomfortable. So, instead, we do what we're taught to do. We numb out. With social media. With alcohol. With drugs. With overworking. With shopping. With obsessively working out. With Netflix binges. With anything that distracts us from the real work. Or, we just plain ignore it.

I know—because I've tried numbing out to social media, Netflix binges, not eating, and obsessively working out. It might make life feel fine. But it also blocks the deeper experience—the kind of love, joy, connection, and freedom that only comes when you finally clean up the mess.

And if that's not enough of a reason to face it, I go back to the work of Dr. Gabor Maté.

> **The way unresolved trauma manifests in the body—**
> **In addiction. In autoimmune diseases.**
> **In chronic stress.**
> **In anxiety and depression.**
> **We carry more than we realize.**
> **And if we don't deal with it—It finds a way to deal with us.**

Truthfully, after the break-in, I second-guessed whether I wanted more kids. Kyle and I had always dreamed of having three, but after everything we'd been through, I couldn't imagine bringing another child into this crazy world. I also didn't know if I had it in me to be a good mom to more kids when I had been treading water for so long.

But about a year after the break-in, even though I still wrestled with intrusive thoughts, the idea of another baby suddenly *felt* right. It was exciting—something to set our minds and hearts on, something good to focus on: the future rather than the past. My intuition, the same one that had been spot on before, sank in, and I just *knew*. Not long after, Kyle and I were beyond excited to find out I was pregnant. It was exactly the kind of news we needed. And Lyla was thrilled.

As soon as Lyla was old enough to engage with toys, she was naturally nurturing. My mom and Mary constantly bought her baby dolls, and she loved every second of it. I have a video of her, taken shortly before I found out I was pregnant, where she's sitting in our empty bathtub surrounded by ten little baby dolls. She had them all laid out on blankets, tucking them in one by one, telling us their names, and giving a full play-by-play of how they were doing. So when we told Lyla the news, she gasped, covered her mouth with both hands, her eyes squinting as she gave the biggest grin, and said, "I get my own baby!"

After finding out I was pregnant, I immediately called my psychiatrist's office. They noted my pregnancy and assured me I was fine to continue my antidepressant. When I went in for my eight-week OB appointment, I was excited—not just for the pregnancy, but to see my doctor again. She had been with me through my pregnancy with Lyla, and after seeing her almost weekly for so many months, I felt close to her. She had also been one of my best friend's doctors, and between that connection and our history, it felt like we had our own little special circle. To this day, even though she's retired, we still keep in touch.

As I sat on the exam table in my gown, staring out the window, I couldn't wait to surprise her. After everything that had happened, this was such positive news and left so much excitement to focus on. When she walked in, she gave me the biggest hug. She had reached out after the break-in and already knew it had been quite a journey since the last time she saw me was when Lyla was born. As we caught up, I didn't even think twice when updating my medical history and mentioning I was on an antidepressant. But then I noticed her pause.

My heart started racing and my smile faded.

I watched as she soaked it all in—the weight of what had happened, the reality of how it had altered my life.

She took a breath and said, "Tennyson, it's OK. The antidepressant is a Class C drug. It's safer for you to stay on it than to risk the impact of going off."

I felt hot. Like, physically fuming hot—from the inside-out.

Until then, I hadn't spent much energy feeling angry about what that man had done. I had been too focused on trying to sleep, feel normal again, and just get through each day. But this—this hit differently.

The thought that his actions could now impact the innocent baby growing inside me made me furious. It made everything feel so much more real. The ripple effects of that one horrific night weren't just affecting me and Kyle anymore. They were extending into this new life I was carrying.

I left the office, trusting her advice but still needing to shift my focus to something positive.

Decorating isn't my thing, but I thought it might help to control what I *could* control and to focus on what was to come as I worked on the nursery.

After finding out the sex, I immediately started pulling together a little boy's nursery. It felt exciting. He would inherit Lyla's white crib, the changing table I had scored on Craigslist, and the world's most comfortable nursery glider. But I painted the walls a light grayish blue, added a five-foot-tall giraffe (a gift from one of my best friends), and splurged on a wooden elephant cutout from Pottery Barn Kids. I stacked my favorite baby books next to the glider, books gifted to me by my mom and from my baby shower with Lyla. The room felt cozy, inviting, and sweet—ready for our sweet little boy. As my belly grew, Ludo would rest his head on it, cuddling me and our sweet boy. The thought I had in the bathroom hadn't returned, friends no longer had to stay with me while Kyle was gone, and the worrying thoughts and nightmares I would have were still present, but at least not overwhelming. I was alright. I was finding myself again.

Skyler was born perfectly healthy and impossibly sweet. He rarely cried and seemed to come into this world with a built-in smile. Unlike Lyla, who had been born with a full head of dark hair, Skyler was completely bald with barely-there blonde fuzz. He was a total snuggler (and still has his moments I hold on to at nine years old). As much work as a newborn is, there was something healing about nurturing a baby. The endless cycles of diapers, feeding, bathing, and laundry kept me busy—and that distraction was exactly what I needed.

And then there was Lyla. Watching her with Skyler was almost ridiculous—like something out of a storybook. She would hold his tiny hand and snuggle up next to him on the couch as he lay in his newborn lounger. When I nursed, she would "nurse" her own baby dolls. When the bottle came, she demanded to feed him, cradling him in her lap as she held his bottle. Seeing them together made me realize just how much life was coming together, how our dreams were literally unfolding before our eyes.

Even on the day we brought Skyler home, Ludo knew. He walked right up to the car seat, sniffed him, and gently licked Skyler's one-day-old face. From that moment on, he watched over our kids like they were his own.

I had been grateful before, but this was different. This was alignment. Kyle and I had always wanted kids. Now, Lyla had a brother. And Skyler had a sister. We were stepping into the bigger picture of our lives. The one we had imagined before the intruder. And that, more than anything, felt like something to be grateful for.

12

TRUSTING MY INTUITION

After reading *The Gift of Fear* by Gavin DeBecker—the book our homicide detective recommended when I was arrested—I gained a much deeper understanding of fear and where it comes from. DeBecker and his security firm have been hired to protect presidents, the CIA, the Secret Service, and some of the world's most high-profile celebrities. The front of the book boldly claims, "This book can save your life." And now, after reading it four times, I fully believe that statement. Honestly, I think this book should be required reading—especially for women.

Hearing someone hired to protect presidents explain the power of instinct and intuition helped me finally make sense of what happened that day. Fighting for Kyle's and my life was instinct. That deep knowing, that voice inside me whispering, "He's coming back," was intuition.

One of the things I loved about this book is that it gives you permission to *trust* that small inner voice—the one we so often dismiss. I was honestly scared to read it. It took me months to work up the courage to open it because, at the time, nothing about fear felt like a gift. But the more I read, the clearer it became—every detail that had felt off now made sense, leading me to realize he was coming back.

DeBecker explains that women are disproportionately victims of violence and makes it clear that "to be politically correct would mean I am being statistically incorrect."

Still, it's a book everyone should read. Over the years, I've noticed that a lot of men assume intuition is something women have—but that couldn't be further from the truth. This book doesn't just teach you to recognize intuition in yourself but also to understand how it shows up in the people around you.

DeBecker not only speaks about intuition regarding personal threats but in real life, everyday situations that can be a matter of life or death. One of the most heartbreaking stories in the book is about a mother who took her young son in for what was supposed to be a routine, low-risk surgery. When the doctor walked in for pre-op, something felt off. He wasn't warm or reassuring. He was cold and dismissive. The boy sensed it, too. He knew something was wrong. His feelings were dismissed as pre-surgery nerves. His mom had the strongest feeling that they should cancel the procedure. But she talked herself out of it, convincing herself to trust the professional instead of her gut. She ignored the deep knowing inside her—and her son's surgery hit complications and, devastatingly, he never made it out of surgery.

While re-reading the book this year, one quote stopped me dead in my tracks:

"What many others want to dismiss as a coincidence or a gut feeling is, in fact, a cognitive process faster than we recognize and far different from the familiar step-by-step thinking we rely on so willingly. We think conscious thought is somehow better when, in fact, intuition is soaring flight compared to the plotting sluggishness of logic. Nature's greatest accomplishment, the human brain, is never more efficient or invested than when its host is at risk. At those times, intuition is catapulted to another level entirely—a height at which it can accurately be called graceful or even miraculous. Intuition is the journey from A to Z without stopping at any other letter along the way. It is knowing without knowing why."

Read that again.

Before all of this, I didn't think much about intuition. I had heard the phrase "trust your gut," but I never really felt anything in my gut. Maybe I'd get a pit in my stomach now and then, but I never thought of it as some divine message.

Even though I knew he was coming back, I was still shocked when he actually did. It left me wondering: *Where did that thought come from? How in the world did I know? Maybe it was just a coincidence.*

After hearing law enforcement say over and over that break-ins like this never happen twice, I remember questioning myself. *Maybe I was just being paranoid. Maybe I was crazy.*

Clearly, I wasn't.

But here's the problem. PTSD had rewired my brain. I was stuck in constant fear. And since I had been right before, I started to believe that every fear I had would come true. That every intrusive thought was a premonition. Reading DeBecker's book opened my eyes to the power of intuition. But at the time, I only understood it as something that could alert me to danger. I had no idea it could be so much more than that.

Three years after the break-in, *CrossFit Journal* published an article on our story. They flew out, spent a couple of days interviewing us, visited our gym, and gathered all the details to tell the full truth about that night. By the end of our time together, the writer kept saying, "You need to connect with Tony Blauer."

Tony, internationally known for his self-defense work, has spent decades studying fear, violence, intuition, and danger. He's trained military personnel, law enforcement, and civilians worldwide—but at his core, he hates violence. His life's work is about making people safer. After hearing our story, he personally offered to come to our gym and host one of his CrossFit Defense seminars—something he rarely did. Our gym was filled with military members, law enforcement, and CrossFitters who not only knew who he was but deeply respected him. I was one of the only women in the room.

Tony kicked off the two-day seminar by making a point about real violence. "Who here has actually killed someone?" he asked.

Silence.

Here we sat in a room of fifty with mostly trained, jacked, battle-ready men who looked around. Then, Tony turned to me. I awkwardly raised my hand. I was the only one. A 125-pound, 28-year-old blonde woman in a room full of guys who looked way more prepared than I did to kill someone.

His point was clear: Violence doesn't discriminate. Tony's system teaches people to use their body's natural mechanics to defend themselves—no fancy moves, just instinct, refined. It makes self-defense accessible for everyone. But I'll admit, despite how much I admired Tony and wanted to take it seriously, I struggled. The drills felt awkward. Pretending to knee someone in the groin or shove their face into a wall? I felt ridiculous. I kept laughing nervously instead of going all in. And that's exactly why I'm sharing this—so many people avoid learning skills that could save their lives simply because it's uncomfortable. But avoiding it doesn't make the danger disappear.

Two years later, Tony invited me on his *Know Fear* podcast. What neither of us realized was that I would be a terrible guest. Just months before, I had reached out to the detective and shared the message I had received from what seemed to be a stalker with serious intentions. At the time, it felt like I had finally made my way out of PTSD only to be thrown back into all my old patterns. While I sat through the interview, my body was back in full-blown survival mode. For months, I studied every person I walked past, making sure they were not a potential threat. I couldn't sit with my back to the door at restaurants. I checked my backseat before driving. The nightmares returned every night. I even made Ludo do full home inspections before I went inside the house.

My thoughts were in constant analysis mode. *Am I safe? Is this a threat?* And I hated it. It had been five years since the break-in. *How is this a constant all over again?*

I wanted so badly to show up for Tony, someone I deeply admired, but I didn't realize how much my answers reflected someone who needed help.

What triggered it all? A single social media message: Where a random stranger sent me something that immediately set off every alarm in my body.

When I showed it to Kyle, his response was different: "Wow. That's messed up. You should just block and delete him."

I wanted to do that, but this was the same feeling I had about the guy coming back. It was *so* strong. I was still learning to understand instinct and intuition, but there was no doubt in my mind that this message was more than just a delete and block.

I had gotten hateful messages before—things like "You're a whore. You should have died." I had learned to brush those aside. But this was different. I couldn't explain why, but I knew it wasn't just a troll being hateful. So I did something I had never done before. I pulled out the detective's business card who had recommended "The Gift of Fear" and called her. I had no idea if she'd answer or if I was overreacting, but she gave me her card for a reason, and if there was ever a time to take her up on her offer, this was it. Shockingly, she picked up.

I read her the message and waited.

After a long pause, she said, "Tennyson, that sounds like a death threat to me."

My stomach dropped. I didn't want to be right. But I was. Again. Panic set in. Everything I had worked so hard to overcome came flooding in.

I can't share all the details, but figuring out how to handle the situation was terrifying. What I can say is that this was the first time I recognized that my knowing—the same instinct that had told me he was coming back—was still working. Even if others didn't see what I saw, or Kyle didn't feel the same urgency, my intuition was right. This is why listening to that small voice inside you matters.

So why do we ignore it? For me, it was a lack of awareness.

I didn't realize those "random thoughts" might actually be something more. But I also think we live in a world full of distractions that drown out intuition. Notifications, texts, emails, to-do lists, and a never-ending cycle of go-go-go make it nearly impossible to hear ourselves. We're conditioned to rely on logic and external validation instead of trusting our own wisdom. It wasn't until later, when I started working with a therapist, that I realized how much my nervous system was affecting my ability to access intuition. The PTSD and healing work we did—things like breathing exercises, grounding, meditation, body scans, and tapping—wasn't just helping me heal. It was helping me hear that voice within me. Intuition isn't just about sensing danger; it's about knowing anything before logic has caught up. And it's always there. We just have to learn to listen.

Albert Einstein's quote perfectly articulates this: **"The intuitive mind is a sacred gift, and the rational mind is a faithful servant. We have created a society that honors the servant and has forgotten the gift."**

Hearing our intuition is one thing. *Applying* intuition was another. Even when I strongly felt something, acting on it was hard—especially if it wasn't logical or if it went against what others thought. I've always cared too much about what people think, so disagreeing or stepping outside the norm felt uncomfortable. But intuition, like any skill, strengthens with practice.

A friend once told me, "Intuition is like a muscle—the more you use it, the stronger it gets."

She was right. Over the years, I've learned it's not just for safety or for "woo-woo" people; it applies to everything in life.

One of the first times I was aware of intuition outside of

survival was five years after the break-in, when a former gym member and business mentor approached me about buying an insurance agency.

"Tenny, I think you should buy this agency."

Insurance? I thought. *Absolutely not.*

The word insurance immediately brought to mind a sleazy salesperson. I had zero interest. But I respected him, so I agreed to hear him out.

At lunch, Kyle and I listened as he laid out the opportunity. The more we talked, the more I realized it wasn't about sales tricks or being pushy—it was about helping people.

I kept saying, "I just don't want to do anything unethical."

When I realized I could do it my way—with honesty and integrity—I stayed open to the idea. I'd always loved working. I had watched my mom run a business successfully, proving that women could build something as powerfully as men. And while I loved being a mom, I had a nagging feeling there was something more I was meant to explore. As I dug into the details, every potential roadblock—securing a loan, moving the agency's location, selling the gym—effortlessly resolved itself. My father-in-law offered to fund the loan. Farmers Insurance approved relocating the agency out of the town where the break-in had happened (which I had zero intention of stepping foot in daily). And, as if on cue, one of our head trainers wanted to buy the gym.

With everything falling into place, I was left with one lingering thought: *Will I enjoy this?*

I had never worked a nine-to-five job, never sat at a desk all day, and knew nothing about insurance. But Kyle and I both agreed. *What's the worst that could happen?* If I hated it, I could sell it. Looking back, I was following my intuition the whole time. The agency gave me the resources to write this book, which may not have happened otherwise. It challenged me as a leader, business owner, and individual and forced me to trust myself.

At first, I knew nothing about insurance. I could barely explain coverages and had no experience in managing full-time employees. Cold-calling was out of the question, so I committed to building relationships instead. One coffee meeting at a time, I awkwardly fumbled through conversations as I worked to find people I connected with. I was good at connecting with others, as it was something I genuinely enjoyed. It was uncomfortable, but I found the right connections—and six years later, I had quadrupled my business without making a single cold call.

My intuition continued to show up in hiring decisions. I once interviewed a woman with the right experience, motivation, and knowledge—yet something felt off. My mentor thought she'd be a great fit, so I ignored my gut and hired her. Within weeks, I regretted it. The same thing happened again with another candidate. He was respectful, had experience, and seemed like a safe bet. But I knew something wasn't right. I dismissed my feelings and hired him anyway. Again, a mistake. I finally realized I was the only one who truly knew what felt right for me. Even those with more experience couldn't override my instincts. It was a turning point for me as I was tired of losing resources and, more importantly, energy on people who weren't the right fit. It was as if the Universe was giving me these experiences to scream at me to learn to have faith in myself. I was finally seeing both instinct and intuition play out in my life and how things unfolded when I listened and how they did when *I didn't*.

In time, I became more curious and dove into books and

podcasts on intuition.

I learned about the clairs—different ways intuition shows up:

clairvoyance (clear vision) – *Seeing* images

claircognizance (clear knowing) – Just *knowing*

clairaudience (clear hearing) – *Hearing* an inner voice

clairsentience (clear feeling) – A strong *physical* sensation

Everyone experiences intuition differently. I had always heard, "Trust your gut," but I had never felt intuition in my gut. It turns out that my primary intuition was claircognizance—I just *knew* things. It was as if a thought would come into my mind that would end up being accurate. That realization was a game-changer. Once I recognized how my intuition spoke to me, I started practicing trusting it more. Whether it was hiring, business decisions, or small daily choices, I learned that whatever was coming up—however it showed up—was worth listening to. Over time, it really has become a muscle that I have strengthened and acting on my intuition became second nature.

13

THE COURAGE IT TAKES

I'll never forget when Kyle and I read *The Five Love Languages* years after the break-in. Things were great between us, but I was always looking for ways to deepen our connection. I had watched my parents' marriage unexpectedly fall apart and had seen so many couples slip into the trap of living like roommates. That was not the marriage I wanted. I was devoted to the idea that we would be that cute, wrinkly, gray-haired couple, holding hands in our recliners while our great-grandkids played around us.

When we took the test in the book, my highest score was "Words of Affirmation", while Kyle's was "Quality Time" (the others are "Acts of Service", "Receiving Gifts", and "Physical Touch"). After discussing the results, Kyle set the book on his lap, looked at me, and simply said, "I don't know about all this. Honestly, Tenny, I just want you to be happy."

At the time, I wasn't that happy, upbeat girl Kyle had fallen in love with. The social media message had triggered my PTSD and sent me twenty steps backwards. Things were still rocky with my mom. I was overwhelmed with the stress of owning a brand new business by myself. And I sure loved our new baby, Skyler, but he sure liked to wake up in the middle of the night *every night*. For eighteen months. To the outside world, I held it together, but at home, where I was safe to feel what I was feeling, the weight of it showed. Kyle was always logical and handled things differently than I did. While I processed through *emotions*, he worked through *thoughts*. And though he supported me fully, my emotions were heavy for both of us.

Even with the antidepressants, sleep routine, and everything I had done to heal, I still wasn't feeling the joy I had hoped for. Kyle had found his way to process, but here I was, struggling again to figure it out. I wanted to be happy. I wanted to be a joyful woman, a present wife, and a fulfilled mom. I wanted to feel peace without the constant zoo of thoughts in my head. And I realized—if I was going to be with myself for the rest of my life, I needed to make this life experience one I truly enjoyed.

Healing is no small thing. It takes courage—real courage—not just to want to heal but to actually *do* the work. Facing yourself, unpacking trauma, and stepping into discomfort are some of the bravest things a person can do. And yet, for years, I overlooked another kind of courage, the courage it took for Kyle and me to survive that horrific night. People always tell us how brave we were to fight back. I appreciate the kind words, but for the longest time, I didn't think of that night as an act of courage. It was instinct, adrenaline, and pure survival. But over the years, I learned that what we did was rare.

Our detective told me, "Tennyson, let me put this in perspective. If you and Kyle were on an airplane that went under attack, statistically, you two would be among the ten people on that flight who would fight back."

She wasn't trying to flatter me—she had decades of experience. I later learned that of people attacked in the way we were, only 5% fight back. And of that 5%, only 3% survive. Those numbers stunned me. It felt surreal to be in that percentage.

I like what Nelson Mandela says: **"I learned that courage was not the absence of fear but the triumph over it. The brave man is not he who does not feel afraid, but he who conquers that fear."**

I won't downplay what Kyle and I did that night, but my hardest moments weren't then.

They were afterward—sitting alone in a room, forcing myself through exposure therapy. Lying in bed next to that enormous window, fighting the urge to check the locks. Walking through a grocery store, hyper-aware of every person around me. Taking that first antidepressant and fearing what it would do to me. Sleeping alone for the first time after months of needing someone with me. These are the moments that didn't make the headlines but required the most courage. Over time, I started to see courage differently. Before, I imagined grand acts of bravery—soldiers running into battle, firefighters racing into burning buildings, survivors speaking out. But there's another kind of courage—*soft courage.*

The kind that isn't flashy. The kind no one sees. It's the courage to tell your spouse the truth about something weighing on you. The courage to call someone who hurt you and say how you feel. The courage to sit with your past wounds, face them, and give them the love they never received. It's small, everyday bravery that no one claps for but matters just as much.

Looking back, I see that my journey through PTSD wasn't just about healing—it was about uncovering who I truly was. It forced me to look at parts of myself I had ignored: perfectionism, overthinking, fear of saying the wrong thing, and unworthiness. It led me to this moment, writing this book and sharing this story. In a life where all I have done is worry about what other people think of me, this, too, is one of the biggest acts of courage.

For years, I wrestled with the meaning of life. Is this it? We're born, we have fun as kids, we work jobs we may or may not love, we raise families, and then we grow old and die? But one day, while driving and listening to EDM music (which, for some reason, helps me visualize things clearly), the answer came to me: The purpose of life is to experience *Heaven on Earth*.

It felt like the clouds parted and the sun beamed through. That's what I wanted. That's what this entire journey had been leading me to. Heaven on Earth meant deep connection with Kyle—not just a good marriage, but a great one. It meant treasuring my kids, experiencing life through their eyes, and soaking in the beauty of simple moments together. It meant traveling the world, standing on Santorini's cliffs at sunset, drinking wine in Tuscany, and taking boat rides on Lake Como. It meant deep, meaningful friendships, laughing, and feeling seen, supported, and inspired. It meant loving my work so much that it didn't feel like work at all because you know you are making a difference in the world in your own unique way.

Every decision I make now aligns with this vision. I don't always get it right, but I do my best to move closer to it every day.

It's not lost on me that this story could be told as a true-crime documentary. In fact, an episode was made for a TV show. The final scene shows us in the kitchen, just hours after the attack, sipping coffee and smiling, relieved that he would never come back.

And then, it ends.

The problem is—that's where everything begins—the pain, the fear, the healing, the growth, and the wisdom. *That* is the story I want people to remember. The chapters that follow share what helped me move from feeling stuck, not just from PTSD, but from other patterns I learned over my life that disconnected me from truly being my authentic self. It's not just about healing from trauma. It's about learning to live in alignment with your true self and the freedom, peace, and happiness that comes as you do. There is no one-size-fits-all approach. Take what serves you and leave what doesn't. Just don't give up. We all have a purpose. We all have gifts no one else has. And the world needs them.

14

BREAK FREE

Looking back on this journey through healing, there wasn't one big *aha* moment where I suddenly knew I had figured it out. It was a collection of moments—small steps layered over time that slowly started to make a difference. Exposure therapy, community support, medication, Ludo, time, the gratitude that we were still alive, and the courage to take even the tiniest steps through discomfort…each played a role in teaching my body that I was safe. And even though I had started the work, I was (and still am) a constant work in progress. Every day, I cycle through awareness, intuition, curiosity, and soft courage to work through the triggers that still linger from that Mother's Day.

All of these things were necessary. But what I didn't realize for years was that beneath the layers of trauma from *that night*, there were deeper patterns—things I had never thought to question. Through my work with my therapist, Jeff, I came to see that processing the big T trauma of the attack had cracked open something even bigger: an awareness of the thousands of little moments, the small t traumas, that had subtly shaped who I was. These weren't earth-shattering events but tiny experiences that had built up over time, influencing how I showed up in the world, shaping my beliefs, and, ultimately, holding me back from fully embracing my most authentic self.

I had never considered how much these moments accumulate—how they condition us without us even realizing it. Whether big or small, they shape the lens through which we see ourselves and the world. As Dr. Gabor Maté puts it, **"No one escapes childhood unscathed. The question is not "Did you experience trauma?" but "How did the environment around you shape your beliefs about yourself?"**

I didn't grow up in a horrible environment. Quite the opposite. My parents were kind, loving, and supportive—something I know isn't the case for many. And yet, despite that, I still absorbed beliefs that shaped me in ways I wasn't fully aware of.

As I got older, I realized just how much I filtered myself in every interaction, constantly worrying about what people thought of me. To those around me, it may have seemed like I was shy or indecisive. But the truth? I was afraid. Afraid of saying the wrong thing. Afraid of making someone uncomfortable. Afraid of being *too much or too different.* So, instead of speaking up, I held back. I played small. I molded myself into whatever version I thought people expected me to be.

I didn't see until much later how my past experiences had wired me to seek approval over authenticity. But as I worked through these patterns with Jeff, I started to question why I had been that way. And, more importantly, how I could break free from it. Because the truth was, I was exhausted from constantly adjusting myself to fit what I thought was expected of me. More than anything, I just wanted to be *me*. I found a story that epitomizes the message of our conditioning, written by an unknown author:

As my friend passed the elephants, he suddenly stopped, confused that these huge creatures were being held by only a small rope tied to their front leg—no chains, no cages. It was obvious that the elephants could, at any time, break away from the ropes they were tied to, but for some reason, they did not. My friend saw a trainer nearby and asked why these beautiful, magnificent animals just stood there and did not attempt to escape.

"Well," he said, "when they are very young and much smaller, we use the same size of rope to tie them, and, at that age, it's enough to hold them. As they grow up, they are conditioned to believe they cannot break away. They believe the rope can still hold them, so they never try to break free." My friend was amazed. These animals could break free from their bonds at any time, but because they believed they couldn't, they were stuck right where they were.

Like the elephants, how many of us go through life hanging onto a belief that we cannot do something simply because we failed at it once before? How many of us are being held back by old, outdated beliefs that no longer serve us? How many have avoided trying something new because of a limiting belief? Worse, how many of us are being held back by someone else's limiting beliefs?

In 2020, I found myself facing some old programming. It was seven years after our Mother's Day event, and I felt the nudge to start a podcast. Here, that inner voice came up again. It was a neutral and random thought: *What if I started a podcast?* It always bugged me that media outlets had only focused on the events of Mother's Day and nothing about what life looked like after such a traumatic event. I get it. It is an extreme and unique story. The shock of the story is what grabbed everyone's attention. We have all heard of break-ins, but you don't usually hear about an intruder coming back on the same day only to have a couple fight to save their lives and then a woman stabbing a guy in the middle of her family room in a safe suburban neighborhood.

Like I have already said, I wanted to share the *full* story, as our story is so much more than that. While I wasn't ready to share about it right after it happened, I was now ready to be in a place where Kyle and I could vocally share the whole truth of the event in *our own words*. Even if that podcast didn't go anywhere, it was my way of sharing what really happened that night and what it was like afterward, with no one else's misinterpretation or slant on a story. Our media world is good at showing breaking news and the shock of events, but ultimately, we are people whose lives are forever changed and who have pieces to pick up and figure out how to put back together. That is where the real story lies and inspiration comes from.

When the idea of starting a podcast came up, my first thought was, *Ummmm, who the heck am I to start a podcast?! No one cares. There are millions of podcasts out there, and I have nothing interesting to add to the mix that hasn't already been said.* The beliefs were clear.

I know I'm not the only one to think this way, and boy, are we hard on ourselves sometimes. But this brings me to my point. For some reason, a part of me was showing up that didn't feel interesting enough, smart enough, talented enough, articulate enough (a big one for me), or worthy to do something that felt like such a big deal. And since one of my biggest fears is coming across as arrogant, I thought everyone around me would think I was this self-absorbed a-hole who just wanted attention. So, I immediately justified to myself the reasons it wasn't a good idea and tried to move on.

Months later, while working with my good friend Stacy—a highly intuitive person—on branding for my insurance agency, something unexpected happened. Stacy has this rare ability to mix openness, acceptance, wisdom, directness, humor, self-deprecation, and honesty in a way that instantly makes you feel safe. When she looks into your eyes, it's like she knows—sees straight through you, past the surface, into what's really going on. With her, there's no need to hide. Not that I could if I tried.

That day, we met to brainstorm creative marketing strategies for my agency. As we went through her slides, she suddenly pulled up an idea for *a podcast*. She suggested I start one—interviewing local businesses, building community connections, and creating something engaging beyond just insurance. I just sat there, shocked and silent. *Coincidence? Or divine timing?* Because just days before, the thought of a podcast had crossed my mind—but in an entirely different context. And now, here it was, staring back at me on Stacy's screen as if the universe was putting the idea right in front of me and saying, *Are you paying attention?*

Crap, I thought. *I have to tell her.*

Nervously, I shared with her how I had thought of starting a podcast months prior. Then, I stepped way outside my comfort zone (a moment of soft courage as I was about to say something aloud that I already felt unworthy, self-righteous, and arrogant for thinking). I shared how interviewing local businesses did not feel right, but rather, I felt like it was time to share my story. As ridiculous as I felt admitting this out loud, as I sat with her,

I knew this was a moment where I could start quieting all my doubtful voices and beliefs and take the first step into genuinely trusting myself.

Stacy paused.

She already knew that was the story that needed to be told. But the annoying (and great) thing about Stacy is that she won't always give you the secret. She'll tee you up, but *I* have to be the one to say it. It's been one of the biggest gifts (and challenges) as I learn to explore and voice what *I* really want.

She looked at me, smiled, and nodded. Then, smirking, she agreed, "Yes, yes, it is."

I'm not sure I knew how to respond. I was excited that my thought wasn't totally crazy, but I also knew it would mean I would do something about it, even though it was way outside my comfort zone. I knew Stacy wouldn't allow me to sound like a total fool, but I was also terrified to share with others that I was starting a podcast, as most people around me are not into putting themselves out there so publicly. But neither was I.

We immediately started planning the first season, including who we'd interview and other details. I knew I wanted Kyle on, and then the only two guests I could imagine inviting were my therapist, Jeff, for his profound wisdom on trauma and healing, and Tony Blauer, to share his insight and expertise on fear and intuition. The interview with Kyle went better than I expected. He has a natural ability to always be calm and, even if nervous, remain articulate. I envy him for that, as I do not have that gift. I trip over my words, second-guess myself, and then beat myself up for it in the hours that followed. I loved listening to him open up about his experience, which he rarely did.

The interviews with Jeff and Tony would be a challenge

for me as I had never interviewed someone in my life before, and here I would be interviewing two masters in their fields. The interview with Jeff went as well as I could have hoped for my first-ever interview. Jeff and I had been working together for two and a half years and therefore, he could pick up where I fumbled, knowing my intention and heart of a question. The interview with Tony didn't feel quite as smooth. I stumbled, not having the confidence to interview someone so public and well-known.

I left the recording studio, after the interviews, in tears. I felt like a total idiot. I could tell by looking at everyone's faces around me that they agreed with me that my interview with Tony had fallen flat. *What the hell was I doing? Who do I think I am to be able to interview people?* Tears rolled down my face, my heart-raced, and I couldn't stop spinning with how dumb I felt to have thought I could do a podcast.

Out of nowhere, the thought came to mind of a recent conversation I had had with someone who encouraged me to create three affirmations whenever I was stepping into something new. At the time, the idea felt awkward—honestly, cheesy. I couldn't wrap my head around how simply repeating words could make a real difference. It seemed unrealistic. But I appeased him by coming up with three: **I am Brave. I am Authentic. I am Worthy.** In my desperation to feel even the slightest bit better, I decided to give it a shot. I didn't want to say them, but I told myself, *Tenny, you have got to get it together here.* So I went for it and reluctantly repeated the affirmations: "I am brave. I am authentic. I am…." and stopped. I couldn't say it. I could bring myself to say *I am brave and authentic,* but I couldn't even *think* the words I am *worthy.*

At that moment, I became highly aware that that was weird. *Was this a belief I had about myself? Why?* I cognitively understood I was worthy, but why couldn't I say it? Even worse, I couldn't even *think it*.

I had done enough therapy by that point to realize something deeper was going on, but I didn't fully understand the depth of my feelings of not feeling good enough, or not feeling worthy enough. It reminded me of a quote by Brene Brown that lands personally, but also my observation of not only myself but our community as a collective: **"If you put shame in a Petri dish, it needs three things to grow exponentially: secrecy, silence, and judgment. If you put the same amount of shame in the light of empathy, it can't survive."**

I had fallen into patterns of constantly judging myself, holding myself to impossible standards, and expecting perfection just to feel like I measured up. While I was naturally empathetic toward others, I rarely extended that same kindness to myself.

At first, I didn't take any immediate action with this realization. But what it did give me was a new level of awareness—an understanding that there were deeper layers to uncover, more parts of me that needed healing. I didn't know how to "fix it," but simply recognizing it shifted everything. Maybe our traumatic experience wasn't just about learning how to heal from trauma. Maybe it was pushing me toward growth in other areas of my life. The fact that I struggled to say, "I am worthy" felt significant, and I wanted to explore why.

I started doing guided meditations that directly addressed my limiting beliefs. I practiced cope-ahead strategies, mentally preparing for situations that made me nervous so that when they happened, my nervous system didn't overreact, sending me into a shame spiral. I worked with my inner child to love and care for the girl who had experienced tons of little moments that left her feeling not good enough. And slowly, over time, the weight of unworthiness began to lift. To feel something so deeply ingrained start to change is indescribable. It's a feeling money can't buy and no one else can give you. I didn't expect to notice a difference—but I did.

Progress isn't neat, nor is it immediate. I'd love for it to be linear, but accepting the inevitable ups and downs has been one of my biggest lessons. We are all conditioned from birth to act, think, and behave a certain way. A large part of this conditioning comes from our primary caregivers, but it also comes from friends, family, teachers, society—the world around us. As children, we absorb everything: how our parents communicate with others, how they speak to us, whether they express affection, whether they say "I love you," whether emotions are welcomed or suppressed, and whether patience or reactivity is the norm. We grow up internalizing these cues, and then, without even realizing it, we model what was modeled to us.

The Power of Conditioning

While conditioning often refers to the limiting beliefs and patterns that hold us back, it's also important to acknowledge the positive programming that shapes us in the best ways.

Growing up, there were phrases my mom repeated so often that they became woven into the fabric of my thinking: "Every cloud has a silver lining" and "You can be anything you set your mind to." I heard them so many times that they became truths I carried with me. My ability to pivot in difficult times and search for meaning in hardship? That wasn't just some natural resilience—I was conditioned to do it. Without that belief system, I'm not sure how I would have survived the break-in, let alone done the work to heal from it. And for the record, during the months and years of navigating my trauma, I never consciously reminded myself that every cloud has a silver lining. If someone had said that to me in the middle of my healing, it would have felt so invalidating and crushed my spirit. But at a deeper level, that belief gave me an inner knowing—there are hard times, and there are good times, and I was determined to find my way back to the good.

Another phrase ingrained in me: "Girls, remember the Golden Rule: Do unto others as you would have them do unto you." I heard it so often, and now, what do I do? Repeat it to my kids. I was once asked in a business group what motto I live by, and if I had to choose one, this would be it. We all have our own struggles. What I have learned is that whatever the conditioning may have been, we all want to be seen and feel loved. This motto helps me do that for others in the small way that I can. And that brings me such fulfillment. And then there was "Where there is a will, there is a way." I'll be honest, this one annoyed me growing up. I'd hit a roadblock, grunt with frustration, and my mom would swoop in with this phrase. After rolling my eyes behind her back, I'd try to explain why I couldn't do something—only for her to come up with a different angle, a new idea, or a fresh perspective. As much as it frustrated me then, it's one of the things I appreciate most about her now. It taught me how to pivot and how to seek solutions when one doesn't work. That mindset has helped me in healing, business, relationships, marriage, and parenting.

My dad had his own words of wisdom: "Count your blessings."

This whole book has reminded me of that phrase.

Looking back, these messages shaped me. They showed me how powerful words are, how deeply they influence beliefs, and how important it is to be intentional with what we pass on—especially to our children. Even with all the positive conditioning I received, life still layered on its own experiences. I picked up patterns like perfectionism and people-pleasing, watching my parents juggle the overwhelming demands of their business while also witnessing my sister struggle with her own challenges. Subconsciously, I learned to stay out of the way, to avoid being a burden. If I was perfect, maybe things would be easier for everyone. Maybe that's how I'd earn love.

15
SUNDAYS WITH JEFF

Jeff and I have talked almost every Sunday for six years.
　　I remember anxiously awaiting my first call with him. It had been five years after the break-in. Even though I knew I was having some challenges, it wasn't as extreme as things were immediately after the incident. I had been off Xanax and antidepressants for a couple of years, and even with triggers still impacting my feelings of safety, I didn't realize how much I had learned to just live with it. I was having the thoughts of the gas station next door to my office exploding, killing me, and my family learning I died as they heard about the explosion on local news. It's intense but true. I still triple-checked the locks every night and occasionally looked under beds, showers, and closets in every room on nights when Kyle wasn't home. Some nights, I contemplated getting a ladder and poking my head into the attic opening in our bedroom closet, just to make sure nobody had snuck in during the day and was hiding there. As I

started to figure out the logistics of finding a ladder or stacking things on top of each other to be able to reach it, it got too complicated, so I at least gave up on that one.

The nightmares, though… those were different. Those were becoming a real problem as they happened nearly every night and ruined the rest of my sleep. I knew where they were coming from. I just didn't understand why the nightmares weren't going away and they had become every night as this was the time I had received the alarming social media message. Or, as the detective assessed, *a serious concern*. I started hating when bedtime approached, knowing the likelihood of what I was going to experience. It was frustrating living this way, but I assumed that was just going to be what life was like with the experiences I had had.

I had had my fair share of trauma therapists, including visiting the best local trauma center in Seattle, and multiple other therapists I worked with post-event, but I also had therapists when I was a kid when my mom forced my twin sister and me to learn to talk through the dynamics of being a twin. It was such an intentional and supportive idea, and was just one of many ways my mom exposed me to experiences that laid the foundation for who I am and what I value. Little did I know how much my exposure to therapy, and therefore, openness to it, helped me now.

Even at a young age, I enjoyed having a professional to talk with. It was nice having someone to express my feelings to, as I always had so much going on in my head. It was as if I could dump all my feelings and struggles on a neutral person, and even if their advice didn't land, releasing my feelings and getting them out always made me feel better.

Although, even with all these years of therapy, I had yet to ever have a therapist where I truly felt seen and that all of me was understood. They had all been lovely and well-meaning and often somewhat helpful, but even as awful as my memory is, I can still see the younger me that sat in all these different therapist offices over the years—there always seemed to be something missing. I didn't realize it then, but it felt like parts of me were overlooked by me and by them.

My first call with Jeff started with me sharing our story and what happened. But more so, he inquired about the years after and how I was doing at that time. One thing that stood out is that I will never forget the *feeling* I had talking to Jeff. I didn't have the language then, but I felt *safe* talking to Jeff. My body was calm and relaxed, and there weren't the natural walls of protection or apprehension that I often felt with other therapists. Even though I hadn't seen him since we were only talking by phone, something about his tone of voice, his questions, and how he would pause to be intentional with his word choice made me feel safe, validated and seen. I listened to him and couldn't get over how this total stranger knew all the inner workings of what my mind and body were doing and could put words to it. I had never talked to someone who showed me such genuine compassion. He validated why those feelings were coming up for me, allowing me to *not* feel crazy. It was in what he said and explained to me and what he *didn't say*. He wasn't giving statistics to convince me to think or believe a certain way, and wasn't jumping in to solve the problem. He was patient with getting all the details, very intentional with articulating the significant impact that something like our experience leaves, got genuinely curious, and gave me so much grace that the conversation didn't feel clinical. It was the easiest conversation I had ever had with a therapist who clearly had so much expertise in helping others through all kinds of trauma.

Jeff's approach was reassuring, warm, and even humble. I believe there is a particular energy exchange when you meet someone you connect with, and it caught me off guard how different this conversation felt from the past. He spent a lot of time explaining why my body was reacting the way it was and why it made complete sense, which was an entirely new concept for me. I had heard about *The Body Keeps the Score* before, but only in my own research, not with therapists. It was shocking to me that he was the first person to make the connection of how trauma impacts someone from a physiological level. My psychiatrist had explained the hormonal process, but not the nervous system. And also not in a way that I could have tools to work through it myself, in a way that only medication would support. Hearing this information and understanding why my body was doing what it was doing, *and* that there were tools that could help, gave me a sense of hope I had never felt before.

Since he lives on the other side of the country, our appointments were always by phone, and I wanted to put a face to a name, so I Googled him before our call. Zoom wasn't as popular at this point, and I didn't realize it, but not having to *see* someone when I shared all my deepest vulnerabilities made it better for me.

That first call, he added a new word to my vocabulary: *amygdala*. I won't even try my hand at explaining the parts of the brain and their importance, but I learned this little sucker is an important part of how our brain functions, particularly in response to threats. The amygdala is critical for your sense of survival as the primary emotion it controls is fear. It processes what you see and hear and then determines whether a situation is dangerous or not. I didn't know this, but hearing him explain it and how my little amygdala was constantly firing, even when I was safe, gave me an unexpected sense of relief. There were finally words to explain the internal challenges I had been having for years but didn't know why.

An hour went by in what felt like fifteen minutes.

Even though I knew he had a waitlist of clients signed up to see him, he surprised me at the end of our call by graciously offering to make time the following Sunday as there was more information he wanted to learn, and more that he said he wanted to explain.

As we said goodbye and I put down the phone, I was shocked. All I could think was, *What the heck just happened?*

It was crazy. I wasn't looking for a therapist, but now all I could think of was my little amygdala. Plus, I was now aware that maybe I was living with more than I had realized. It was the first time I remember thinking that *maybe things like nightmares, uncontrollable body sensations, and constant anxiety don't have to be a forever part of my life.*

On the second call, Jeff gathered more details while continuing to educate me on other parts of my brain and the nervous system. I had to work hard to understand science in school, but this science actually was helpful, and it all related to what I was internally experiencing. It was the first time I remember anyone explaining what was happening in my nervous system, which is shocking considering the PTSD Kyle and I had faced. Even though I wasn't being attacked, my system thought so. I was so dysregulated that my body was constantly in fight mode all day, responding to anything that felt like it could be a threat (i.e., even nearby gas pumps that have the potential of exploding but likely will not). On this call, I grasped a bigger picture of how I was *really* doing. I realized how unaware I was of accepting to live with these challenges and that there was something I could do about it. I could actually change.

At the end of the second call, Jeff was noticeably torn about what to do. He had a more than full schedule, so he had to squeeze in time for me on his weekend. I joked that maybe I'm just really good at manipulation (I am not), and he always joked that he would be too smart to be manipulated. I guarantee that is correct.

I'll never forget what he said at the end of this call, "Tennyson, I get the feeling you are someone who gives to everyone around you, but I'm not sure that you have been given that back. I would love to continue working with you and can make time on Sundays if it's something that you also think is a fit."

I froze for a second as my heart started racing, and tears filled my eyes. I had never received such an observation about me like this. I couldn't help but notice that the language he used in his offer wasn't because of the unique event I went through but tied to how he saw me, deep down. Not only did he see something in me, but he also wanted to help me and was willing to make time on the weekend, which was so unexpected. I knew this was a big deal, and part of me didn't feel I could accept his offer, but I also knew he wouldn't have offered if he hadn't meant it. Relief, hope, and excitement flooded me because someone understood the suffering and fear I was trying to manage alone. He was optimistic, and I could tell he knew he could help me. There was no way I could pass up this opportunity. Little did

I know that working on the big Trauma was going to lead to what it did.

And so began our routine. Every Sunday, we would have our scheduled phone calls.

Working on regulating a nervous system didn't happen overnight. Having a conversation about the tools he was teaching was one thing; implementing them was another.

Our initial months together, we were working on big T trauma aftermath things, like all the anxious thoughts I was constantly having, the nightly routine of getting out of bed to double and triple check locks, always looking under the beds and in closets, dealing with the nightmares and, even as much as an idiot I felt saying it out loud, the worries about the gas station blowing up.

I never knew what cocktail of therapies he used with me on our calls, but he always took the time to explain the various approaches to me, how they helped, and even where they fell short. As someone who had become skeptical because previous therapies had not always worked out, or the modality was just plain awful (ie: exposure therapy), I didn't realize how important the education component was for me. There were CBT (Cognitive Behavioral Therapy), DBT (Dialectical Behavior Therapy), IFS (Internal Family Systems), and meditation, mindfulness, and awareness techniques. But the most important foundation of all is the Polyvagal Theory, which is all tied to our nervous system and feeling safe—and what I have learned is the most critical for our mental health. It was evident that he knew so much, and had the most extensive toolbox of any therapist I had known.

It still is mind-boggling to me that I did not learn anything about my nervous system or the concept of helping my body to learn it was safe in the years after our event, even with as many mental health professionals as I saw and resources I looked into. I suppose that shows how much our society still has to learn about trauma and mental health. That said, I cannot express enough how crucial this has been to feeling genuine change and improvement. The best part is that the work itself is not retraumatizing (like exposure therapy or talk therapy can be); it is grounding, comforting, and immediately relieving.

There is a quote from Dr. Stephen Porges: **"If you want to improve the world, start by making people feel safer. Connection is the antidote to the isolation that trauma creates. Through connection, we find safety, support, and the possibility of healing."**

Safety comes down to our connection with others and our connection with the Self. I now recognize the people I genuinely feel safe around—not necessarily safe physically, but safe with my thoughts and feelings. Those are the relationships and the people I will surround myself with as I see how critical it is for my own mental health. And for those who are not that, my work is to be better at creating boundaries, and honoring how best to support myself around those types of people.

I still can't believe how fortunate I am to have connected with Jeff and worked with him for over six years. We used his many different areas of training and expertise, but the Polyvagal Theory, Internal Family Systems, meditation, and a simple (but not so simple) sense of Awareness have been the most life-changing.

I often think back to the quote, **"If you want to improve the world, start by making people feel safer."** This is exactly what Jeff did for me in our work together. It was why I felt the way I did on our first call. And it's what I hope you feel reading this book.

It was time to do the work.

16

WHATEVER IT TAKES

In our initial session, Jeff was well aware that this big T trauma was very much still impacting my everyday life, even though it was five years post-break-in. He also immediately sensed little t's I had been holding onto, as well, but that would come later. My nervous system was so dysregulated, our work focused on getting it to calm down and not have to stay in "fight" (in polyvagal terms, dorsal) mode so much of the time. I will probably butcher this as I am not a psychologist and will not pretend to be, so please take my explanation with a grain of salt.

Dr. Stephen Porges is the man you want to research to learn from the expert himself. Jeff explained how the Polyvagal Theory is based on the vagus nerve, our one main nerve that wanders through the whole body and hits every major organ. It starts in the brain and then webs through the neck, goes to the heart, lungs, stomach, and kidneys, and whenever you get nervous, your brain thinks, *I'm not safe.* Thus, when you feel unsafe, whether that is physically or even if it is someone looking at you wrong at a party, your vagus nerve fires, dumps cortisol and then symptoms like IBS (Irritable Bowel Syndrome), headaches, heart rate, sweating, flushing of the skin, inability to articulate words and other things, come up. Physiologically, the same thing happens in our body if we see a cougar versus someone looking at you wrong in a certain context. That was wild, but it made sense to me.

A funny but interesting side note is that Dr. Stephen Porges connects his research with the vagus nerve back to thinking of himself and how he was also a clarinet player. To him, playing a woodwind instrument is like pranayama yoga, as it is all about the breath. All my years of working hard at the clarinet were, unknowingly, laying a foundation I would pull from later. I have learned that no experience is random, and I'd be lying if I said it didn't make me more aware of encouraging my kids to have this foundation as well.

Things like the constant thoughts, my heart immediately racing when things caught me off guard, and the nightmares were the main challenges I struggled with. I was having the same version of a nightmare almost every single night where the scene was a psychopath or terrorist who was chasing me with the intent to rape me and then kill me. The nightmare would end almost at the same point in the story every night, where I would be running and hiding. When I thought I was safe, I would turn to escape and suddenly, he'd see me and catch me. I would start fighting back…and that's when I would wake up in a complete panic, sweating, my heart racing, and my mind going one million miles an hour as if the dream had actually happened. And now that we have firearms, I worried that I may do something completely unknowingly in my sleep with a gun. It horrified me to think I could respond to an attacker when really it was Kyle or the kids. I'm incredibly embarrassed to admit it, but I actually have Googled something to the effect of "Can you kill someone with a gun while you're sleeping?" Jeff assured me that the fact that I even had this concern proved it was *not* something I would do. All of this fell in line with the level of anxiety and my dysregulated system that I was experiencing. And, I suppose, PTSD that still existed.

Our first attempt to calm my system down was to implement breathing techniques. Jeff gave me the homework so that when I woke up from a nightmare, I could focus on my breath and count my in and out breaths. The intention was that focusing on my breath would pull my focus off the nightmares and a mindfulness technique that helps calm the nervous system, signaling *I am safe*.

I remember lying on my back in the middle of the night and getting to my third or so breath but then getting confused about what count I was on. Jeff told me this would happen, and even though he did, I was annoyed that I wasn't able to follow a simple assignment of being able to count my breaths. Thoughts of the nightmare would pop back in, along with thoughts of whether I should get out of bed and recheck the locks. So I tried to start counting all over and then would get frustrated when I, yet again, couldn't figure out how to count my darn breaths. When I started to count, the nightmare would come in, and then I'd lose track of the number I was on. I just could *not* get out of my head. Eventually, I grabbed my phone and scrolled for a distraction. It seemed to be the only thing that got my mind off of it until I got so tired that I would fall asleep. I was disappointed in myself. I hated failing an assignment that felt like it should have been relatively easy. I didn't want to tell Jeff I failed, and not only failed but pulled out a device, which I know is an awful habit, but I knew I needed to as I was back to feeling stuck on what to do.

The breathing technique is one of the most approachable mindfulness techniques, which is probably why he started with it. When it didn't quite do the trick to get my mind off the nightmare, lucky for me, he had more options. Intense exercise.

In one of my sessions, Jeff talked about ways to calm the vagus nerve firing in that hyper-arousal state. These could include cold water on the face, breathing techniques, a cold shower, and time.

Yes, you can try and just "wait it out." Yet, with time, a minute can feel like an eternity, and as he told me, "Who the heck wants to sit there in torture waiting it out?"

I couldn't agree more. The time post-nightmares and trying to wait it out was awful.

I would think back to that day. I would see *him* and experience him grabbing me all over again, bending me over the couch, and pressing his body against mine as he yanked on my hair and covered my mouth. I'd see him stare at me with his black eyes and the hateful energy I could feel from him that represented how intensely he wanted to hurt me and potentially all of us. *His 1:30 am silent and strategically planned break-in into our home. The duct tape. The camera. The tripod. The gardening gloves duct taped to his wrists...* Just writing this right now makes me want to say—what a f-#$%.

Even though reality would eventually kick in after thoughts like this, that he was no longer alive, it only made me worry about someone else wanting to find me and kill me. So, yes, I preferred a different option than "time."

I can still sense Jeff's delivery with his second recommendation around intense exercise was like he knew this was going to suck and wasn't ideal, and he almost felt bad bringing it up. This idea of physical exercise came with clarifying that it had to be intense—things like sprints, push-ups, jumping lunges, and so forth.

Jeff paused and then asked, "Alright, Tennyson. What is one exercise that you could do that is not only intense but also easy to do when you step out of your bedroom?"

Immediately, one of the worst exercises came to mind—*burpees*. I didn't want to admit it or say it out loud, though, because I knew where this was going.

A burpee is an intense full-body exercise that begins in a standing position before quickly dropping into a squat, planting your hands on the ground. From there, you kick your feet back to land in a plank, perform a push-up (or just throw your body on the ground), and then jump your feet forward again. In one fluid motion, you rise and explode into a jump, reaching your arms overhead, only to land softly and drop right back into the next repetition.

They're the worst.

He knew I thought of something and didn't want to say it. Somehow, even though I didn't want to share it because I knew what it would entail, I felt drawn to it. I could sense he would find a way to help me attempt it while not making it completely unbearable. I trusted his advice.

Finally, I responded, "God, okay. It's gotta be burpees." I laughed-sighed.

Jeff laughed. "Of course, the CrossFit trainer picks burpees. Haha!"

He continued, "I know it sounds awful, but the next time you have a nightmare, I want you to step outside your bedroom so you don't have to worry about waking Kyle, and do twenty burpees. You're going to go into the burpees thinking about the nightmare while still in the hyper-aroused state. As you start to do the burpees, your mind can't help but focus on the exercise because of how intense it is, which will, as crazy as it sounds, take your mind off the nightmare." He paused, as he knew I was soaking it all in. "What are your thoughts?"

I took a moment to have an intentional response. As soon as he asked, my competitive nature came out, and I wanted to prove him wrong. I was up for trying it as I was desperate to have a regular night of sleep again. All of his advice had been spot on so far, but part of me struggled to believe that burpees in the middle of the night after a nightmare would relieve me of the hours of agonizing that came after a nightmare. So, I said, "Yeah, I mean, that makes sense. I can definitely try it."

But secretly, I believed I would be reporting back, "This didn't work for me."

Per usual, the nightmares continued. Let me first say I was absolutely not excited to get out of bed and do burpees. Outside of it being one of the worst physical exercises in the daytime, it takes a ton of willpower to willingly leave a warm, cozy, soft, comfortable (did I emphasize that enough?) bed in the middle of the night and choose to do twenty burpees. So, when the nightmare rolled in, I didn't do it. I woke up as usual, panicking from the places my mind had gone, but I thought how incredibly awful it sounded to get out of bed to do twenty burpees. I started to reason with myself. *How about I go back to the breathing Jeff first recommended? Maybe I didn't try hard enough. Sure sounds a heck of a lot better than burpees. Let's just pass on the burpees. I'll try the breathing again.* I now had more buy-in to that idea, which meant I could stay in my warm, cozy bed.

So, I gave the breath work another try: "One" on the in-breath, "two" on the out-breath, "three" on the in, and "four" on the out.

I'm not going to lie. I was bored. I continuously lost count and got frustrated, immediately judging myself by thinking, *Seriously, you can't just count some simple breaths?*

I was so tired, frustrated, and exhausted from my sleepless nights and failure to figure out my breathing that I went back to my bad habits and distracted myself again with my phone. I knew it wasn't what would genuinely help me, but I knew it would at least do it for the time being. I just wanted to sleep.

The next night, the nightmares showed up again. *Can we just stop already?* It's wild what comes up when I haven't found a way to figure it out. It's like the nightmares grew to be more and more intense. Annoyed from the night prior of breathing practices not working, I lay there thinking about Jeff's recommendation for the burpees. I was worn out from my failed attempts at finding a way to sleep. Something had to change so I could stop thinking about this monster.

While lying in bed, I hoped that by some random miracle, this might be the night I might just snap out of it once I was awake, but I didn't. Just like all the other nightmares, it triggered my biggest fear—before falling asleep, I lay there thinking that someone, somewhere out there, aligned in the worst ways with this guy and wanted to finish what he had started. That led me to think about our kids' safety—would someone crawl up a ladder, place it against their bedroom windows, and then try to climb in? Would someone break in, shoot our dog, which was our main line of defense, and then blow right past him to get to us? I immediately jumped to the thought, *I need to check all the rooms in the house, even the bathrooms, and look under the bed, behind the shower curtains, in the closets.* But there was no miracle where I was able to shake it off. The particular nightmare I had on this night scared the hell out of me. In this one, I saw the exact same eyes as I did from the guy who attacked me. A feeling of pure evil. He was chasing me with a knife. I was hiding behind boxes and then scrambling from room to room. It was so vivid that I felt like I was watching a scary movie in which I was the main character. And in this dream, he caught me. Right as I started to fight back…I woke up.

My body was in complete overdrive, flooded with thoughts of the man who would have tortured me and devoured every second of it. I forced myself (as hard as it was) to get up and followed Jeff's advice. As I dragged myself out of my warm bed and into the hallway to do burpees, I started getting pissed. *Five years later, and here I was—up at 1:30 am, forcing myself to move just to convince my body it was safe.* It was wild to think that in just twelve hours, he had done something that still took up so much space in my life, years later.

I stood in the hallway, looking down at the carpet and preparing for my first burpee. I couldn't help but look at Skyler's bedroom door, which was cracked open. The thought of being next to a sleeping toddler felt comforting and sweet. I knew he wouldn't wake up because of how sound he slept (*finally*), so I entered and positioned myself right in the middle of his room, right next to his crib and took a moment to just stare down at him and soak in the sweetness of him sleeping. He lay there, with his head facing up, his arms spread out like someone scored a goal, and his mouth slightly open as he breathed. As much as I hated why I was in his room, I equally felt so much love and appreciation that that sweet little bundle was my son.

Feeling better mentally, I prepared myself. I stood there looking at the floor and then back at Skyler. I glanced at the clock. It was 1:30 in the morning. I thought back to Jeff explaining how the burpees would get my mind off of the nightmare. Still frustrated and so tired of facing so many of the same fears, I dropped to the floor and did my first burpee.

Keep thinking of the nightmare. I have to prove Jeff wrong. Focus— **one burpee.** *Still thinking about the nightmare.* **Two.** *Do NOT forget about the nightmare. (So stubborn)* **Three.** *Ok, this is exhausting and I'm only on rep three.* **Four.** *Dang, why am I breathing hard after only four burpees?* **Five. Six. Seven.** By the fifth burpee, I had completely lost track of the nightmare. It was all I could do to keep count of the burpees. There was no way in the world I wanted to do a single burpee more than was required.

Freaking exhausted and breathing heavily, I took a quick peak at Skyler to make sure he was still sound asleep. He was. *Ugh, and so cute.* I walked back to our room and tried to be as quiet as possible as I climbed back into bed. I worried Kyle would wake up and hear my panting. While laying in bed, still panting, I wondered what the heck just happened. I was still aware of the nightmare, but I was more focused on the fact that I had just done twenty burpees in the middle of the night. I couldn't help but recognize how out of shape I felt, and how exhausted I was after doing them. Twenty burpees shouldn't have been hard for me. But, doing them after waking up from a dead sleep, jacked up after a terrifying nightmare, and at 1:30 am was a different experience. It leveraged my body's natural response from an intense workout to calm down, which simultaneously calmed down my nervous system.

Jeff was right.

I lay there, aware of my body and my breath slowly coming back to normal, and without realizing it, I ended up falling asleep and woke up to my alarm clock in shock.

Oh my God, I thought. *It actually worked.*

I had to do burpees a few more times as the nightmares showed up, and it was always shocking how they consistently calmed my nervous system. In a way, I thought the first time was a fluke. Even the second. But each time I did it, I climbed back into bed panting as my body slowly calmed down, and I fell fast asleep before I knew it. After that, when I had a nightmare, I almost willingly jumped out to get the burpees over so that I could climb back into bed and fall asleep.

Burpees were a pretty extreme measure to help my nervous system calm down, but fortunately, I didn't have to continue doing them for too long. And after several nights of burpees to help calm me down, I went back to attempting breathing techniques and was finally able to see progress since my system had become a bit more regulated.

There are many other ways to help the body switch from a sympathetic "fight" response to a parasympathetic state. Another practice I used for everyday life was something Jeff called "cope ahead." This comes from the world of DBT, which is about Emotional Regulation. DBT was developed by psychologist Marhsa M. Linehan. It's been effective for treating a range of mental health problems.

> *DBT is a type of cognitive behavioral therapy (CBT). CBT focuses on helping people change unhelpful thought patterns. DBT takes those CBT ideas or challenging unhelpful thought patterns, but also adds additional elements like mindfulness, acceptance and distress tolerance, and interpersonal skills to give you more tools for dealing with hard situations. Dialectical (the D is DBT) meets opposites, and comes from the idea of combining two of those ideas - change and acceptance. From: dialecticalbehaviortherapy.com*

Cope ahead is amazing for general situations in life, and it was especially helpful for me when dealing with situations at work. When I first met Jeff, I had bought my insurance agency two months prior. Sure, I had owned a business before owning the CrossFit gym for nearly ten years, but this was completely different. I barely knew anything about insurance and had no other business partner to run the agency. It was all me. I figured a lot out on my own, but I struggled the most with having tough conversations with employees. I hate confrontation and am constantly worried about whether what I was going to say would be perceived as wrong, so having tough discussions was one of the hardest things I could imagine doing. There it was again, this constant fear of saying the wrong thing and therefore tripping over my words. This wasn't just a lack of skills, wouldn't you know it, this too, was coming from conditioning.

There was a point when I had to have a tough conversation with an employee, and I was absolutely dreading it. She was intense, blunt, and didn't have my best interest at heart. On top of that, she was quite a bit older than me, which made it even harder to stand my ground. I brought it up to Jeff, and he gave me the simplest tool—cope-ahead. He told me to expect that I'd be nervous going into the conversation. That's it.

The idea was that when the nerves kicked in, instead of letting them hijack my ability to think or speak clearly, I'd recognize that I had already planned for this moment. Just knowing that I expected to feel this way helped signal to my nervous system that I wasn't actually in danger, so it didn't fire as intensely. It seemed almost too simple to be effective, but when I put it into practice, it actually worked. And that gas station blowing up? We used this tool for that.

Another tool that has been critical to apply is co-regulation. Co-regulation is one of the main principles of polyvagal theory and is explained as when two people come together to regulate their emotions. Imagine a crying baby being soothed by its mother. Or that feeling when you are sad and a family member, friend, or spouse hugs you. It is not just a quick hug; it is the kind of hug you feel like you melt into, and your body immediately starts to relax. The regulated person and their nervous system, because it is in a calm and relaxed place, is soothing the dysregulated system of the other person. It's amazing how everything always seems to tie back to human connection. I can't think of a more profound tool to use in relationships but also with parenting.

"As we co-regulate each other, we feel safer in the space and time that we're in. We become more generous to others, more welcoming and more accessible."- Stephen Porges, PhD

There's so much more to the Polyvagal Theory than just these stories, and there are even tools you can buy that stimulate your vagus nerve to relax, but the nervous system is the foundation for healing, growth, connection, and freedom. And it doesn't just apply to big T trauma. I don't know about you, but the world can be heavy. We are constantly juggling so many things every day, from full-time jobs, kids, their activities, marriage, health challenges, social media, inflation, global crises, and constant distractions. So much impacts our nervous systems, pulling us out of a calm and relaxed state. I know firsthand how a dysregulated system makes it extremely challenging to experience joy, happiness, and freedom. It also cuts us off from our intuition.

Work rooted in the Polyvagal Theory is about connecting our mind and our body and honoring the incredible design we were all created with as a holistic approach. It's not about logically trying just to fix the problem. It's getting to the root of where we hold on to trauma and learning to have compassion and understanding of why our body does what it does and how to support that.

After all I have endured and worked on, I can leave you with this: Honoring and supporting the nervous system is the secret ingredient to everything. When you begin to do so, your world will change.

17

ALL THE PARTS

Sometimes, I'm embarrassed to admit how much therapy I have done. But the truth is, every experience—whether helpful or not—has taught me what resonates and what doesn't. That said, I've never felt a deeper internal shift than I have with IFS.

Created by Dr. Richard Schwartz, Internal Family Systems (IFS) is based on the idea that we all have a core Self surrounded by different inner parts—often younger versions of ourselves—that show up to protect us when we don't feel safe. When these parts take over, we become "blended" with them, making it hard to recognize what's happening. Jeff, who trained with Dr. Schwartz, helped me identify my parts, and I quickly realized how much they had been running my life. They worked so hard to protect me that they kept me from being my authentic self. I had only intended to work through the break-in, but as my nervous system started to calm, these parts of me started showing up in conversations more and more. Unexpectedly, I found myself so excited at recognizing these parts so that I could continue to change the patterns I had lived with my whole life.

As the big T trauma settled, the little t experiences kept surfacing. Jeff helped me see them through the lens of IFS—the perfectionist part, the high-achiever part, the part that didn't feel smart enough, the over-analyzer, the frustrated part, and the part who always second-guessed everything.

With IFS, the goal isn't to reject these parts but to get curious and compassionate, to learn where they come from and what they have to say. In visiting a part, I close my eyes and imagine visiting that part. I ask how old she is. And I wait as my mind settles into the scene of what this part may have experienced. Every part has a story, a memory, and feelings tied to it. The more I listened, the more I understood—and the more these parts trusted me and didn't need to take over to protect me. The authentic version of me— not the perfect, high-achieving, unworthy, self-critical version, started to stand a little taller.

The memories are little t moments, where this part learned to protect me. When you can get curious and hear what this part has to say, validate its experience and feelings, and then show up with compassion toward that part, you are literally reparenting this younger part of you that didn't get what it needed at that moment. By doing this, the part then starts to feel seen and validated. The part feels *safe*. Safe enough to know that maybe they don't have to work quite so hard to completely take over. When I can connect to my Self and see what she needs and tell her *I've got it* there's no need for that part to work so hard to protect me.

One of the biggest things we uncovered was how much being a twin had shaped me—more than I ever realized. My mom worked hard to empower us as individuals, but naturally, there was always comparison and an unspoken awareness of the other. I learned early on to suppress my own feelings, constantly considering how my sister might feel. She was the rebel, always testing boundaries, while I was the rule-follower, trying to avoid adding stress to our family. Without realizing it, I took on the role of being the "easy" one. I also learned to downplay achievements, as if any success of mine needed to be kept quiet to avoid making my sister feel worse. This pattern followed me into adulthood, leaving me (unknowingly) feeling unworthy of attention or support, trying to blend in as much as possible, and constantly prioritizing others' feelings over my own.

We also explored my dynamic with my mom, where, instead of leaning on a therapist or a support system, she processed her unresolved trauma with me. Recently, I visited the part of me that struggled to feel articulate with words. As I have been writing this book, this part has spoken so loud. I actually have asked Jeff on several occasions if he thinks something is wrong with my brain as I know I have quite a bit of knowledge about stuff and don't understand how I trip over my words so easily. When I visited this part, memories started flooding in around the decades of conversations with my mom. Conversations where I tried my best to help, only to walk away with us both frustrated and hurt. There was a part of me that learned that *when I was vulnerable, I upset others.* Then it hit me: the act of writing this book has been one of the most vulnerable things I have ever done. This part of me, the part that so deeply worries if my words will upset others, has been trying to silence me—making me trip over my words to protect me from being hurt again. This work is not just little *aha's*. These are major beliefs I was uncovering.

Through IFS, Jeff helped me see these weren't just feelings—they were parts of me. The frustration? *That was a frustrated part of me.* The sadness? *A sad part of me.* And for the first time, I had a therapist who got excited when I expressed anger or frustration because these were emotions I had suppressed for far too long. I had no idea that feeling frustrated or angry could actually be a good thing.

What I appreciate about IFS is its simplicity. The term "part" is easy to use, as it's already in our everyday vocabulary. IFS has given me the most accessible way to work through something instantaneously or notice big shifts in an area I have struggled with for decades. One of the most incredible things is that you can do it independently—no therapist required.

It's wild to think about because I've never been much of a journaler. My hand cramps, it takes forever to get my thoughts out, and I never really went back to reread what I had written. I didn't see the point—until now. When I first started journaling, I had this nudge that I should do it in case I ever wrote a book. My memory has never been the best, so I figured it would be useful to have a record of my thoughts and feelings. It also became a way to prepare for my calls with Jeff, jot down what I was struggling with, and track my progress—especially as I started working through parts of myself.

One of the most powerful entries I wrote came after an emotional visit with the scared part of me. Jeff and I had been discussing my habit of double-checking locks and making sure no one was hiding in the house. It was the first time I visited a part entirely on my own, and I wasn't sure if it would work. Jeff had prepped me, but I doubted whether a memory would actually surface or if I'd get anything insightful from it. Boy, was I wrong. In less than five minutes, so much came through. I couldn't believe it.

Journal entry 9/26/2021 (eight years post-break-in):
Notes from the call with Jeff:

When I'm scared…(checking locks, checking under beds, dimming lights)—I go to the scared part and love up on it. Then, I work with the scared part and encourage strength. I see what this part wants to tell me.

Heads up…it's going to want to say some scary stuff. I have to reassure that part that I'm ok, I can listen, I have done all this work and I want to listen. When I have those thoughts and don't listen, it squashes them and tells them it's not important. Acknowledge that scared part.

Homework: Sit at the end of the bed, breathe, and love up on that part and see what the part says. Go towards the part with:

1. *Curiosity*
2. *Compassion*
3. *Connectedness*

Then, give it an update and let it know how you're doing.
When I visited the Little Girl:

- *She was crying—so scared she could barely breathe through the sobs.*
- *She kept repeating, "What if someone else comes? There was no one there to protect us. He was so big and strong, and I'm no match for that."*

- *I gave her endless compassion and reassurance, reminding her that what she did protected her and her family.*
- *She said, "I have no idea who he was, and I did nothing to him to deserve this."*
- *Again, I agreed with her, validating that she had done nothing wrong. I told her how incredible, brave, and strong she was to do what she did. I reminded her that she had powerful intuition—she knew something was coming, and she was right. And now, she knows how to be even more aware and trust it.*
- *She started to calm down.*
- *I asked her if there was anything she wanted me to know. She shook her head slightly in a not really kind of way.*
- *I then asked if there was anything I could do.*
- *She asked me to check back on her.*
- *I promised I would.*
- *Then she cried again and begged, "Please, never leave me. Don't go!"*
- *I reassured her I would never leave. I am always here and always will be.*
- *I reminded her—again—how brave and incredible she was. That when faced with the unthinkable, when most people would have frozen, she attacked. No one told her to. No one demanded her to. She did it all on her own.*
- *I told her how much people have learned from her. How I have worked so hard every day to heal and move forward. That I have met incredible people who have helped me and will continue to be there.*

Lastly, I let her know how much better things are now:

- *I can sleep at night alone, without music or medication.*
- *I can work in my office alone if I have to.*

Then she asked again, "Well, what if someone you don't know is like him...since you didn't know him?"

I reminded her: Yes, I walk through life with kindness, but I also walk through life with strength. Awareness and intuition are now a part of me.

When I came out of that session, I was shocked at how naturally the conversation had flowed. My whole body relaxed—my heart rate slowed, my breathing deepened, and for the first time in a while, the voices in my head settled. It's wild to go from feeling completely overwhelmed by an emotion, like fear, to spending just a few minutes closing your eyes, showing yourself the same love you'd give a child or a friend, and feeling relief almost instantly.

Even though it only took a few minutes, something had shifted. I've had to revisit that part of myself many times since, and as Jeff reminds me, I probably will again. But because I've taken the time to check in, I don't get as scared as I used to. And when fear does come up, it no longer feels unmanageable. I can't overstate how much this has impacted my life.

The start of writing this book exposed another part of me. When the idea of writing it first came up, I immediately thought I needed a ghostwriter. *I'm not a writer.* I need a professional. That was my default. I started looking into it, but for various reasons, it didn't work out, and instead, I was encouraged to write it myself. That terrified me. I had no idea how to write a book, but deep down, I knew that if I wanted this story to be exactly what I envisioned, I had to do it myself.

At first, it was a slog. Sometimes, I'd get into a flow, but most of the time, I felt stuck, convinced my writing was boring and no one would care. Being aware that this may be a part of me, I realized there was a part of me that worried my writing was boring. Knowing I didn't want that part to continue to show up if I was going to get this book written, I got curious, having absolutely no idea where the worry about being boring would come from. I closed my eyes and set the intention to visit that part of me. It's wild how quickly something pops into your head—sometimes a memory you've long forgotten, other times something you pushed away.

For me, it was middle school, riding the bus to a basketball game. I wasn't good—I mostly sat on the bench—but I loved being part of a team and the social time that came with it. Around that same time, I had a new best friend. We were inseparable, spending almost every day together. But after a few months, I noticed a shift. She had started gravitating toward the popular crowd. I wasn't uncool, but I wasn't in *that* group. And suddenly, she stopped answering my calls, making excuses, and eventually, she just disappeared from my life. I was devastated.

Somehow, I found the courage to write her a letter—poured my heart out, told her how much I missed her, and hoped we could still be friends. I folded it up, built up the nerve, and handed it to her on the bus. She smiled, took it, and that was it. She never wrote back. Never mentioned it. Just passed me in the halls with a polite smile as if none of it had ever happened.

I hadn't thought about that moment in decades, but as soon as it surfaced, it made so much sense why I had this fear of putting myself out there. I had done it before—written something deeply personal—and was met with silence. Rejection. My younger self had learned that sharing my feelings through writing meant that I was not interesting.

This is what's fascinating about this work. That fear wasn't just about writing—it was a pattern I had been carrying for years, affecting *so* many areas of my life. But now, instead of just noticing it and moving on, I did what Jeff taught me: I noted what age I was when I felt that way.

I let the memory surface without judgment. I got curious about what that younger version of me needed. I validated her feelings—because, damn, they were real. I reminded her that she's not alone anymore. I introduced her to the me of today—the one who started a podcast, spoke in front of 700 people, ran a successful business, and has an incredible support system.

Even after just one session with that part, writing became so much easier. The doubt still popped up, but instead of stopping me, it softened, too. I came up with a mantra and told myself—*if it sucks, I can always find someone to edit later*. That small shift made all the difference.

If I had let that fear stay blended with me, I might have thrown in the towel and convinced myself I wasn't cut out for this. Or the process would have dragged on, filled with second-guessing and forcing words onto the page. But once that part of me trusted that I had this, it stepped aside—and the words started flowing.

Our parts are a part of us for a reason. If we choose to acknowledge and love them instead of numbing or judging them, I think our deeply hurting world may be in a different place than it is now. IFS truly has the power to change it.

The last part story I want to share is about a part I never allowed myself to express…*anger*. I had mastered managing that part of me. I assumed anger was bad. I'd been mad before, of course, but growing up, I learned to read the room, gauge everyone else's emotions, and adjust accordingly. I became a pro at accommodating, pleasing, and keeping the peace.

Then, a few months into writing this book, Lyla was diagnosed with a second autoimmune disease. Her journey with autoimmune issues had already been incredibly tough for years, and getting this second diagnosis completely wrecked me. I had poured myself into finding ways to heal her—exploring every alternative path possible—so another condition added to the list felt like being kicked when you're already down.

I remember sitting in the doctor's office, just in shock. I was angry, frustrated, sad, exhausted—so many emotions all at once, and yet, I couldn't just "fix it". That night, I had my usual Sunday call with Jeff, and I was fired up, ready to spill every emotion and have him validate them. And while he did, I wasn't prepared for his suggestion.

He pointed out my anger. I knew where this was going, and I wanted nothing to do with it. I told him I was thinking about taking up boxing—something to physically get the frustration out. I thought he'd be on board. Instead, he gently pointed out that I wasn't comfortable feeling my anger, let alone expressing it. That caught me off guard. He was always right, *damn it*, which made me curious—why was I so resistant to this part of me?

When I finally sat with it, memories started flooding in—years of unspoken frustrations I had never let myself process. The first thing that hit me was all those nights in high school and college, sitting on the couch between my parents as they argued, trying to help them find a resolution. Then, I thought about middle school sports, when I had to constantly hitch rides with friends because my parents were too buried in their business to be on the sidelines. I understood why, but I still wished they had been there. And then, there was my mom and our conversations always turning into a disaster.

This part of me was angry that she never had a normal relationship with her mom. She was angry her family had fallen apart. And in that moment, I was angry, too. Memory after memory spilled out, years of bottled-up frustration finally coming to the surface. And when it was done, when I had felt it all, I asked that part of me how she felt. Her answer? "Fucking GOOD."

I literally wrote that in my journal, which is interesting because my go to's were "effing" or "freaking." But the release was real. And beyond that, I realized something—I liked this part of me. She was strong. She was powerful. She wasn't filtered. And for the first time, I saw her for what she was: a protector. As I had done in other sessions with Jeff, I asked this part of me what she wanted to do with all these memories. I imagined a quiet lakeside scene, sitting around a campfire where she wanted to gather all these memories, load them onto a rowboat, and push them out into the lake. As the boat floated away, a massive ray of sunlight beamed down, bathing the boat in light. It was as if all those heavy memories were being purified and released. The sense of relief was indescribable and overwhelming.

Then, I asked her—Do you want to stay here or come with me? She didn't hesitate. *I'm coming with you. I want to protect you. Like a bodyguard.* I smiled. I thanked her and told her I understood why she was there. But I also reassured her—*I* was doing the work. I was surrounding myself with people who truly loved and supported me. We're a team, I told her. You don't have to fight alone anymore. Just watch how I handle things now.

That moment changed something in me. I didn't just acknowledge that part of myself—I accepted her. With that acceptance came a sense of power I hadn't felt before. Visiting these parts of myself has been surprisingly simple. It doesn't take long, and I can do it on my own. But that doesn't mean it's easy. It takes a quiet (soft) kind of courage—that kind no one else sees. Sitting on my bed, eyes closed, visiting these pieces of myself…it always looked like nothing. But inside, those five to ten minutes were breaking down years of old wounds and letting go of the baggage I had carried for far too long.

18

BEING HERE NOW

One of the tools Jeff brought up to me was meditation. The moment he mentioned it, my gut reaction was *Ugh. Meditation.* I wasn't into it. Never had been. Everyone and their sister raved about it, but I just couldn't get on board. For years, I heard it come up over and over—on self-development podcasts, in books, from people I admired. And I'll admit it—I rolled my eyes every time. I had tried. Really. But it was completely foreign to me, and no matter how many times I attempted to sit still and quiet my mind, all I found was frustration.

I always thought meditation meant sitting in complete silence, legs crossed, hands resting just so—thumb and pointer finger touching, like some enlightened monk floating on a cloud of inner peace. Who actually does that? Seriously. Who can sit in total stillness and *enjoy* it? I didn't get it. Meditation, in my mind, was for monks, yogis, or people way more evolved than me. Still, I gave it a shot once. The *Headspace* app was all the rage, and I figured if everyone was talking about it, maybe there was something to it. I'm sure Andy, the founder, is a wonderful guy—he's helped thousands of people find peace through meditation. But me? I just couldn't get into it. My mind would wander, I'd get frustrated, and eventually, I would throw in the towel. *I guess I'm just not someone who can meditate.*

Then, in early 2020, the world shut down. Everyone was living in a state of fear, myself included. That's when, during a call, Jeff casually mentioned he had been creating meditations for the students and teachers at his school to help them cope with the uncertainty. He wasn't pushing me to try them—just sharing what he had been up to. But after the call, curiosity got the best of me. Not because I wanted to meditate but because I trusted Jeff, and I was intrigued by what kind of meditation *he* would create.

One title caught my eye, *Breathing into Tension.* I had a persistent knot in my upper right back that had been driving me crazy, so I thought, *What the heck?* It was only seven minutes. If anyone could get me to attempt meditation again, it was Jeff.

He guided me to focus on a tense spot in my body for seven minutes and breathe into it. That was it—simple, intentional, and, breath by breath, something changed. When the meditation ended, I realized something shocking—the knot was gone. *Gone.*

I sat there in disbelief. *What just happened?* It felt like magic. My mind wasn't racing. I wasn't tangled in my to-do list. For the first time in a long time, I felt relief—calm, even. And I wanted *more* of that.

Since then, I've logged hundreds of hours meditating. Jeff introduced me to *Insight Timer,* which became my go-to. I started exploring meditations for everything: calming anxious thoughts, grounding myself, heart coherence, morning intention-setting, and gratitude before bed. Even just five minutes could shift my entire state.

Eventually, meditation became a habit—not something rigid or scheduled, but something I naturally wove into my life as I intuitively felt called to. Some nights, I'd fall asleep with an earbud in, listening to affirmations or a body scan. Other nights, I'd let my body decide if I needed stillness or was better off just breathing alone. It wasn't about forcing anything. It was about balance.

Then, one night, something incredible happened. I came home, and my eleven-year-old daughter, Lyla, hesitantly approached me. Almost embarrassed, she said, "Mom, I made a meditation."

A couple of years before, I started introducing her to meditations, hoping they might support her healing journey with her autoimmune condition. I believe deeply in the power of the subconscious mind—people like Joe Dispenza and Dr. Gabor Maté have only deepened that belief. And despite what traditional medicine says, I choose to believe she *can* heal. If listening to meditations that affirm her body as strong, vibrant, and whole can help, I will play them for her every night.

She loved them from the start. As I tuck her in every night, we recap the day and choose a meditation together. But this time, she had created her own. I could see the perfectionist in her, hesitating as she pulled it up, but she let me listen. And then I heard it…five minutes—five minutes of pure beauty. In her sweet, innocent voice, her recording guided me through breathing, gratitude, and a technique Jeff had taught me: *So… Relaxed*, a polyvagal exercise to calm the nervous system.

And then, she *wrecked* me. Softly, she said, "Now repeat

these affirmations out loud or in your head: **I am unique. I am brave. I am honest. I am kind. I am beautiful. I am confident. I am smart. I am loved. I am me, and I can do anything.**"

As a parent, I know I've conditioned my kids in ways I *never* intended—just like all parents do. I worry. I remind them to *be safe, call me when you get there, and watch out!* I know I've probably instilled fears they wouldn't have had otherwise. But I've also spent years doing the work—therapy, meditation, self-development—to heal my own unhealthy patterns so I can show up better for them.

Hearing Lyla's voice guide me through those affirmations… I felt something deep. I don't often say I'm proud of myself. But in that moment, I was. I was proud of every hour I've spent untangling old wounds. I'm proud of every meditation I've done. Proud of the healing I've worked so hard to bring into my life—because now, I can see it rippling into hers.

In our first sessions, Jeff mentioned that there are two different kinds of trauma. He shared, "I believe that every little experience we have is a little t. And I think we are made up of millions of little t's, and that's key in how we operate in the world. How we can learn to respond to them, deal with them, become resilient, and develop grit is how we grow and learn to deal positively with these little t's."

Gabor Maté, distinguishes between "big T" traumas and "small t" traumas in his work:

> **"Big T" traumas refer to significant, often singular events that profoundly and immediately impact an individual's life. These could include experiences like physical or sexual abuse, natural disasters, or witnessing violence.**

On the other hand, "small t" traumas are more subtle and cumulative experiences that may not be as dramatic but still significantly affect a person's well-being over time. These could include neglect, emotional abuse, ongoing stress, or other adverse childhood experiences."

Maté emphasizes that both types of traumas can have long-lasting effects on individuals, potentially leading to various physical and mental health issues later in life. He often explores how these traumas shape a person's beliefs, behaviors, and overall health outcomes. Maté's work underscores the importance of recognizing and addressing big and small traumas to promote healing and resilience.

As I mentioned before, the thing about small t trauma is that you could still have lived in a wonderful and supportive household and still experience little t's. Maybe there was a situation when you were a kid, and you said the wrong thing and were told to go to *time out* when you just needed to be heard and given a hug. Maybe someone told you you were stupid when you couldn't figure out a math problem. Maybe you spilled something, and your parents reacted by yelling, getting upset, or telling you to go away instead of saying, "It's ok. Mistakes happen." All these little moments in life shape who we become and slowly create our belief systems over time.

Awareness allows us to see these patterns, thus being able to do something about it. Jeff told me that everything comes back to Awareness. When I asked him how he would explain awareness, he described it as a complete *checking-in* of where we are. He explained, "Sometimes, it can feel overwhelming because we're dealing with many emotions. But becoming aware is the first step. Awareness allows you to give something back to yourself."

I still have nightmares sometimes. I still check the locks—frequently. I haven't felt the radical urge to climb into the attic in a while, but it's not like the thought is *gone*. And while the fear of the gas station exploding isn't something that haunts me daily, it still sneaks in every now and then.

The truth is that triggers still show up. Life has a way of pressing on old wounds when I least expect it. For a long time, I believed I could overcome them—that if I just did enough work, healed enough, and *tried* hard enough, one day, they'd disappear. But I'm learning to accept that healing isn't about making them vanish. It's about making peace with their presence.

Awareness opens the doors to our inner world, allowing us to honor what's going on inside. With awareness, you can get to the root of your pain, challenges, and struggles. When we are aware of this, we can take courageous steps to heal from these experiences, big or small.

In my experience, to become aware, I had to get regulated. Things like journaling, working out, meditating, breath work, taking a warm shower, or just even small moments in the day where I paused and got grounded—becoming aware of my feet on the floor, butt in the chair, back against the back of the chair. These were moments that helped shift my nervous system to a relaxed state, thus allowing me to be aware of how I am *actually* feeling and be present in the moment rather than just spinning around in my head. The Polyvagal Theory also references moments like these as *glimmers*. The opposite of triggers. Positive moments that spark feelings of safety, joy, and connection support the nervous system to relax. These moments could be things like soaking in the sun, hearing the birds chirp, a smile from a stranger, a hug, a particular song, the fresh scent of coffee in the morning. Moments we often overlook.

While working with Jeff, I became aware of who I truly am and *why* I am that way. I didn't know where the incredible journey would lead me, and I didn't realize it would take years of work, but I was committed to peeling back the layers and letting go of patterns that weren't allowing me to be the best version of myself. I was aware that others around me did not struggle as I did, and I wanted to live like that. I wanted to experience the vision I had for my life, *To Live Heaven on Earth*, and feel like I had a purpose. I didn't have a plan or know what to do, but things were definitely different inside, making me more curious than ever.

19

DOES IT MAKE YOUR TAIL WAG

"Breathe...." she said.

I was beyond excited about getting on this Zoom call, but a huge part of me also felt like I was doing something wrong. *She's telling me to breathe....crap. She totally knows I'm nervous. Oh, God. She's an intuitive. Is she reading my mind? Can she see I'm running around the house like a crazy person because I'm so nervous? Good grief, why am I doing this? I feel like an idiot. Ok, Tenny, take a breath.*

I thought back to how this call came about. It was early in 2021, and I was listening to one of my favorite podcasts, PaleOMG. The host, Juli, was someone I had followed for a while. She had always intrigued me, given she had been in the CrossFit community and was passionate about all things health and wellness, nutrition, skincare, and pop culture, all of which were interests I was passionate about as well. Plus, she was intelligent, making the information valuable and entertaining while being extremely witty. I had no idea how she could talk for forty-five minutes and keep it so entertaining. I admired that confidence and skill. I'm not one who laughs easily at jokes or funny stories, but her podcasts elicited rare moments where I would laugh out loud. Mainly because she would often say things that we all think…but don't often say out loud. Whether those were stories of throwing herself under the bus or calling someone else out, it was always stating the obvious in a way that I never would have the boldness to do.

While I aligned with so many of her interests, I felt different from her. I'm a traditional astrological sign of Cancer who is sensitive and often described as empathetic, so a lot of times, I couldn't relate to having the guts to just say things so bluntly. While it was sometimes direct, I respected that she was bold enough to say what was on her mind, as I couldn't have felt farther away from being able to think, let alone *share* thoughts like that.

After listening to her for a year, I was surprised when the tone of her podcasts started to shift. I noticed a softer side of her that I enjoyed seeing come out, where she shared more vulnerabilities and started to have more understanding for others. Her podcast titles shifted to things like *Attitude Change, Mindset Shift, Always Learning, Can't We All Just Be Nice,* and *Check Your Judgy Self* (referring to herself).

As the months progressed, it was like I was personally hearing someone transform. She was no longer making as harsh of comments but rather sharing her efforts to be better, more understanding, and compassionate. She started leaning into more spiritual practices and alternative healing tools. Things like *Human Design, Astrology* readings, having her birth chart read, and doing an *Akashic Record* reading. All of which helped her see an entirely new perspective of herself and those around her. This new perspective gave her more grace towards others, and was helping her learn about herself in ways that she was excited about and had never experienced before.

Everything she was exploring was completely foreign to me. But I was deeply curious. I found myself counting down the days until her next podcast episode, eager to hear what unconventional thing she was trying and what she had learned from it. Every discovery, every deep dive—fascinating. But what captivated me most wasn't just the experiments themselves. It was *her*.

She was changing. Growing. Expanding. Becoming more open and more vulnerable. I was watching her transform in real-time. And as I was on my own journey healing parts of myself while learning to express myself authentically, I couldn't help but wonder—*could everything she was trying somehow help me, too?*

Divine timing is a funny thing. Right around this time, Jeff and I were digging into the deeper layers of my self-worth—the parts of me tangled up in what others thought of me. Not in a vain way, but in a way that touched every aspect of how I showed up in my life. I wasn't facing the same struggles as Juli, but in my own way, I was still as stuck. My habits, my patterns—they held me back. I was constantly criticizing myself, questioning my thoughts, second-guessing what I said in conversations, and even doubting the things that genuinely interested me! I hadn't realized just how much this controlled my life. Once again, I had been completely unaware.

The grief of losing our family, as I once knew it, ran deep.

As a child, I admired my parents' love. They seemed happy—like they truly *enjoyed* each other. My dad would playfully slap my mom's butt, flirting. They shared a love for music—holding hands while sipping wine, the lights off, candles flickering, lost in their favorite songs in our beloved music room. They'd even dance, completely present with each other. But life happened. A lost business. A tragic death in the family. Divisive political shifts. And little by little, it all crumbled.

Losing that shattered something in me. It wasn't just their marriage that fell apart—it was the pieces of my childhood that I had cherished most. The music room went silent. The movie nights—sitting together on the couch, each with our own bag of Pop Secret popcorn and Cherry Coke, watching the Oscar nominees—were gone. Holidays and family celebrations in that space would never happen again. I couldn't believe how much it unraveled. And what stunned me even more was how, even as an adult, I was still struggling to process that loss.

Jeff helped me take steps through it. With every session, he guided me deeper—helping me see the connections, understand the impact, and slowly begin to heal. It was patient work—therapy sessions filled with vulnerable conversations and homework on my own. Hours spent doing *parts work* and *nervous system regulation*. And learning to actually sit with my emotions through meditation. And many, many private moments where I let myself break down and just *cry*.

I didn't realize it at the time, but all of this was preparing me. Bit by bit, I was untangling the patterns that had kept me stuck—patterns that left me overwhelmed, frustrated, and sad. I was taking baby steps toward something new. Toward a shift, I couldn't yet see, but could *feel* coming.

I'll never forget the moment that truly changed the course of my life. Maybe it's because it's Washington, and we barely see the sun for nine months, but I remember how it was a beautiful sunny day, and I was driving to my office. I was at a stoplight while listening to one of Juli's podcasts when she said it. She declared that instead of a New Year's resolution for 2021, she was claiming a word for the year. Her word was....*curiosity*.

As soon as I heard it, my body completely lit up. A wave of excitement immediately flooded over me. Stacy, my intuitive friend who encouraged me to host my podcast, gave me this analogy, so I can't take credit for it, but it's *that feeling when a dog wags its tail in excitement*. That is exactly how I felt. I had an imaginary dog tail, and I could feel it wagging like crazy at the idea of following my curiosity. I immediately knew what that feeling and knowing was—*my intuition*. Having now a little more practice under my belt with intuition, I knew it was a sign trying to tell me something.

In that moment, full of excitement and high vibes, all I could think was that I wanted to make a deal with myself. I decided to do exactly what Juli had done and make 2021 my year of curiosity. To make sure I followed through, I felt the urge to make rules for myself. I committed to doing anything I was curious about that I could afford and that wouldn't negatively impact others.

Curiosity is such a simple thing. But it's crazy that I had not even given myself permission to truly explore all my curiosities. If I was curious about things that seemed unorthodox, I always defaulted to thinking I was weird, I wasn't being realistic, or other people would *think* I was crazy. Somehow, I had gotten trapped, thinking someone else always knew better than me.

While worrying about others' opinions may not necessarily be your thing, I realized there are many other ways we hold back from truly being authentic and getting curious. Here are a few examples:

- **Fear of doing it wrong** – *What if I mess this up and everyone sees? What if I follow the wrong advice? What if I make a fool of myself?*

- **Fear of wasting money** – *What if I invest in this, and it doesn't work out? What if I spend money on something I don't end up using? What if I could have used that money for something "more responsible"?*

- **Fear of being too old… or too young** – *What if I'm too late to start? What if I missed my chance? What if people don't take me seriously because I'm too young/inexperienced?*

- **Fear of not being smart enough** – *What if I can't figure it out? What if I don't understand the information? What if I try, and I just feel stupid?*

- **Fear of change** – *What if this shifts my life in ways I'm not ready for? What if I lose relationships because I change? What if I don't like the new version of my life?*

- **Fear of rejection** – *What if they say no? What if I put myself out there, and I get ignored? What if I'm not accepted or wanted?*

- **Fear of getting hurt** – *What if I open my heart, and I get betrayed? What if I take a risk, and it ends in pain? What if I let my guard down and regret it?*

- **Fear of failing** – *What if I give it everything I have and still fail? What if I look like an idiot? What if I prove to myself* (or others) that I wasn't good enough after all?

- **Fear of success** – *What if what I want actually happens? What will I do? What will people think of me? Will I lose it all, once I have it?*
- **Fear of the unknown** – *What if I step into this, and I have no idea what comes next? What if I lose control? What if I make a choice and everything changes in a way I didn't expect?*

Here's what I have found: The mind loves certainty, so when we don't have it, fear fills in the blanks with worst-case scenarios. But *what if* we did a reframe? As someone who tends to still struggle with worst-case scenario thoughts, this is a reframe I have learned from mentors and those I admire.

- *What if I do it right?*
- *What if this investment changes my life for the better?*
- *What if my age is actually my advantage?*
- *What if I learn and grow in ways I never imagined?*
- *What if change leads to something even better?*
- *What if I get accepted?*
- *What if it's worth the risk?*
- *What if failure isn't the end, but the next step toward success?*
- *What if the unknown holds something amazing waiting for me?*

Be thankful for closed doors, detours, and roadblocks. They protect you from paths and places not meant for you. - Unknown

Fear is loud, but curiosity and possibility are just as powerful—if we choose them.

I had lived through so many of these fears, and honestly, I was just *over it*. I watched people I admired creating the kind of life I *knew* I was capable of, yet I kept letting doubt hold me back—telling myself my dreams weren't "realistic" enough. And for what? Because I was worried someone might think I was crazy? I was tired of playing small, of letting fear dictate my choices. I didn't want to settle for a life that felt safe but unfulfilled. I wanted to know what it felt like to be *free*. **Year of Curiosity. Let's goooooooo.**

Not long after I made this commitment to myself, I was listening to another one of Juli's podcasts where she shared her experience with a Human Design reading. I had never heard of it before but was immediately interested. It combines astrology, quantum physics, the chakra system, and other things that take your name, birth date, birth time, and location of where you were born. It translates into a chart showing a blueprint and design of the qualities that make you, *you,* and how you operate best in this world. Not only this, but your design helps show you what you are created for and how your unique design is meant to impact others. All things I was in desperate search of. As Juli discussed the insights from her reading and how many of the things that showed up completely aligned with her now-experience, I was immediately *curious* about what my chart would say.

As I felt the pull to explore Human Design, my Christian upbringing chimed in loud and clear. *Am I a bad person for being interested in this?* The thought hit me instantly. I felt like I *shouldn't* be curious about something like this, like I was tiptoeing into territory I had no business exploring. I tried to reason with myself—*It's probably not a big deal. Just a silly reading.*

How could my birth date, time, and location possibly reveal anything meaningful? But no matter how much I tried to dismiss it, the curiosity wouldn't go away.

Juli had experienced so many breakthroughs through Human Design, and as I was deep in my own search to understand myself—who I was, what my purpose was—I couldn't stop wondering: *What if this could give me something I hadn't considered?*

Then, I remembered the promise I had just made to myself—to follow my curiosity. To stop shutting things down just because they didn't fit neatly into what I had always believed. If I was this excited and drawn to it, there had to be a reason.

The thing I love about curiosity is that it's low-stakes. It's not a commitment. It's not a massive life change. It's just exploring. So, I pulled up the show notes from the podcast where Juli had linked her Human Design resource, clicked the link, and started reading everything I could about a woman named Althea—the length of the session, the cost, and every little detail on her website. And instead of feeling hesitant, I felt even more excited. I knew what I had to do. I booked the session.

In the days leading up to the appointment, I felt like a giddy teenager getting ready for a first date. My session was scheduled for 9:30 am After dropping the kids off at school, I came home and tried to settle myself—grounding, breathing, preparing to be fully present for whatever was about to unfold. I had never done anything like this before. I had never met with an *intuitive* or sat down for a session that claimed to reveal my unique design and purpose. And honestly, I had no idea what to expect. *How could something as simple as entering my birth details give me any real insight?* How accurate could this really be? But, damn, was I curious.

When I finally sat down at my computer and logged onto the Zoom call, my heart was pounding. Althea had already sent me a copy of my chart along with some notes in our email exchanges—just enough to make me even more intrigued about what was about to unfold. In her email to remind me of our call, she included my chart and responded, acknowledging the healing work I had already been doing in response to such a life-changing event, revealing that I am on a path to impact others. She referenced my chart, revealed aspects of family expectations and where I could be holding back, and how that fits into a greater design —that it is part of my purpose.

I had shared a little about our event—just enough so she had some context and it didn't feel like I was dropping it on her out of nowhere. I'm always sensitive about that (and still am). I never know how sharing our story will land—whether it will resonate or if it will trigger something in someone else. It's happened before, and I hate that feeling. At the same time, I knew I *needed* to share it with her. I had always felt that our experience was tied to my purpose in some way—I just hadn't quite figured out how.

So when she acknowledged it as part of my path, when she spoke about tendencies and family expectations, it *hit*. It felt like a quiet validation of something I had always known deep down but not quite trusted. For once, I didn't have to explain myself. I didn't have to justify my feelings or overexplain my reasoning. She already saw it.

"Breathe..."

For the next two hours, I sat there listening—completely captivated—as this woman, a total stranger, told me things about myself that were shockingly accurate. Not just surface-level things but deep, soul-level truths. The kind of things I had always felt but never fully put into words. The things no one could possibly know because they lived inside me, unspoken. I barely said a word. I just sat there, listening, taking it all in.

It's funny that I had been nervous to have this session with her. The moment she started speaking, the nerves melted away. She articulated things about me in a way that made me feel seen and understood. She had the words to explain why I operated the way I did, why I felt the things I felt. I had spent years unpacking layers of this with Jeff, but this was a different angle—one that added a whole new depth. It was one of the most validating, encouraging messages I had ever received. She wasn't telling me who I *should* be. She was reminding me of who I *already was*.

Again and again, she reinforced that my purpose wasn't about striving to be something different—it was about fully embodying who I was created to be. That leaning into my natural gifts and intuition wasn't just the path to the most fulfilling life possible—it would also inspire others to do the same. And that whenever I felt frustrated, stuck, or unhappy, it was likely because I was trying to be something I wasn't—following what I *thought* I should do instead of what truly lit me up....*makes my tail wag.*

And then, she dropped something that caught me completely off guard. "One of your superpowers is hearing what's *true* when people speak. They may say one thing, but you know what they really mean."

I blinked. I had never had anyone tell me this before. Especially not someone I had just met. I had always known I was intuitive. That I was highly sensitive and deeply empathetic.

But no one had ever put it into words like this. I paused. *How would she know that about me?* It was something I had felt my whole life but had second-guessed, over and over, because no one else ever talked about this kind of thing. Then, she told me something else—something I *definitely* needed to hear. Because I feel things so deeply and pick up on other people's emotions, I need to work on creating boundaries. She explained that there's a difference between seeing a problem and trying to fix it.

Good grief. How does this woman know me so well?

Boundaries have always been a struggle for me. I *want* to solve people's problems. I *need* to make things better, even when it's not my responsibility. And in doing so, I sometimes overstep—offering advice that wasn't asked for, taking on emotions that weren't mine to carry. Hearing her call this out so clearly made me be aware of how I can start taking a step back.

Then came one of the biggest *aha* moments of the entire session.

"No shoulds. No yeah, buts." She explained that if I caught myself saying, "*I should* call that person, *I should* work out today, or I really want to take that trip, *but* I can't afford it," it is a red flag. A sign that I wasn't following my intuition. That I was operating from obligation or fear instead of desire.

So, this was great information for me to hear. She then told me, "Basically, if it's not a **"HELL YES,"** it's a **"HELL NO."** *Whoa.* That gave me some serious context to help start applying to situations where I still wasn't trusting myself.

After that call and contemplating all the times I just went with the flow without considering what direction I wanted to really go in, I decided that if something excites me, if it gives me that tail-wagging, can't-wait-to-do-this feeling—that's my inner guidance saying *go for it*. Anything outside of that? Not for me. After all, booking this call had been a perfect example of listening. She reminded me that when I lean into what I love, I naturally uplift others just by being myself. That alone was a *huge* perspective shift and another reason to live this way.

I immediately thought about all the times I had forced myself to do things because I *should*. Hearing her break it down like this made me realize just how often I operated from obligation instead of genuine desire. And the moment I gave myself permission to *not* follow every "should," I felt an *instant* weight lift off my shoulders.

Another thing she told me? My strongest sense is *touch*. I hadn't really thought about it before, but it made perfect sense. I feel most connected when I'm holding hands, hugging, or even playfully wrestling. It's my natural way of expressing love. I realized I do it all the time—reaching out to touch someone's arm during a conversation, pulling my kids in close, wanting to sit next to Kyle or put my head on his shoulder so I can feel that connection.

Then, she touched on something else—my willpower (or lack thereof). I laughed when she said it because, well... *yeah*. I've always been hard on myself for not having stronger discipline in certain areas. She used working out as an example, which was, ironically, perfect timing. I had transitioned out of my CrossFit days, where I used to work out six or seven times a week. Now, I sat at a desk all day, squeezing in workouts on the Peloton or with weights at home when I could. I was still consistent—three or four times a week—but nowhere near where I used to be. And I had been beating myself up for not sticking to a strict routine.

But then she told me something that, again, was not advice I was used to hearing between all the self-help and wellness-focused content I was consuming. I wasn't meant to force myself into rigid schedules. My body operates best when I *listen* to what it needs. Some weeks, that might mean five workouts. Other times, maybe just one. Maybe I work out in the morning one day and at night the next. I don't thrive on fixed routines, and that's okay. But other people do need routine. The fact is, we truly all do have our own unique design.

Hearing her say that felt like *permission* to follow what I had already been doing—except now, I could trust that it was actually the *right* approach for me. It went against everything society pushes about discipline, habits, and routines, but it felt accurate for me.

She also told me how intuitive I am—and then challenged me to use it and to start speaking up when I felt something. To trust my instincts. To practice tapping into what I already knew but hadn't fully embraced. I had never had someone believe in my intuition so openly before. I certainly knew I was able to tap into it—especially on *that* Mother's Day, but it was time for me to start believing in it in my everyday life, too.

Not everything she said landed, but most of it did. And that's the beauty of any tool—just because some things don't resonate doesn't mean the rest isn't valuable. I walked away from that session feeling **Seen. Encouraged. Excited. Hopeful.**

And it was only the beginning.

20
ANGELS & SPIRIT GUIDES

I scheduled a follow-up session with Althea because, as she predicted, questions were already surfacing. Now that I had this new framework to understand myself, I was seeing things through a completely different lens—and I needed help figuring out how to apply it in real life. The follow-up kept the momentum going, reinforcing all the insights she had shared while giving me space to process and integrate them.

These two sessions, along with Althea's warmth and encouragement, gave me something I didn't even realize I needed: *validation*. Validation that I wasn't just *different* for the sake of it—I was meant to be different. That my uniqueness wasn't something to fix or suppress, but rather the very thing that would allow me to make an impact in this world.

I would never be Oprah. Because *Oprah is Oprah*. And *Oprah isn't Tennyson*. That realization hit me hard. I had spent so much time measuring myself against others, questioning whether I was doing life *right*. But this made so much sense. There was still a long road ahead to fully own who I was, but now I had tools—little steps I could take to start embodying my true self. And looking back years later, I can say with complete certainty: this session was one of the best things I ever did for myself. Not just because of what I learned, but because it created momentum. It sparked a new way of thinking, a new way of trusting—not just in external frameworks, but in my own curiosity.

Mind blown and now completely obsessed with Althea and Human Design work, I couldn't wait to see what Juli was diving into next. It felt like I was vicariously living through her, watching her transform, and wanting to lean into anything that had helped her along the way.

And then, she shared about another healing session she did called an Akashic Record reading. A *what* reading? I had never heard of it. I could feel myself leaning in, intrigued, but this felt even more "woo woo". *Oh God, I'm going to hell.*

The Akashic Records, as she explained, are an energetic library of the soul—a record of past lives, present incarnations, and future possibilities. If Human Design was something I could logically categorize, like a personality test, this felt like a whole different ball game. This felt like stepping into the world of psychics, which had been ingrained in me as something *wrong* to even consider. And yet... here it was again. That same pull. That same curiosity.

Juli had so many powerful takeaways from her session, sharing how it was different from everything else she had explored. And no matter how much my rational mind tried to push it away, I *felt* the excitement bubbling up. *Crap. Here we go again.*

One of the things I want to add about every "energy healer" I have worked with is that they have all been the most encouraging, kind, supportive, and loving individuals. There are a few that I didn't feel a strong connection with, but even if there is a session I did that didn't totally land on the mark, it's been worth it because, with every person I have worked with in what some call a "woo woo" setting, has felt like an uninterrupted time of self-love. These sessions, along with my therapy sessions with Jeff, are the times in my life when I have felt the least amount of judgment. Rather, it's been the opposite of judgment. It's been a level of acceptance, compassion, and encouragement of my potential that I so needed.

I didn't grow up attending church, as I shared at the beginning of the book, but I did start going in high school to find more of a social circle. And, well, some good-looking guys attended the local youth group, so I sacrificed myself to give it a shot. I didn't think I would find something deeper while attending, but I did. I remember having a moment when I was leaving youth group one day and I had tingles all over my body. I had never felt anything like that before, and it was the first time I had ever felt connected to something bigger than myself. I believed in that, and since have had faith in it.

While I have appreciated what I have learned and aligned with so many of the biblical teachings, it's also been a place where I have had my own challenges in feeling judged. There have been several experiences in my years where it was pointed out what I did wrong over what I was doing right. As someone who fought so hard to be a rule follower and, frankly, learned to put themselves second to the needs of others, this confused me and strengthened feelings of not feeling good enough. It also never made sense why things like swearing were looked down upon, but then the same person who doesn't believe in swearing is, on the same day, snapping at their spouse, yelling at their kids, or making fun of someone who is not like them. That felt worse to me than using a swear word.

The truth is that there are incredible people I know who don't go to church and incredible people I know who do. Frankly, it doesn't matter to me. I just want to surround myself with people who show love to others, who are open-minded, who I feel like I can be my authentic self around, who I'm celebrated for doing so, and who ultimately make me feel better when I am around them.

When I first started exploring what some might call the "woo-woo" world, I found something unexpected—a space that felt deeply loving and free of judgment. There was no focus on pointing out failures, shortcomings, or sins. Instead, there was an understanding that mistakes, challenges, and even the hardest moments are all part of a greater plan—a path meant to teach us, stretch us, and expand us into who we're meant to become.

For me, there is no doubt that something greater than us is at play. Whether you call it God, Spirit, Source, the Universe, the Divine, or Buddha—it doesn't matter. What does matter is that you define it in a way that resonates with *you*.

I *felt* it the night of our break-in. That night only strengthened my belief in a higher power. There were far too many details—small, specific, perfect details—that lined up in our favor. The fact that Kyle's truck was gone made it seem like he wasn't home—when he actually was. The fact that our dogs woke up at the exact second they did. The fact that he passed by Lyla's room and ours, finding Kyle in the hallway instead. I can't even begin to imagine what it would have meant if he had gone into one of our bedrooms. And then, the clarity for me was there in my own knowing—the feeling, the certainty—*he's coming back.*

That wasn't a coincidence. That was divine protection.

Since that night, my eyes have been opened to all the ways the divine weaves through our lives—not just in life-or-death moments, but in the smallest, most ordinary ones. The synchronicities. The whispers of intuition. The moments that feel too perfectly aligned to be random.

As I have said, one of the hardest things about writing this book has been quieting the voice that worries about what people will think. *Will they judge me for sharing these experiences? Will they misunderstand my intentions?*

But here's the truth—this isn't about me telling anyone what path *they* should take. It's about sharing *my own* in the hope that it encourages you to find the one that feels right for you. Maybe the specific experiences I've explored don't interest you. Maybe they do. But at the core of everything I've done, every risk I've taken, every belief I've questioned, is one simple truth: I am relentlessly devoted to finding purpose. To living the most fulfilling, joy-filled life I can. And that? That is something I am deeply proud of.

If these things aren't for you, I completely understand. But if nothing else, I hope you'll read this with an open mind—and more than anything, I hope you see my heart. My only intention is to heal, to grow, and to live as authentically as I possibly can.

Ok, back to the Akashic Record reading. In preparation for the session, I was asked to write a list of questions for my angels or spirit guides—whatever I needed guidance on, just write it down.

I had no idea what "spirit guides" even meant. And the thought of asking questions to someone who wasn't human?

Honestly, it felt awkward. *What kind of questions do you even ask angels?* But after the profound insights from my recent Human Design reading—and seeing how much Juli raved about her experience—I did my best to quiet my ego and just roll with it.

Thirty minutes before the call, I found a quiet space to calm my body and focus on where I needed direction. At least this time, I wasn't running around the house frantically before the session. At this point in my life, I was deeply confused about my career. My insurance agency was successful—thriving, even—but something was missing. I had built something I was proud of, yet I wasn't fulfilled. The thought of spending the rest of my life selling insurance made my chest feel tight. *Was this really what I was created to do?*

I realized how much it killed me to sit all day. I missed movement. I missed the deep connection and community we had built at our CrossFit gym—the hugs, the check-ins, the small moments of encouragement that made people feel seen. I missed sensing when someone was struggling and being able to support them in real-time. I missed introducing people I just *knew* would hit it off. I missed being the overenthusiastic cheerleader, screaming through gross workouts, giving high-fives, and celebrating small victories. I wanted more of that.

Around this time, I had just launched my podcast—my first real step toward exploring what might fill that missing piece in me. But I still felt lost. I didn't want to fall into the trap of settling for a career that checked all the "success" boxes but left my soul starving.

I had always believed in the idea that you should love what you do. One of the only things I remember from my 11th-grade chemistry class was a Mark Twain quote taped to my teacher's desk: **"Find a job you enjoy doing, and you will never have to work a day in your life."** I read it every single day. It made sense to me. Even back then, I think I subconsciously recognized the toll my parents' business stress had taken on them. That belief had stuck with me for years, but when I shared it with others, I was often met with skepticism: *That's not realistic. Work is work. There's no such thing as a job you love all the time.* I understood their perspective. But I didn't agree. Of course, nothing is *always* sunshine and rainbows. But I had felt that deep sense of purpose before—when we ran the gym. And I wasn't willing to accept that it wasn't possible again. So, I sat down and wrote my list of questions for my spirit guides:

- **What is my purpose in life?** (Might as well start with the big one.)
- **How can I have more fun, be more spontaneous, and feel happier?**
- **What is the best self-care for me?**
- **What's the best way to improve my posture?**
- **How do I create the business and career goals I truly want?**
- **I feel bored at work, even though it's going well. What am I meant to do with my career?**
- **Sometimes, I feel brain-dead—I forget things or trip over my words. Should I be concerned, or how can I improve it?**
- **How can I deepen my connection with God or myself? I sometimes feel lonely.**

As I wrote them, I felt ridiculous. But I was committed to going all in—no matter how weird it felt. If a question popped into my head, I wrote it down. *Yes, even my question about posture. Why not?* I had spent years trying to fix it—chiropractors, alternative therapies, yoga, foundation training, posture braces, you name it. If my spirit guides had any advice, I'd take it at this point.

Then, I met Kimber. From the moment we started talking, I felt safe. She radiated love, kindness, and pure acceptance—the kind of presence that makes you feel like you can exhale and just be. You know when someone is fully present with you, with no personal agenda? That's what it felt like. I immediately relaxed, ready to receive whatever messages came through.

As she spoke, I scrambled to take notes. Here's what my spirit guides had to say:

- Purpose: To be 100% Tennyson. Radiate that light. My career is an expression of who I am. Vulnerability and light go hand in hand. Take action on what excites me the most—no attachment to the outcome. Whatever happens, trust that it's meant to be.

- Boredom is just really good information. You're clearly being guided to explore different paths.

- Self-care: Yin Yoga, breathwork, and full yoga breaths help release the analytical side of my brain. Also, use magnesium spray!

- Transitions make you feel "dumber" because you're in a beginner's mind.

- Posture: Don't focus on posture. Focus on heart-opening. Your shoulders roll forward because you're unconsciously protecting your heart.

I took pages of notes. It was another session that left me feeling seen, understood and encouraged. Many of the messages echoed what Althea had told me—which was wild, considering these two women didn't even know each other. *Coincidence? Maybe.* Or maybe it was just another reminder of what I already knew deep down but hadn't fully trusted yet. And maybe, just maybe, I had found two more people who were unknowingly part of my journey to uncover something bigger.

Fueled by these experiences, I started embracing curiosity in a whole new way—trusting that each "what if" could lead somewhere unexpected. It was curiosity that led me to hire a business coach for my insurance agency. Within minutes of asking myself, *I wonder if I need outside help,* I saw a Facebook post asking for recommendations. I read through the comments, found someone I resonated with, and hired them.

That decision led to me speaking on stage for the first time—standing in front of 700 people and sharing our story. I was so nervous that I couldn't stop burping backstage. (Gross, but true.) I felt like I might even throw up. But I knew—deep within—that this was what I was meant to do. Afterward, I was stunned. A line of women formed, along with a few men, all waiting to talk with me. Women with tears in their eyes, who simply wanted to hug me, to tell me they saw themselves in my story. That moment was proof. Proof that our story had value. Proof that following curiosity—even when it scared me—was leading me exactly where I needed to be.

Tony Robbins has a quote I love: **"The quality of your life is dependent on the quality of questions you ask."**

I often wonder—are we asking the right questions? The

kind that opens doors instead of shutting them? Instead of *Why is this happening to me?* What if we asked, *Who can help me?* Instead of *When will things change?* What if we asked, *How can I make a change?*

Looking back, I realize that curiosity had always been my greatest tool—especially in the years after our trauma. Instead of getting stuck in *Why me?* or *Why did this happen?*, I was unintentionally asking better questions. *Who can help me? What else is out there? How do I get through this?* Those questions led me to new therapists, alternative healing, and small but meaningful steps toward feeling like myself again.

Curiosity pushed me to explore Dr. Joe Dispenza's work, opening my mind to the science behind thoughts shaping reality. It led me to *The Magic* by Rhonda Byrne, a book that transformed my view on gratitude and manifestation. At the time, my insurance business wasn't performing like I was used to. I wasn't doing anything differently, yet I heard "no" more than ever.

The book's assignment? Write down ten things I was grateful for every single day. And not just write them down, write them down and *feel* that gratitude. It sounded simple—until day five, when I found myself scribbling things like, "I'm grateful for sticky notes" just to fill the page. But something repositioned. I started noticing gratitude in everything: red lights that prevented accidents, the warmth of my coffee, and the comfort of cozy socks. Within a month, my sales doubled. *Coincidence? Maybe.* But even if it was, I didn't care—because I also felt happier.

Fueled by this, I enrolled in a six-month manifestation course. Not to manifest material things (though, let's be honest, I was curious about that too), but to fully lean into what it meant to *create a life I loved*. The course echoed so much of what I had already learned—breathwork, mindfulness, meditation, even nervous system regulation—but it also gave me permission to dream without limits, to follow my excitement, and to trust that small nudges could lead to big things.

I started asking myself a new question. *"What's the worst that could happen?"*

It became a filter for decision-making:

- Curious about a Human Design reading? *Worst case—I'm out a couple hundred dollars.*
- That new strawberry matcha latte sounds weird but interesting. *Worst case—it's gross, and I'm out six bucks.*
- Considering a manifestation course? *Worst case—nothing manifests and I'm out the time and money I had committed.*
- Felt the nudge to write a book but doubted myself. *Worst case—I explore ghostwriters, realize it's not the right fit, and, well… end up writing it myself.*

In most cases, the stakes are so low. And yet, people hesitate. I see it all the time—people holding back, not because they can't do something, but because they don't believe something small will make a difference. But it does. While writing this book, I kept asking myself: *If there was one message I could scream from the rooftops, what would it be?* There are so many, but I keep coming back to this: *Be curious.*

Curiosity is exciting. It's fun. It's empowering. I truly believe that our intuition speaks through curiosity—and when we listen, it never leads us in the wrong direction. So if you're feeling the nudge toward something—trust it. You never know where it might lead.

21

HELL, YES

I had the opportunity to practice a "HELL YES" in action.

One day in late 2022, I felt the nudge to stay home from work. I wasn't sick, the kids were at school, and every logical part of me screamed that it was lazy and irresponsible to stay home when I didn't have a "reason" to. But something deeper was pulling me to take space—to pause. The night before, I had stumbled across a podcast where a woman described her solo retreat in Sedona, Arizona. She spoke about working with healers, having life-changing epiphanies, and feeling completely renewed. This was clearly right up my alley. I had been dipping my toes into the "woo-woo" world—Human Design, Akashic Records, manifestation—and was still on my mission to uncover my purpose and make it a reality. The thought of sitting among Sedona's red rocks, receiving guidance, and gaining clarity felt magnetic.

When I woke up the next morning, still thinking about it, I

knew this wasn't random. I wanted to learn more. But taking a day off just to follow a feeling? It went against everything I had been raised to believe about hard work, discipline, and success.

Yet, I had been practicing something new—listening to my intuition— and all the nuggets of wisdom that had come from my Human Design reading. And when I heard myself try to reason with myself that morning that I *should* go to work, I recognized it as a signal: my intuition was actually telling me to stay home. So, I did.

I started researching the retreat company the woman had mentioned, eventually working up the courage to call. I braced myself for a pushy sales pitch but was met with warmth, curiosity, and genuine interest in what I was looking for. When I was paired with a guide to customize my experience, I was sold. Every healer, every session, every piece of it felt like a hell yes. Except for one thing. The cost.

This was, by far, the biggest financial investment I had ever made in myself. I had just completed a manifestation course that already stretched me outside my comfort zone, and now I was considering spending double that. My mind was a mess—excitement battling fear, trust wrestling with guilt. *Was I being irresponsible? Was I being scammed? Would this be worth it?* And, of course, the ever-present mom guilt—leaving Kyle with the kids while I went off on some "spiritual retreat."

But as I talked it through with Kyle, I kept coming back to one question: Would I regret **not** doing this?

You know those moments when an opportunity excites you, but you talk yourself out of it? And later, you wonder for weeks, months—sometimes years—*what might have been?* Well, I knew this was one of those moments. So, I went through my process:

- Am I genuinely curious about this? *Yes.*
- Can I afford it? *Yes.*
- Will it negatively impact the people I care about? *No.*
- What's the worst that could happen? *At worst, I'd get a much-needed break and some amazing weather to recharge.*

With Kyle's support, I leaned in. Within a week of hearing about Sedona, I had booked my retreat, secured my flight, and was counting down the days.

What surprised me most was that, despite my deep-rooted fears around safety, traveling alone didn't even phase me. Our home has become a fortress—gates, fences, an alarm system, guns, a dog, and even a fan to block out noise, so I'm not lying awake analyzing every sound.

Even when we travel, I request a higher-floor hotel room (for safety, not the view) and one far from the elevator so I don't overthink every passing voice in the hallway. Kyle packs a travel fan because silence at night still feels unsafe. And after eleven years, we still haven't stayed at an Airbnb alone as a family. I used to judge myself for these things. But I've learned to offer myself grace. Whenever I start to question it, Jeff reminds me, "Doesn't it make sense that you feel this way, given everything you've been through?" *Yes. It does.* And that's part of the journey—learning to honor where I am while still following the hell yes moments that pull me forward.

I couldn't believe I was actually thinking of traveling alone. A couple of years ago, before my work with Jeff, this would have been unimaginable. The fact that I was even contemplating it felt monumental. In my initial conversation with my guide, I openly shared my concerns about feeling safe and how critical it was to understand the community, who these providers were, and where I would be meeting them. One detail that immediately put me at ease was learning that the average age of residents in Sedona is 70. It's a peaceful place with its own police force, where the most common calls are for speeding tickets. Sedona is well-known as a community of healers, attracting people from all over the world who seek to deepen their spirituality, experience breakthroughs, and find peace. If there were ever a place to travel alone for the first time, Sedona would be the perfect choice.

Since it was an individual retreat, I was responsible for booking my own place to stay. While most people stay at an Airbnb or rent rooms in people's homes, I knew there was absolutely no way I could sleep in a house with other people living there. No way. I felt much safer in nicer hotels. Part of me wanted to save money and be like everyone else who could rent a room from someone and feel completely fine, but I knew that staying in a shared space would only make my fears, worries, and anxiety worse, making it impossible to relax. So, I found one of the nicer hotels in Sedona and booked my stay.

In preparation for the retreat, you are paired with one of their coaches to set your intentions for your trip to be the most intentional and impactful trip possible. Looking back at my journal, here are some of my notes in preparation for this meeting:

- Clearing Limiting Beliefs
- Not worthy enough
- Not smart enough
- There are already amazing people out there
- A dream life is possible for others but not for me

- Get clear on the vision for the life I want to create in Business
- Clear Money Blocks:
- Believing what I desire is possible
- Not feeling greedy for wanting more
- Clear things that are holding me back
- Release as much trauma as I can
- Book?/Speaking?//How am I making income?
- Connectedness to patience and faith for things unfolding
- Are signs a thing??
- What's up with Angel Numbers??
- Healing Thoughts for Lyla
- Clarity on Tools to use and how often (I often feel like I'm doing the kitchen sink right now):
    - Therapy
    - Meditation
    - Gratitude Practice
    - Visualization
    - Hypnosis
    - Music
    - Journaling
    - Energy Sessions
- Strengthening my Intuition and learning more about my intuition
- Direction for Career

As the days counted down, my excitement was next level—the kind that felt like being a kid waiting for Christmas morning. I had traveled before—trips with Kyle, girls' weekends with close friends—but never something entirely for me. The idea of flying to a stunning place, immersing myself in eight sessions with some of the most gifted healers, and diving deep into strengthening my belief in myself in unconventional ways? I could barely put it into words. It felt like I was about to step into a moment I'd never forget.

There's something so freeing about making a decision that is purely *for you*.

As Kyle drove me to the airport, I checked in and saw an upgrade to first class for $100. I had never flown first class before and for this trip? It felt like the perfect way to step into the highest energy possible. Another Hell, Yes.

I didn't realize first-class meant being addressed as "Mrs. Jacobson" or being served drinks in actual glassware. And eating my first veggie omelet 30,000 feet in the air? *Pure luxury.* I took it all in, completely aware of how lucky I was to be here, heading into an experience I had only dreamed about.

I closed my eyes, put in my headphones, and let my favorite EDM playlist transport me to another world—one where I could see my goals and feel the life I wanted to create. I imagined having the most incredible trip, setting my intentions, and leaning into the unknown with complete trust. I had no idea what was ahead of me. And I couldn't wait to find out.

22

THE VORTEX

Sedona, Arizona, is often called one of the most magical places on Earth—a place of breathtaking red rock formations and energy vortexes. I had to look up what a vortex even meant, but apparently, these are powerful energy centers where the earth's energy either flows inward or radiates outward. The four major vortex sites—Cathedral Rock, Bell Rock, Boynton Canyon, and Airport Mesa—are said to have transformational energy. Some visitors claim they can feel the energy moving through their bodies.

I had briefly visited Sedona once before, in 2021, on a quick day trip with Kyle while we were in Scottsdale. We hiked up Cathedral Rock, standing in silence at the top, just taking it all in. The deep red and orange rock formations looked almost unreal against the bright blue sky—it was like stepping into a painting. The twisted juniper trees, the crisp, fresh air, the way the sun cast moving shadows across the canyons—it was perfection.

People around us were meditating, fully immersed in the energy of the place. It felt sacred, like time had paused, and everyone respected that. I remember feeling a pain of regret that we hadn't planned to stay longer. Even then, I knew I'd have to come back. *And now, here I was.*

But the moment I landed in Phoenix, reality hit. I was completely alone. As I got into my rental car, a wave of panic rolled over me. *What the hell am I doing?* I had just committed to driving two hours into the desert by myself, in a place I barely knew, with no one nearby. *I'm such an idiot*, I thought. *How could I not even consider how scary this would feel?* Before I even left the airport, doubt flooded in. I had hyped this trip up in my head, and told Kyle how life-changing it would be, and now, I wasn't just afraid it would be a waste—I was afraid it would be a complete failure. I didn't feel safe. I didn't feel adventurous. I felt alone. And before I could stop them, the tears came.

I sat there in my rental car, overwhelmed, realizing just how far I had pushed myself outside my comfort zone. I had been so focused on the magic of this trip that I hadn't considered what it would actually feel like to step into the unknown—completely on my own.

I loved traveling with Kyle, the kids, and our friends. *So why in the world did I need to do something alone? What was I actually doing?* The question hit me hard as I cranked up the AC, trying to cool myself down. I caught my reflection in the rearview mirror, running through a dozen different scenarios in my head. But one thing was certain—I couldn't turn back.

I forced myself to focus, leaning on Jeff's advice for calming my nervous system. I reminded myself why I was here and how excited I had been about this trip. I took deep breaths, grounding myself in the seat, feeling my back press into the cushion and my feet firmly planted on the floor. Slowly, the flood of emotions started to settle. And then, almost unnoticeably, a thought popped into my head—I was proud of myself for being here. It was small, but it was something. I knew there would be more of those moments. After all, I came here to discover my purpose, strengthen my intuition, and embrace the experience as fully as possible. Even if the thought of driving into the middle of the desert alone still scared me, I turned up my visualization playlist and decided to picture the best trip ever—challenges and all.

Pulling into the hotel parking lot just before dinner, I exhaled in relief. No crisis. No flat tires. No horror-movie scenario of being stranded in the desert, reliant on a stranger's mercy. Just me, about to begin four days of complete solitude.

At check-in, I confidently gave them my last name.

"Yeah, I'm so sorry, we don't have any reservation under that name," the front desk clerk said.

My heart dropped. What? My mind raced—where would I stay? I had been so intentional about choosing this hotel. There was no way I could just wing it and feel safe. "Are you sure? Try my first name—Tennyson?"

The clerk frowned at the screen. "No, I'm really sorry. I don't see anything."

Panic crept in. I was alone. In the desert. With no room. I frantically pulled up my reservation on my phone, proof that I had, in fact, booked a stay.

The clerk double-checked the computer. "Hmmm, I just don't see—" Then she paused. "Wait. We do have a "Tenny Cell." Could that be it?"

Oh. My. God. I dropped my head onto the counter in

immediate relief. Of course. Apple Pay. It must have autofilled my contact name as "Tenny Cell." I laughed at myself and explained the ridiculous mistake to the front desk team, who had now become invested in solving the mystery.

They felt so bad that they offered me a complimentary bottle of wine from their amenities room. Not just the house wine. *Any* wine I wanted out of about thirty options. I appreciated the kindness, especially since the mistake was entirely mine. Small gestures like that make a big difference, and their generosity didn't go unnoticed.

Once I settled into my room, I heard something that immediately caught my attention—live music echoing from the hotel restaurant. *My favorite.* Just the sound of it sent me back to my childhood: years spent playing the clarinet, summer band camps, and late nights in the music room. That deep, familiar pull made me want to go downstairs and listen. But there was one problem—*I was alone.* I had never gone to a nice restaurant alone. Ever. The thought of sitting at a table by myself made me unreasonably uncomfortable. And yet, I knew I wanted to go. I debated with myself: *You have this nice bottle of wine. You could just stay in the room and enjoy that.* But then, the real voice in my head—the one I was here to listen to—chimed in, *Tennyson, get real. This is literally why you came here. Are you really going to miss out on the live music because you're too afraid to sit alone?* I knew the answer. So, after several minutes of internal tug-of-war, I mustered up the courage to go.

Not gonna lie—the first hour was painfully awkward. I sat at a cozy spot, ordered a glass of wine, and stared at the menu as if I were preparing for a final exam. I wasn't hungry, but I needed something to do. I scrolled through Instagram, pretending to read something fascinating, even making little facial expressions like, *Hmmm, interesting*. It was ridiculous.

But I stayed. I pushed through the discomfort. And slowly, something shifted. The music was perfect. The atmosphere was warm. And I felt a small spark of pride. It wasn't a huge, life-altering moment, but it was another little victory—a rep of courage. And that mattered.

The next morning, the real work began. After checking in at the retreat's main office, I was invited to choose a crystal—something to represent me during the experience. Holding it in my hand, I closed my eyes, repeated my intentions, and let go of any expectations.

My first session was with a woman who had spent nearly fifty years working with *Highly Sensitive People*, helping them release trauma and integrate their mind, body, and soul. Years ago, I had taken the Highly Sensitive Person test and scored high, so her insights weren't a surprise. But our conversation on marriage struck a chord. She encouraged me to appreciate how grounding Kyle is for me. I tend to live in my thoughts and emotions, expecting Kyle to fully understand my inner world—sometimes unfairly so. Her perspective reminded me of the balance we bring to each other.

We also talked about my career—how I felt unfulfilled, and how I craved clarity. And then she said something that stopped me. "Release the need for a clear vision." She explained that clinging too tightly to the question, "*How* will this happen?" actually blocks the flow of opportunities. The real work is in trusting the process. It wasn't the first time I'd heard this message, and it wouldn't be the last. As I left, she smiled warmly. "Tell Kyle I already feel like I know him, and let him know he's a lucky man."

Her words didn't unlock some groundbreaking realization. But the way she looked at me—the way she truly saw me—stuck with me. People always say it's not about what someone says, but how they make you feel. And in that moment, I felt understood. Seen. Encouraged.

I didn't realize it, but this trip was already working its magic.

Heading into my second session that afternoon, I couldn't help but feel excited. This was one of the sessions I had been looking forward to the most. As I approached the house, I hesitated for a moment, confused by the two front doors. Wandering along the paths, trying to decide which one to choose, I suddenly heard a cheerful voice call out, "Tenny! Tenny."

I froze for a second, surprised. *How did she know I go by Tenny?*

"You're getting warmer!" she added, her tone playful and inviting. I followed her voice, drawn in by its warmth, and found my way to the right door. Standing there was a petite woman, probably in her late 60s or early 70s, with light blonde hair and the sweetest outfit—a flowy skirt, a button-up blouse, and a delicate lace collar. She radiated pure joy, and I couldn't help but smile before I even stepped inside.

She opened her arms wide, beaming at me like I was a long-lost family member finally coming home. There was something about her presence—so full of light-heartedness and warmth—that made me feel instantly at ease. Despite being a total stranger, she made me feel like I was visiting a grandmother who had known me my whole life and was thrilled to see me again.

Her home had an old-fashioned charm, with light baby-blue

carpet that immediately reminded me of my grandparents' house—a single-story, mid-century modern home still frozen in time. The color triggered a wave of nostalgia, taking me back to my grandma's bathroom, which had a similar light pink carpet—a quirky detail I had been strangely fascinated by as a kid.

She led me into what seemed like a second living room, and my eyes widened. Every wall was completely covered in trinkets. Floor-to-ceiling shelves lined the space, packed with books, plants, figurines, baskets, signs, and toys—each object looking like it had a story to tell. At the center of it all sat a table with a large tray filled with sand and two open chairs, adding to the room's eclectic, cozy feel.

As we sat down, she looked at me with bright blue eyes and asked about my journey—why I had come to Sedona, and what I was hoping to find. I opened up about my desire for clarity in my life's purpose, my hope for healing energy for my daughter's autoimmune conditions, and my need to release what no longer served me. I shared the trauma I had been through, explaining how it felt like part of a larger story I was meant to tell—but how I was still struggling to understand how I would use it to help others.

She listened intently, nodding with a deep understanding that made me feel instantly seen. There was something remarkable about her. She wasn't just warm and goofy—she was incredibly sharp and intentional. She carried wisdom in a way that made you lean in closer. I wanted to catch every word. Then, we began the session.

"I want you to walk around the room and choose anything that catches your eye," she instructed. "When in doubt, pick it out."

Her words made me laugh—simple, yet exactly what I needed as an overthinker.

The first thing that grabbed my attention was the book *Love You Forever*. Without hesitation, I picked it up. That had been a childhood favorite—one my mom read to me over and over again. Then, I noticed dolphin figurines. One was a bright blue pair, playfully leaping together, while the others were neutral-toned and solitary. My instinct was to go for the bright blue dolphins, but a familiar voice in my head whispered that I should pick the neutral ones—because I always go for neutral colors. *When in doubt, pick it out*, I reminded myself, reaching for the playful blue ones instead. Next, a one-million-dollar bill caught my eye. I hesitated, feeling a twinge of guilt for wanting to grab it, but I did anyway. Then, I noticed several butterflies and chose the most colorful one.

One by one, I continued gathering objects that pulled at something inside me: a feather, a laughing pink Buddha, a tiny chair that read *The Boss*, Gumby, an old McDonald's mini Barbie from the '90s—the exact one I used to get in Happy Meals. A volcano, an airplane, a firetruck, a Teenage Mutant Ninja Turtle, a small yellow tennis racket, a dreamcatcher, a figurine of a snow-covered house, a stuffed animal almost identical to my childhood Mr. Bear, a Princess Diana Beanie Baby, the Genie from *Aladdin*, bright green sunglasses, a monkey figurine with huge, ridiculous eyes that made me laugh, a vibrant blue masquerade mask, and a scroll of holiday-themed sheet music.

By the time I was done, I had collected an entire pile of seemingly random objects. Placing them in the sand tray, I arranged them where they felt right, adjusting them until everything seemed to belong. She then asked me to walk around the table twice, studying the arrangement.

"What's the first thing that comes to mind when you look at your tray?" she asked.

I wanted to have some deep, insightful revelation. I wanted a breakthrough moment, a realization about my life's path. But as I stood there, looking at my absurd little collection, the only thing that came to mind was... *this looks really fun.* Feeling a little disappointed, I admitted it out loud. "Honestly, it just looks like a lot of fun."

She paused, then met my eyes. "Tenny, how much fun do you actually have?"

The question hit me harder than I expected. I immediately thought of Kyle. How effortlessly he turns everyday moments into play, how he can be silly with the kids in ways I admire but rarely emulate. I've always thought of myself as laid-back, someone who doesn't take life too seriously, but when I really considered it... *How often do I actively choose fun? How often do I let go, just for the sake of joy?*

She gently pointed out how we sometimes close off parts of ourselves after going through trauma. *Had I shut down my playful side without realizing it?* I didn't think so—not entirely. I could still be goofy, still crack jokes, still make people laugh. But true, unstructured play? That was different.

She asked about my childhood—whether fun had been encouraged or if things had been more structured. I told her my mom had always prioritized learning. She read with us constantly, played classical music, used flashcards, and signed us up for music lessons. Sure, I played with Barbies and spent time outside, but there was always an underlying focus on growth. She smiled knowingly. "I want you to color outside the lines."

The irony wasn't lost on me—I've never liked coloring outside the lines. She encouraged me to make room for spontaneity. To add more color to my wardrobe. To take the kids outside and draw with sidewalk chalk. To start art projects with no plan. To grab Kyle and the kids on a weekend morning, hop in the car, and go somewhere *just because*. "From there, the answers may come," she said with certainty. As I gathered my things to leave, she looked at me one last time, her expression soft yet firm. "I can see how your story can help so many people. This isn't just important for you... it's time to share it."

I nodded, knowing she was right. I just wasn't sure how it would all unfold. I had come into this session expecting to shed old beliefs or receive some profound spiritual insight. Instead, my biggest takeaway was: have more fun. It seemed almost too simple. But maybe the simple things are the most profound. And, honestly? Out of all the personal growth work I had done over the years, this was the first time I left with homework that told me to "go have fun!" I loved the deeper inner work, but this was refreshing.

That evening, I decided to catch the sunset at Cathedral Rock, one of the four vortexes. With sunset at 6:32 pm and the time already 6:20 pm, I had about a half-mile walk to the spot. Not wanting to look like a crazy person sprinting through the desert but not wanting to miss the sunset, I started walking as fast as I could, eventually breaking into a light jog as the minutes ticked. I found a spot on the red rock and took in the breathtaking view as the sun set. Sitting next to a small creek shaded by pinyon trees, I looked up at Cathedral Rock—the enormous red formations that looked like pillars reaching to the sky, catching the sun's last light as it set. It was truly one of the most beautiful scenes I've ever witnessed. I put in my earbuds, turned on a grounding meditation, and sat cross-legged, fully absorbed in the moment as the sun slowly dropped below the horizon and the red rocks turned dark.

I felt grateful for trusting myself to come here alone and for that last-minute decision to run. I'll never forget that sunset—it felt like a perfect ending to my first full day. I made a mental note that I would need to do this again. I hadn't received any magical answer to my intentions, but there was no denying it was a great day.

When I returned to the hotel, I hit the bar again for the second night and enjoyed the same live guitarist while eating dinner. This time, I felt a little more confident and comfortable, not needing to look at a menu or my phone, and I was surprised to see that shift.

I brought my journal to the bar to capture everything about my first day—only in Sedona would journaling in a bar seem completely normal. I ended up sitting next to two lovely ladies who were life coaches. To my surprise, one asked me what I was journaling about (again, only in Sedona), so I shared that I was on a personal retreat, as the retreat company calls it, a "soul journey." They were incredibly intrigued and began asking me questions about what drew me to take this trip, my sessions, and how I was finding the experience so far.

As we talked, I mentioned our story and how I had started a podcast without knowing what I was doing and that I was now working on a book. One of the women was particularly interested. She told me how her husband, who had been in law enforcement, was in an altercation that led him to have to kill someone to protect his partner. This happened shortly after the nationwide unrest in 2020 following George Floyd's death. His department struggled with supporting him while navigating the sensitive issues that were, and still are, very real. The trauma of taking a life to save someone else's, and then feeling unseen and unsupported eventually led him to leave his career. She shared that his therapist had told him that very few people could relate to what he had gone through. She believed I was one of those people and was eager for him to hear my podcast, hoping he might feel understood and find a connection in our shared experiences. It was good for me to hear her mention this. It was like seeing a glimmer of what it would mean to put myself out there and share my story. I was mainly here in Sedona to find confidence in my life's purpose…but maybe I was already being given clues. Even with this, though, that didn't stop all the doubts from coming.

Is what I really want possible? There are so many incredible people out there who know and understand trauma better than me. Why do I think I have anything new to add to the mix? Can I really help someone like her husband?

The synchronicity of this conversation wasn't totally lost on me. It reminded me that what I have to share does have interest and potential value. *How* all that looks was just not clear yet.

After I unloaded everything I was experiencing in Sedona onto them, I asked if they had any recommendations since they had been there for a week and it was their last night. I had learned these women to be bright, professional, and open-minded, so I was curious about their suggestions. They told me about a woman who does Animal Card readings, which they said was, hands down, the best thing they'd done. Animal Card readings? *Oh God*, I thought to myself. I was skeptical, but their enthusiasm was undeniable and I knew I needed to add that to my list.

I went to bed that night with the biggest smile on my face. I had sessions with two amazing women who genuinely supported and encouraged me. I witnessed the most ridiculous sunset in the most beautiful setting. For my second night, I enjoyed a solo dinner with the best ahi tuna tacos, a glass of wine, journaling, and great company. I was finally starting to get the hang of things.

23

I AM

Going into my second day, I had a Core Belief Transformation Session—a practice that combined bilateral stimulation and hypnosis to help shift deeply ingrained beliefs. The facilitator handed me a list of core beliefs and asked me to rate how true each one felt to me.

Some of the beliefs included: **I am worthy. I am deserving. I am lovable. It is safe to be my authentic self. I can make mistakes.**

As soon as I saw the list, I immediately thought of my work with Jeff and recognized these as 'parts' through the lens of Internal Family Systems (IFS). I felt some hesitation. These weren't just simple affirmations—they were the deepest wounds most people carry. The moment took me back to that experience in my car when I couldn't bring myself to say I was worthy.

I had support in working through this outside of the retreat, but I wondered about people who didn't. *Would this experience open wounds they weren't ready to face?* And if I was being honest, part of me felt protective of my work with Jeff. I respected him too much to fully lean into another approach. But I was here and decided to stay open—to take what I could from the experience without overthinking it.

I rated most of the beliefs pretty high, but when it came to *it's safe to be my authentic self* and *I can make mistakes*, I couldn't bring myself to give them a high score. Those hit differently. The facilitator handed me two small vibrating devices—one for each hand. They pulsed back and forth, gently alternating from right to left as I focused on the beliefs I had struggled to embrace.

"Where do you think these beliefs come from?" he asked.

Tapping into these memories had become second nature to me, so I let my mind wander. But as I did, a different thought crept in—*What would Jeff think about me doing this? Would these Sedona sessions interfere with all my progress with him?* I didn't want to undo everything he had helped me work through. So, I decided to approach it like IFS. I let the memories surface, validated them, and showed compassion to the younger parts of me who had learned that it wasn't always safe to be myself or to make mistakes.

The session didn't bring any earth-shattering revelations—it was work I was already familiar with—but it did bring up parts of me I hadn't fully explored. By the end, when I was asked to re-rate my beliefs, I wasn't surprised to see how much they had improved.

The facilitator must have picked up on my lukewarm reaction because he gently reassured me, "Not every session has to be life-changing. Sometimes, it's just about being present with what comes up."

I knew he was right, but I still felt a little frustrated. I had come to Sedona expecting major breakthroughs—some profound moment of clarity that would make everything click. I had made a huge financial investment, taken time away from my family, and had the courage to embark on this trip alone. Of course, I had high expectations.

He smiled, sensing my resistance. "Maybe what you're looking for isn't in a single session. Maybe it's in the experience *as a whole.*"

Ugh. That wasn't what I wanted to hear. But deep down, I knew he was right.

Before my next session, I decided to clear my head with a hike at Airport Mesa, a shorter trail known for its vortex, which is said to help release fear and worry. The hike was stunning, offering a 360-degree view of Sedona. It felt like the perfect place to reset. I wanted to fully embrace the Sedona experience, so I decided to meditate in the vortex. But the moment I sat down, self-consciousness crept in. There were so many people around. *What if they think I look ridiculous?* Then I reminded myself—*If there's anywhere people would understand this, it's Sedona.* So, I went for it. I pulled up my favorite meditation app, *Insight Timer,* and chose a session specifically focused on clearing fear. With each breath, I felt myself settling in, letting go, and absorbing the energy around me. I was already pushing myself outside my comfort zone, so why stop now?

The view was too breathtaking not to capture, but I hated taking selfies. The idea of drawing attention to myself, seeming vain or self-absorbed, made me cringe. I could easily take photos of the landscape, but I knew I'd regret not having any with me in them. I took a deep breath and forced myself to do something that felt even more uncomfortable—ask a stranger to take my picture. I scanned the crowd, searching for someone who looked approachable. I felt awkward. I second-guessed myself. Then, finally, I did it. And you know what? It was fine—more than fine. They were happy to. And it was actually nice to have a small interaction with someone, given I was here alone. It was just another small act of courage—stacking on top of all the others. Traveling alone, dining alone, meditating in public, asking for a photo—all these seemingly insignificant moments were building something bigger. I could already feel a shift. The fear of what people thought was still there, but it was loosening its grip.

I blasted music in my car and rolled my windows down, riding that wave of confidence all the way to the session I was most excited about—Life Purpose through Hand Analysis. From the moment I booked this retreat, this was the session I had been anticipating the most. I tried to keep my expectations in check—nothing had completely blown me away yet—but I couldn't help but hope. Unlike a traditional palm reader, my facilitator had studied at the International Institute of Hand Analysis. This wasn't intuition-based—every fingerprint and hand line correlated to a specific aspect of life, a serious craft backed by years of study.

As I pulled up to her house, I half-expected someone draped in shawls and covered in rings, looking like a character from a movie. Instead, she was polished and confident and carried a quiet strength that immediately made me respect her. She explained that the Navajos believe fingerprints are the marks of the soul—unchanging—while the lines in our hands are shaped by our life experiences. It was poetic, and I was intrigued. After studying my hands, and taking notes, she said something that took my breath away. "Your purpose is to experience a deep, deep, *deep* sense of fear."

I stared at her. Without knowing anything about me, she looked at me as if she knew I had experienced something incredibly painful and life-changing... She asked, "Is there any experience in your life where you deeply felt fear?"

I nearly laughed. *You could say that.* For the next hour and a half, she broke down what my hands revealed—my gifts, my purpose, and the struggles I was meant to overcome. Every detail aligned with what I had worked through in therapy, what I had uncovered in Human Design, and what I had journaled about for years but never fully understood. It wasn't just *accurate.* It was *validating.*

As I processed everything, she told me something that landed deeper than anything else: "Stop trying to plan your life. No five-year plan. No one-year plan. Just take it one day at a time. Follow what excites you, what feels like a HELL YES. The Universe has a far greater plan than you can imagine, but you have to trust yourself."

I wrote it in my journal immediately after, *"I already have it in my hands. Success and abundance are already done. But I have to stay aligned with myself. Trust. Let go of ego. Follow what excites me. Enjoy the journey."*

For years, I had forced myself into goal-setting, believing that structure equaled success. But deep down, I had always resisted rigid plans. Hearing someone else tell me to trust my instincts—to move through life guided by excitement rather than habits and expectations—felt like another permission slip to embrace my own unique way. I left that session feeling lighter. Stronger. More confident than I had been in years.

Every experience in Sedona had led me to this realization: I had been looking for answers *outside* of myself when, all along, they had been *within* me. And for the first time in a long time, I trusted that was enough.

24

THE WONDER OF THE WOO WOO WORLD

I had heard about the best crystal shop ever and that it was a must-visit in Sedona. I wasn't exactly sure what to do there and what crystals were about, but I knew I would not get the whole Sedona experience if I didn't check the shop out. After picking out a few crystals and selecting a few for my family, I backed my rental car out of the parking spot and noticed a building next door that said, "Aura readings." *Oh man, should I?* I thought. I could feel my curiosity bubbling up, but then my logical side chimed in again: *Really, Tenny? An aura reading?!* I sat there with my foot on the brake, debating whether to go in. I felt ridiculous that I was considering an aura reading. But then I reminded myself: *Tenny, you're here alone. You flew all the way to Arizona by yourself for this. You get to do whatever you want—no one's watching. Are you really going to let the fear of feeling weird stop you? No one in Sedona will judge you, and most importantly, will you regret not trying it? Yeah, probably.* So

I parked the car and went in.

The experience was interesting, but again, not life-changing or blow-your-mind kind of takeaways, but I recognized they were more little reps—small moments of intuition, curiosity and courage that were stacking up, helping me to not just reflect things to me that I already felt but lean into my path more and more. One thing I took away from the aura reading was that we're all made of energy, and science has shown that our bodies emit frequencies. An aura is simply an energy field; when it's read, you can see where you might be blocked. I learned about the body's seven chakras (energy centers), each with its own color. If one color is dim or missing, it often correlates to a physical, mental, or emotional issue. When she read my chart, my heart chakra, the green chakra, was extremely bright green.

On the other hand, my sacral chakra, or root chakra, which is tied to safety and feeling grounded, was tiny. It showed as a little knot, whereas the heart chakra was super expansive and cloudy-like. It was helpful to see this on the printout she gave me. She told me that this visual representation of the heart chakra meant that I felt incredibly loved and was extremely empathetic. *That tracks.* And for my root chakra, it was rather stuck. She said I still lacked a sense of safety and feeling grounded—a*lso, tracks.*

I ended the day by taking a recommendation from the ladies I met at the restaurant to do an Animal Card reading. This was going to be more new territory. I certainly was curious and, by this point, warmed up to doing unconventional things to see my takeaway, but it also didn't take away from how awkward I still felt approaching these experiences. But, I sure was having fun trying new things and having the courage to do so.

Out of a deck of 152 cards spread face down, I ran my hands slowly over them, trying to "feel" which ones were calling to me, and I picked three and flipped them over: *the Badger, the Marmoset, and the Cougar.*

The first card I pulled was the Badger. Its message was, "Now is the time to be assertive and persistent in your self-expression without fear of judgment." It reinforced the idea that this is my time to focus on being authentic without worrying about others' opinions. "Be yourself unapologetically, and you'll attract the right people who align with your vision." *Wow, if this wasn't a theme I had been struggling with.* It ended with, "The world needs authentic leaders like you to speak your truth and be an example for others." Since this was the time when I started writing this book, I couldn't help but smile.

The second card was the Marmoset. It said, "Let go of feeling stuck by moving in a new direction and following what brings you the most joy." The reader explained that the Marmoset is all about fun, exploration, and discovering new things, which exactly echoed my second session with Sand Play. The card added, "Now is the time for your imagination and childlike nature to come to life." *The message that kept popping up throughout my trip.* The final line read, "It's never too late to start something new. Let go and let your heart guide you."

Finally, we got to the Cougar card. Everything she'd explained about the Badger and Marmoset hit home, so I was a bit nervous about what the Cougar card would bring. It felt bold and powerful—qualities I'm still working on embracing. But it didn't quite feel like the '*me*' sitting in that store.

Here's what the book said about the Cougar card: "Cougar– Step into your power confidently while balancing assertiveness with patience. Cougar is a feminine symbol of power, intuition, and strength. Solitary and silent, Cougar is a skilled hunter who possesses excellent patience. She knows how to get what she wants and does so in a way that balances assertiveness with the grace of receiving. While she waits patiently in the background, she asserts her power confidently, striking only when the moment is right. When Cougar comes to you, it's a sign that you've come into your power. Now is the time to take charge of your life. Make space for solitude and deep introspection as you prioritize your evolution and self-mastery. Balance your newfound strength with gentleness, letting your intuition and inner wisdom guide you. This will ensure that you remain grounded yet confident as you progress on your truest path of empowerment. When the cougar comes to you, it is a sign that you have come into your power. Now is the time to take charge of your life."

As she read this, I felt chills all over my body. I looked at the card and reread, "*When the Cougar comes to you, it is a sign that you have come into your power. Now is the time to take charge of your life.*" It was crazy. It seemed like everything clicked into place for me. I could sense the truth in the reading, even if it was hard to admit and fully embrace.

She explained that the cougar was the most powerful card in the deck, giving the example that cougars are at the top of the food chain. It was her favorite card due to the soft but incredible strength a cougar embodies. I couldn't help but notice her excitement as she lit up about the card. I set my ego aside and appreciated this moment, acknowledging that maybe I did have more power than I give myself credit for. Not to mention, it was the perfect example of the intuition, patience, and courage that I had come to believe in.

Did I feel ridiculous pulling animal cards for life advice? *Yeah, I did.* But was I having fun? *Heck, yes.* It was so freeing to have fun doing things I'd never do at home. And it didn't matter if the cards didn't apply or if they did. You take what you want from it and leave the rest. These cards highlighted a consistent theme I had heard from this trip and only reinforced my true trust in myself. After this reading, I'd be lying if I didn't say I felt a shift in myself—a real sense of letting go and totally enjoying the experience. A feeling like this would've been foreign to me in the past, but here I was, finding my groove, having so much fun meeting new people, eating wherever and whenever I wanted, exploring the vortexes, and following whatever I felt like doing. Something was definitely changing within me.

The next day started with a session I was super curious about. I had heard it was one of the most profound healing experiences at the retreat—Issues from the Tissues. The name alone intrigued me. It was about releasing stuck energy and trauma stored in the body. Even though I had spent years in therapy working through my trauma, I had never experienced a practitioner who did somatic work directly on my body.

The most powerful takeaway from the session was a realization that hit me harder than I expected: I had been approaching healing as if I needed to cleanse myself of trauma. Even my meditations had been focused on clearing fear, clearing worry—like I was something that constantly needed fixing. It suddenly became clear: I wasn't broken. I didn't need to keep clearing things out of me—I needed to learn to just be. To sit in stillness, to listen, to trust myself rather than constantly trying to fix myself.

At one point, she placed her hands on my feet, closed her eyes, and took a deep breath. "Wow. There is *so much* power here," she said. "I'm not going to stay here long, but I feel so much power within you."

Immediately, I thought back to the night before—the Cougar card. It felt like another confirmation, another nudge from the universe telling me the same thing over and over again.

Her final encouragement before we wrapped up was this: "Stop trying to clear yourself. Instead, invite in your own power. Call in your gifts, your inner guidance, your higher self. Lead with unconditional love. And remember—every experience is part of your learning."

I had expected the session to be heavy and full of deep emotional processing, but it was the opposite. It was light. Empowering. It left me feeling inspired rather than drained. It was exactly what I needed.

After the session, I felt energized and decided to squeeze in another vortex hike—this time, Thunder Mountain. I followed it up with lunch at Tlaquepaque Shopping Center before heading into my next session: holotropic breathwork.

Truthfully, I was terrified. I had done this kind of breathwork before, and it was intense. Holotropic breathing involves keeping your eyes closed, your mouth open, and breathing rapidly for the entire session while listening to music designed to shift your consciousness. It's not some woo-woo concept—it's backed by science. The breathing pattern increases CO_2 in the body, shifting brain wave frequencies from "beta" (our everyday thinking mode) to "theta," which is associated with deep relaxation, intuition, and a stronger connection to the subconscious. I knew this. I believed in the science of it. But that didn't make it any less intimidating.

For forty-five minutes, I would have to keep my mouth open,

breathing rapidly. My lips would dry, my body would tingle, and sometimes, people even experienced their hands clawing up from the energy release. I still *hated* the idea of losing control, and breathwork pushed me past my limits. Still, I reminded myself that I was in the hands of a professional—a highly trained expert—and decided to surrender to the experience.

Getting started was just as awkward as I had thought it would be, but I eventually found a groove and became incredibly relaxed. It was amazing to see what my mind explored in such a calm state and truly finding a place to let go of rational thoughts and feel free in my head.

I noticed that all I wanted to keep doing was focus on calling in light, love, trust and truth and letting go of worry, fear, not being good enough, not worthy enough, and all the other limiting beliefs I was still working through. I can't say I walked away wanting to sign up for more intense breathwork sessions, but the experience was undoubtedly powerful.

I've learned a lot about breathing over the years, and while I'm no expert, I know firsthand how powerful breathwork can be for regulating the nervous system and connecting more deeply with your heart and body. After all, it was the first thing Jeff had me try when I was experiencing my awful nightmares.

In the Bible, breath is a symbol of the Holy Spirit. In Latin, spirit comes from the word spiritus, which means breath. There's no denying that breathwork is a major component of overall wellness and a reminder of where we come from.

While holotropic breathwork may not be my thing, there are more approachable methods, like box breathing, 4-7-8, the breath of fire, or Wim Hof, which I have tried and enjoy. But I have to admit, this session took things to another level. If you're curious, look for a professional and proceed cautiously—this isn't right for everyone.

On my final day, I had my last session with a guided hike called Letting Go on the Land. I assumed it would be a typical hike, but it turned out to be the opposite. The purpose wasn't for physical exercise, which admittedly challenged me, but rather to really notice the nature around us. I was surprised at how much being on a "hike" made me feel like I had to "make it worth it." The guide walked very slowly, pointing out every tiny detail—birds chirping, the breeze shifting, and the sound of a woodpecker in the distance. She even stopped to observe a little lizard that had died, belly-up between two rocks. At first, I was impatient. But then, something clicked. I was rushing through the experience. I was so focused on getting to the end goal—the summit—that I was missing everything that was right in front of me. So, I let go. I slowed down. And I started to see—*really* see—the details around me. It was another lesson in presence. Another lesson in letting go.

I wrapped up my trip with a two-hour massage designed to let me do nothing but receive No digging into my past, no deep emotional processing—just pure nurture and support. It was a reminder that I deserved it and that it was a choice to accept it.

The length of the retreat was perfect. When I woke up on my last day, I was excited to go home—to see Kyle, to be with my kids. I felt refreshed, loved, and supported.

Before heading out, I made one last stop at the Life is Good store to grab Kyle a t-shirt. If there was one brand that he wears more than anything, it is this. Well, that and his old CrossFit competition shirts—the ones that were way past their prime but still too comfortable for him to part with.

As I stood there, taking in the last moments of the Sedona landscape, I felt an overwhelming sense of gratitude. The people here had been so kind, so present. No one was glued to their phone, lost in distraction. People saw each other here. I would miss that.

On the two-hour drive back, I tried to piece together how this retreat had changed me. I knew friends and family would ask, "What did you do? What did you get out of it?" And honestly? I wasn't sure how to explain things like animal card readings, aura readings, holotropic breathwork, and vortexes to my more traditional circle at home. Would they judge me? Probably. I knew it would still bother me if people had opinions about it, so I protected my experience and was careful with how I would share it. Because this experience wasn't for them. It was for *me*. And when I thought about what I had gained, one word came to mind: **empowerment.** I had been looking for some life-changing advice, but I realized it was never about one moment or one healer. It was the entire experience—becoming aware, staying curious, embracing the small moments of courage, using my intuition, trusting, and choosing to believe in myself. I still had layers to work through, but for the first time, I wasn't focused on the when or the how. I was finally trusting that it was all leading me exactly where I was meant to go.

25

PUTTING IT ALL TOGETHER

"Do you forgive him?" she asked.

It was the last episode of the podcast series I released in 2021, and Stacy, my producer and highly intuitive friend, was interviewing me for it. I was completely caught off guard by the question.

We were live, but I took a long pause, not knowing how to answer her. Forgiveness was a message I had heard preached so many times over the years. I witnessed people who went through incredibly traumatic experiences share their testimonies of forgiveness. A part of me always wondered if that was how they truly felt, given their shared experiences. I just couldn't understand it. I knew forgiveness was not for the person who hurt you but rather for yourself, but it was hard to wrap my head around how people could forgive people who did such awful, disgusting, and horrifying things. At this point, I couldn't truthfully say I felt forgiveness toward him after all the struggles

Kyle and I faced and how monstrous he was and would have continued to be.

"Honestly," I paused, "I'm not there yet," I responded.

Her question stuck with me, and it wasn't until after this interview and starting IFS therapy on my own parts that I started to be at a place where I could find my version of forgiveness. Because visiting parts often takes you to memories of when you were a child and where a situation left you hurt, I started to think of our intruder as a little boy. I didn't know his past, but I couldn't help but think of him as this young boy and wonder about the moments he faced that hurt him deeply. I couldn't help but want to forgive that young boy.

While finishing this book, I had been working with an energy healer to help Lyla with her autoimmune disorder. She had been experiencing awful and painful rashes on the backs of her legs for years, and I had learned about someone who did energy work and was incredibly successful with rashes. After three years of painful, itchy, and oozing rashes that were only better when strong topical steroids were used but would come back the second we stopped, I was open to trying everything. And it was appearing to be helping.

After five or six sessions working on Lyla, the woman recommended that we do a session together as she could feel how close Lyla and I were and how much my energy also impacted Lyla. This made sense because I knew about the nervous system. If I carry things in my nervous system, it will subconsciously impact my kids as well, especially someone as intuitive and sensitive as Lyla. In Chinese medicine, they often practice, "Don't treat the child. Treat the mom." Just minutes into our session, she quietly tapped into my energy. Then she interrupted the silence. "Tennyson, um, I don't know how to say this, but something unexpected happened," she said.

I had yet to learn where this was going. I was only thinking of Lyla, and maybe we had a new clue about how to help her.

"The guy, umm, the guy who you killed is here. He immediately came in and wanted to share a message with you," she said.

My heart started racing. After forty-five minutes of talking beforehand about my childhood, my parents, my sister, and my relationship with Kyle, we had not even spoken about the break-in. Although she already knew about it, it wasn't something we talked about on this day.

"He wants to say that he is incredibly sorry. He knows what he did caused so much pain for you and your family, and he wants you to know that he apologizes for that. He also feels bad for leaving his family that way but knows it was also better for them," she continued.

I started to cry. A huge part of me questioned whether I could even believe this—whether any of it was real. But another part of me didn't care. It felt good to even consider the idea that he recognized what he had done, not just to us but to his own family as well. It was heartbreaking to think about all of us left in the wake of his choices—his family, his kids, and the ripple effect of pain that went far beyond that night.

Shifting toward understanding and compassion for him felt unfamiliar, almost foreign. But at the same time, it felt lighter. It wasn't about excusing or justifying his actions but about allowing myself to acknowledge his humanity. To consider, for even a moment, that maybe in some sort of reality, he did carry regret.

Walking through the days, weeks, months, and years after everything that happened has been a journey. But doing it with

Kyle, knowing we're the only ones who truly understand the depths of what the other went through, has created a unique bond between us.

Seeing each other fight to save our family's life skyrocketed our trust in one another. But what I didn't expect was how much trust and love I've learned to have for myself.

We recently informed the kids of what had happened on that day. We had to pick Lyla's jaw off the floor multiple times. As for Skyler, who was eight at the time, his response was a calm, "Wow, mom, didn't know you would ever do something like that," as he anxiously waited to get back to throwing a football. While telling them, I couldn't help but notice their little faces, as well as Kyle's, whose eyes were red and filled with tears, and be aware of this bomb that we were dropping on them. My heart broke thinking of this being something that would likely cause them struggles while at the same time knowing the time was right for them to hear it. They had many questions and slept in our room for almost three weeks, but they handled it amazingly well. Of course, we will stay on top of that as the years unfold. We are very aware that not every family has something like this in their history books.

The fight that night and what Kyle and I did were surreal experiences. I can still vividly remember every moment of that early morning and feel every emotion and action that played out. Even as much as it has impacted us in the decade since, it's often hard to believe that was actually reality.

While I hadn't heard of this term—post-traumatic growth (PTG)—I learned it is a real thing. And even further, post-traumatic wisdom (PTW). Research shows we can grow, change, and evolve after traumatic events. This can help us connect more deeply with our values, become more empathetic, and gain profound wisdom that comes from processing these experiences. It doesn't mean we weren't impacted; it means there is a resilience that comes from facing and doing the work to heal from such events.

I know many reading this can't relate to killing someone. At least, I sure hope not. But I do know that every single person reading this has faced trauma in some way. And for many, they have faced so much worse than we did. But the point is that we don't need to compare our trauma against others. The emotions at the root of the experience, whether big T trauma or little t trauma, are universal—grief, shame, anger, sadness, fear, confusion, unworthiness, and many more. In acknowledging these parts and doing the work to heal, we are capable of experiencing joy, happiness, and the freedom that comes from that healing.

The Biggest Takeaways

As I write these final paragraphs and reflect on this entire journey, my biggest takeaways are these:

CONNECTION

I'm no historian, but there's a reason humans started living in villages. We aren't meant to do life alone. We thrive on connection.

In 1979, Lisa Berkman and Leonard Syme conducted a study that found people with strong social ties were three times less likely to die, even if they had unhealthy habits like smoking, poor diet, or lack of exercise. Given today's technology and the epidemic of loneliness, I can only imagine that number is even higher now.

There's also the saying, "You are who you surround yourself with." And while I usually cringe at clichés, I couldn't agree more with this one.

Don't surround yourself with people who dim your light. Seek out those who lift you. Open yourself to new connections and communities that bring you joy. Have the courage to be vulnerable. Give to others, but also know that *you* are worthy of receiving.

Spend time with your kids. Devices have their place, but nothing replaces real connection—the laughs, conversations, and moments that make memories.

Our connections meant everything. Friends. Family. Our firefighter family. The police. Detectives. Therapists. Mentors. Healers. Every single one of them played a role.

ASK FOR HELP

Over the years, I've worked with many people on my journey of growth, personally and in business. I've hired countless therapists, coaches, healers, and mentors to help me navigate whatever season I was in.

Some friends would laugh and say, "Tenny, you're hiring another coach, therapist, etc?"

And the truth is, yes. Yes, I was.

While I've definitely had too many cooks in the kitchen at times, every therapist, coach, healer, or mentor I've worked with has taught me something and they came at the perfect time. And sometimes, the only lesson I received was that someone wasn't the right fit for me. Sometimes, we are afraid it won't work out, it'll cost too much, or we will seem crazy for trying something new. But even in the moments when it didn't work out for me, it still helped me take one step closer to finding what did.

AWARENESS

The most profound lessons I've learned came from becoming aware, practicing mindfulness, and noticing the tiniest details.

Moments of silence. A pause to feel my feet on the floor. A breath to relax the muscles in my face.

Our world is constantly pulling our awareness away. I recently heard a statistic that our attention span has dropped from three minutes to forty-five seconds. That's heartbreaking. And it's undoubtedly contributing to rising rates of depression, suicide, and mental illness.

Find brief moments to pause. To become aware. Then repeat. And then repeat again. Awareness alone can change your life.

CURIOSITY

Life is so much more fun when you lean into curiosity. It leads to growth, expansion, and fulfillment. Be curious about experiences. Be curious about people. Be curious about your spouse. Be curious about your kids.

As Bryant McGill said, "Curiosity is one of the greatest secrets to happiness."

INTUITION

This is where the magic happens.

Your intuition—your gut, your inner knowing, your connection to God/Source/Spirit—will never lead you astray. Maybe it's a whisper. Maybe it's a feeling. Maybe it's a thought that pops into your head out of nowhere. Trust it.

My favorite check-in for intuition is this: Does this feel expansive or contractive? Or Does it feel like love or fear?

Learning to trust your intuition will change everything.

COURAGE

It took me a long time to acknowledge that what I did that early Mother's Day morning was courageous—because in so many ways, the years that followed felt even harder.

But courage isn't about being fearless. It's about feeling the fear, the doubt, the insecurity—and deciding that something else is more important.

The biggest lesson I've learned about courage? It's not just found in the big, heroic moments. It's in the small, everyday choices—the quiet, unseen decisions. The struggle no one else sees.

Becoming aware + trusting your intuition + being curious + asking for help— all require *courage*.

SUPPORT YOUR NERVOUS SYSTEM

Whether you have experienced big T trauma or the millions of little t's we all experience, our nervous system is the *foundation* for healing. Our world is not slowing down, seemingly only getting more and more stimulating. My learning and study has made me realize how much our bodies weren't designed to manage the magnitude of information that comes our way each and every day. Regulating your system is a continued practice, but one that has the most profound effect.

CONDITIONING

We are all a product of how we were raised. You don't have to have had a neglectful childhood to develop behaviors that don't serve you well as an adult.

Dr. Gabor Maté says, **"Trauma is not what happens to you; it is what happens inside you as a result of what happens to you."** That means trauma isn't just about the big moments—it's also about the small, subtle imprints that shape how we view the world, how we respond to stress, and how we learn to survive.

Maybe your family didn't have the tools to acknowledge emotions, so feelings were swept under the rug. Maybe you learned it was better to stay quiet than take up space. Maybe you were left alone to fend for yourself while your parents worked two jobs. Maybe you observed family struggles completely out of your control, yet they left a lasting impact anyway.

These imprints become part of our conditioning. They dictate how we move through life, the beliefs we carry about ourselves, and how we interact with others.

Healing from that conditioning has created the most significant shifts in my life. These will always be parts of me, parts I want to help know are safe to *not* take over all the time. And I know that if you commit to being curious and becoming aware of your own patterns, it can do the same for you.

THE FINAL THOUGHT

I don't know what happens next. I don't know exactly where this journey will lead me. But I do know that every single step—every challenge, every breakthrough, every moment of fear and doubt and courage—has led me here. And here is exactly where I'm meant to be.

And maybe, just maybe, you're exactly where you're meant to be, too.

"Perhaps we spend so much time trying to be 'whole' because we were never taught that our wholeness includes every fragmented piece of us."
— Unknown

EPILOGUE BY TENNYSON JACOBSON

In March of 2024, eleven years after that fateful Mother's Day, Kyle, Lyla, Skyler, and I took our first-ever vacation alone as a family. Lyla was eleven, Skyler was eight. We had always traveled with friends or extended family, never even considering that we could do something with just the four of us. But here we were, stepping into something new.

Wailea Beach stretched before us, its golden sand and turquoise waves more beautiful than I had imagined. It was known for having some of the best body-surfing waves on the island of Maui, and I watched as Kyle, Lyla, and Skyler waded out to their waists, searching for the perfect one to ride. When they found it, they exchanged excited smiles, anticipation building between them. I smiled as they launched into the water, letting the wave carry them to shore.

As they tumbled onto the sand, Lyla wiped the hair from her face, revealing the biggest smile. The boys climbed to their feet beside her, shaking the water out of their hair, their laughter contagious. I wanted to freeze time, to capture this moment—this pure, perfect joy. I knew we were making memories that would stay with us forever.

Earlier that morning, we had sipped coffee on our condo balcony while watching humpback whales breach in the distance. The day before, we had snorkeled just feet away from sea turtles at Black Rock Beach. Butterflies seemed to follow us everywhere, almost as if they were guiding us through something sacred. And then, as I stood there on the sand, Skyler ran over to me, his entire body covered in sand, his eyes bloodshot from what was probably his fiftieth wave of the day. He grabbed my hand, breathless, his face lit up with pure happiness.

"This is soooooo fun, Mom!" Then, without hesitation, he wrapped his little arms around me in the tightest hug. He paused for a moment, pulled back slightly, and in the softest, most sincere voice, he said, "Thank you so much for taking us here."

I melted. This. This was heaven on earth. For the first time, after all the years of processing and healing, I felt fully present. Fully grounded. Safe. Fully happy.

I don't know where you are in life or what you're working through. But I do know that everyone is going through something. Some struggles are obvious, but others are hidden beneath the surface, carefully tucked away where no one can see. We may try to outrun them, bury them beneath distractions, convince ourselves they aren't there—but they always find a way to show up. As Jeff once told me, "Whenever we don't process something, or the brain doesn't think we've fixed it, it keeps throwing it back at us. It's not trying to torture us—it's just trying to say, 'Hey, you haven't dealt with this yet.' And it doesn't say it nicely—it beats the hell out of us."

We've all had experiences that shape us. That mark us. That change the way we move through the world. And for those of you who are searching for healing, for clarity, for peace—I see you.

Healing is messy. It's uncomfortable. It forces us to sit with things we'd rather avoid. But what about the other side of that work? The growth, the wisdom, the freedom? That's what makes it worth it. I don't have everything figured out. I never will. Healing isn't a finish line you cross—it's a process, a practice, a lifelong unfolding. And I'm learning to be patient with that. To accept it. To even appreciate it.

When I look back, I feel like a completely different person from the woman I was before that Mother's Day. Not necessarily different to others, but different in how I experience my internal world. I have never felt more me than I do now.

That night forced me to grow in ways I didn't know I could. It led me to incredible mentors and healers who helped me find my true self—who reminded me that my uniqueness wasn't something to hide but something to honor. It taught me how to let go—of control, fear, worry—and to trust that everything is unfolding exactly as it is meant to.

My only job is to take one day at a time, take care of my nervous system, be aware and love all my parts, stay curious, and have the courage to trust my intuition. I know there will be more challenges. Life will continue to test, stretch, and challenge me to evolve. But I will lean on these practices and do my best to live out the vision I have for this one precious life we get.

Would I ever choose to relive that night and the aftermath that followed? No. But am I grateful for what it led me to? One million percent.

I have found that many people who have faced tragedy or trauma find healing by discovering a deeper meaning in their experiences. Turning such pain into their own unique purpose. It doesn't mean we don't carry scars. It means that we choose to let those scars shape us into something stronger. We always have a choice. We can ignore the pain. We can numb it. Or we can choose the higher path—the one that isn't easy but the one that leads to freedom. Choosing healing is brave. Choosing growth is brave. Choosing to step into the unknown and trust that beauty and meaning can come from the hardest things is the most courageous thing of all. The world needs your gifts. Trust that. If you are suffering, don't give up. Keep going. You—your life, your dreams, your happiness—are worth fighting for.

With love, Tenny

AFTERWARD BY KYLE JACOBSON

Reading through Tenny's account of the incident brings back memories of my experience and, quite frankly, ones that I haven't thought about for years.

It's difficult to explain what it's like when you think you're taking your dogs out to pee at 1:30 am and instead, you find a madman in your hallway. What my body did was something I've never felt before, but I'll try to explain. You've got to remember that I had zero expectation of what was to transpire.

After walking to the front door, the dogs turned around and ran back toward our bedroom, barking. I was confused and annoyed with them because I didn't want them to wake Lyla. That's when the fella came around the corner into the hallway.

Even though I hadn't seen this guy earlier in the day, I knew it was him. The way Tenny had described this guy from her earlier attack might be part of why I knew it was him, but also because I couldn't imagine who else would be in our house. After that first encounter with the guy, I was so pissed that I hadn't been there to protect the family. He gave me a second chance, I suppose. It felt like my body had a bolt of lightning go through it (this is what I mean by never having this feeling before). The thought that went through my mind in just seconds was, *Oh my God, oh my God.* I knew I had to react. And I actually thought, *Well, I better win this, or our family isn't going to live through the night.*

The guy bull-rushed me, but I was able to stay standing up with him. I remember feeling like it was a hockey fight in that I had his shirt in my left hand and was hitting him with my right. I didn't have a shirt, so he had nothing to grab onto. After maybe fifteen seconds of that, we went to the ground, and I was able to get him in a front headlock. I tried to knee him in the face about three times but grazed the top of his head each time. After that, I resorted to just controlling him in the front headlock so that he couldn't do anything.

Tenny was busy giving this guy everything she had - the baseball bat and Raid. She broke the bat over this guy's back, kicked him in the family jewels and sprayed his eyes with Raid. The guy kept slowly crawling forward and inching me backward, which seemed like forever. I had been a competitive wrestler, but this was like nothing I had ever experienced in the energy needed to keep the upper hand. I was so freakin' tired.

At one point, the guy tried to get my hand into his mouth to bite me and then tried to grab my balls with his hand. This was when I realized I might not be able to control this guy for much longer. And I sure didn't want him to get the opportunity to chomp a finger off or squish my sac. That's when I told Tenny I needed help. It was the only thing said the whole time.

The speed at which she went to the kitchen, grabbed a knife, and stabbed the guy was unreal. My head was right next to the guy's (ear to ear) the entire fight once we had gone to the ground. I remember being surprised at how quickly the fight went out of him. I hadn't expected Tenny to grab a knife and stab him, so it was a shock to me. However, that shock went away as quickly as it came up because I was so relieved he was done fighting. I laid on the guy for quite some time, trying to catch my breath, and honestly, I was nervous he would come back to life to fight some more. I managed to tell Rosalyn (Tenny's mom) to let 911 dispatch a medic because this guy was dead.

One of the crazy things that always struck me was that the guy never made a noise besides grunting and growling. Being right next to him, I heard everything. I couldn't believe how tough he was. It definitely made me realize that some folks have immense strength and can disconnect from their pain, which blew my mind. Afterward, it actually threw me for a loop mentally for a long time.

Like I said earlier, I don't think about this much anymore, but I do have two scars on my chest that are a subtle reminder every time I see them. I'm not even sure how I got those scars from the fight.

As Tenny described, I struggled for a long time...with everything, really. I wouldn't turn my back to the open kitchen while washing dishes, didn't want to close my eyes while showering, had the same process of checking the house with our dog before turning in for the night, had trouble sleeping, and I even got nervous walking up to houses while on shift for the fire department, not knowing who would open the door. It was a surreal feeling that I had never imagined possible, and it was shocking how much something that happened in less than ten minutes impacted everything I did. There are many specific stories of these instances, but I don't have the space here to write them. All I can say is that I was in a mental state I never thought I'd be in my life.

However, as time went on, I slowly got out of it. The counseling I went to didn't do it for me. Especially when I told my counselor the whole story, his response was, "Kyle, that's my biggest fear." Now, I'm not a huge therapy guy, but I was pretty sure this wasn't the way it generally goes. Oh well, I tried. What really got me through it was several things - Faith, Family and Friends. I've always relied on my Faith. It helped me through this whole situation. Although it was a slightly different experience than Tenny's, I always felt drawn to our physical church, as the messages made me feel supported and loved. I always left with the feeling that everything would work out—not always knowing what that meant, but it has served me well to believe in that. Over the years, but especially during this time, I always felt lifted when thinking about the teachings of loving your neighbor, treating them like you'd want to be treated, helping those in need, and not to judge others, etc. Truth is, we both know there's a higher power. There certainly was a feeling of being covered the day and night this all went down.

Family—this, of course, is huge for me. This experience brought Tenny and me closer as it was something we both went through and worked as a team to "win." We had to stay a team to work through what came next. We had several people tell us that the percentage of divorce after things like this is exceedingly high. So, we took it seriously to work together, not only on ourselves but also on our marriage. Being with my family brings me so much joy. It's where I can disconnect from the world and just be in the moment with them. This is what life is all about for me. Also, my parents were a huge thing through all of this for me. The love and support they offered our family were unparalleled. Tenny went into the story of us sleeping in their room for months and I think about that frequently. They truly helped me through the event in every way imaginable and I'll forever be thankful to them.

The friends (and coworkers because many of them are my friends) were also an enormous help. Folks at our gym took over all duties for us, friends came over to support us at any time of the day or night, and people were just so kind and supportive once we were able to get back to the gym. I'll never be able to express the gratitude I have for the friends who supported us through everything.

Lastly, the fire department was a huge support for our family. The offerings the firefighters went to were so far above and beyond anything expected and it blew my mind. I'll also never forget the generosity of these folks. I even remember the first time I worked a whole shift when my lieutenant offered to sleep out on the recliners in the TV room with me if it would make me feel more comfortable. We received so much kindness and love; it showed me how meaningful and genuine relationships can be.

I feel like I'm able to compartmentalize things well, probably because of my job. I found what worked for me and I truly am happy. I don't think about what happened to us much anymore. Some things will never be the same for us, but that's okay. Life is unpredictable and I believe in taking everything we go through as an opportunity to get stronger. I sometimes ask myself *if I wish this hadn't happened.* The easy answer is obvious, but I remind myself, "At least he can't do this to anyone else." So, that's where I'm at these days. Life is beautiful and life is good (one of my favorite phrases and clothing brands.) I feel blessed to live life surrounded by my family, a great community and loving friends.

Lastly, I'm so incredibly proud of my wife for everything she has done to heal and grow, write this book and, God willing, be able to help a lot of people. While reading back through this book, there were many times when I teared up reading about how difficult of a time Tenny had at certain times after this event. It was tough to read sometimes and that's why I'm so glad she's found peace in so many areas of her life. All the work she has done on herself to heal, find happiness and a bigger purpose for her life is inspiring. It has reinforced for me the importance of being present in the small moments in life. I am also inspired to be a great listener, as she is, and to ask my close friends questions that allow them to open up to me.

I joke with her that I'm glad she's gotten the story out about what we went through and, more importantly, how hard she has worked to overcome all her feelings and struggles because if she hadn't, this story would have never been publicly told.

I don't talk about this story a whole lot, and nobody would have been helped through our experience if it wasn't for her, so I'm super proud of her! Tenny is an amazing woman who shows love to those around her. She is one of the best listeners I've ever been around and is a loving wife and wonderful mother to our children. Tenny is setting an incredible example for our kids and I'm forever thankful for that.

Love you all and thank you for reading my brief thoughts and the journey this event led Tenny on with her hope to make a difference in this world.

Kyle

ACKNOWLEDGEMENTS

I shared in the book about having the thought of writing a book years before I ever actually did. I now see there were experiences and growth I still needed to walk through in order to write the story I wanted to tell. This growth and healing would not have been possible without those who supported Kyle and me along the way, and those who never gave up on me as they held up a metaphorical mirror to me, reminding me to believe in my potential.

The first of those being my parents. Thank you for believing in me and always reminding me of it. For constantly telling me how much you love me. And for modeling respect, open-mindedness, and growth. Dad, you taught me to count my blessings and embodied deep love for your family, all while having fun and being able to laugh along the way. You appreciate the simple yet most important things in life. It was a foundation I came back to and that inspired me as I found my way. Mom,

I am incredibly appreciative of how hard you worked from the second I was born to dream big. You taught me to never give up and always did everything in your power to expand my limited view, two things I couldn't be more thankful for. You are an incredible mother and I can't thank you enough for all you have done that has inspired me to become who I am and how I now parent Lyla and Skyler.

Jessie, you have been my biggest cheerleader throughout this book. Twins have a unique bond and your love and encouragement through this process are deeply felt, especially given what we have walked through together.

Norm and Mary, thank you so much for all you did for us and continue to do for our family. I'm not sure how we would have navigated all the moving pieces after Mother's Day without your help and support. You anticipated our needs before we needed them and went above and beyond to help us move forward. Not many can say they have been roommates with their in-laws! We are very grateful to have all your support in all ways!

To Lyla and Skyler. Skyler, your energy is contagious and you are a constant reminder to have fun and embrace life. You remind me of the importance of physical connection and how things like hugs or sitting next to each other are some of the most important moments of the day. Lyla, I loved brainstorming titles and taglines with you and sharing ideas for the cover while getting your feedback. I appreciate you checking in on me on how I was feeling and being so excited for me to bring this book to life. But mostly, you inspire me with your awareness of what really matters in life. Time together. At twelve, you are wise beyond your years.

To the crew at Eastside Fire and law enforcement who

responded to both calls on Mother's Day. It can be easy to overlook the impact someone makes when responding to a situation like that. Your professionalism, respect, and sincere care for us will forever be with us, and we couldn't be more grateful for how you treated us during such a traumatic time.

Detective Barlett, I truly feel you were a special gift to us. How you handled the scene that evening and every moment after was done with grace, empathy, and integrity. From the bottom of my heart, thank you for all that you did to make going through that process as painless as possible.

To our firefighter family at Kirkland Fire. It has always felt special to be a part of a unique brother and sisterhood that protects each other—getting to experience it firsthand and how this community comes together and rallies around one of its own in one of the most trying times is nothing short of beautiful. Thank you for the many ways you supported our family and, most importantly, for giving Kyle the gift of time to be home. There are few times I cry when I share our story, but sharing what you did always gets me because of how deeply it meant to us. We couldn't be more grateful to be a part of KFD.

To our Cascade CrossFit community. First, we love and miss you so much. Even though it has been many years since we sold the gym, the relationships, friendships and incredible memories we had together have shaped so much of who Kyle and I are. There is the saying, "You don't realize what you have until it's gone." We realized we had something special, but didn't realize how much we all need connection and community and how critical it is to have a place for belonging. Having a place to come to every day filled with the most incredible people truly did carry us through. I can say thank you for all the things you have done for us, but more importantly, I want to thank you for who you all are, the memories we have of all our times together, and what that has meant to us and forever will.

To Stacy Heller, I can't thank you enough for your friendship, helping me find my voice, and encouraging me to share my story. You've challenged me in the best of ways. You have a rare gift, and your heart is pure gold. Or platinum. Or whatever is most precious. Thank you for teaching me about intuition and helping me practice it, even if I defaulted to wanting to hear it from you rather than myself. I'm not sure I would have had the courage to write this book if it weren't for you always reminding me of my potential. And lastly, thank you for your genius in creating the most perfect title for this book.

Judy Cochrane, you became so much more than a book coach and editor and publisher. You became family. Working together with you through this has taught me so much more than just thinking about the end result. It is about enjoying the ride and who you are riding along with. You taught me that art isn't built under pressure. Art is built when we are inspired, which doesn't follow any sort of timeline or formula. You easily see the depth and heart of a message and I cannot imagine a better person in the world to have helped me articulate mine. Your gift is incredible and it was an honor to share this journey with you.

Jeff, I'm not sure how I can put into words how to thank you for all you have done for me. This book would not be here if I didn't have your guidance and support to heal not just the big T trauma but the little t's that had been holding me back in so many ways. Your wisdom, humility, and compassion are unlike anyone I have worked with. Thank you for seeing the parts of me that needed compassion that I was not aware of and didn't understand. Thank you for helping me find my voice when I didn't think I was worthy to do so. Thank you for helping me understand the importance of mindfulness and for giving me the tools to practice it. And thank you for the incredible gift of self-discovery, which is to slowly start to become aware, love myself, and honor all my parts.

To Kyle. My crush from freshman year in high school and the man who has always made me feel safe and protected. Everything would have been so different that night if you hadn't been there. Your situational awareness, sense of calm, and courage that evening were incredible to witness. But most importantly, I admire your strength of character and profound love for your family. With you, nothing is more important. Thank you for embodying love and generosity to others. Thank you for always making me feel safe and protected. Even if there aren't words, I always feel it. And thank you for your continued support and encouragement as I find my footing in finding my way of sharing not just my story but our story. It is an honor to be your wife. I love you.

To each of you and everyone who has played a part in this journey with me. Thank you. Whether it was a smile as I grabbed coffee at a drive-thru, a sleepover while Kyle was at work, a message of support, or the countless other ways that I have felt encouraged, it all has helped culminate in the ability to write this book.

With all my love and deepest appreciation,
Tennyson

CONNECT WITH TENNYSON

WEBSITE
heyitstenny.com

EMAIL
hello@tennysonjacobson.com

INSTAGRAM
@tennysonjacobson

FACEBOOK & LINKEDIN
Tennyson Jacobson

TIKTOK
@tennyjacobson

www.ingramcontent.com/pod-product-compliance
Lightning Source LLC
Chambersburg PA
CBHW030431010526
44118CB00011B/591

9780997692372